THE
GREAT MIGRATIONS

THE
GREAT MIGRATIONS

From the Earliest Humans to the
Age of Globalization

JOHN HAYWOOD

Quercus

Contents

Left: Polynesian outrigger canoe.
Pages 2–3: Zion Canyon, Utah, settled by the Mormons in the 1860s

Emigrant family crossing Nebraska in the 1880s.

Muslim refugees following Indian Partition in 1947

Introduction

Since humans first left their evolutionary cradle in Africa 100,000 years ago, migrations have been one of the great driving forces of historical change. At no time has this been more true than today, when the forces of economic globalization have set so much of the world's population on the move.

This is an exciting time in the study of historical migrations. New scientific developments in genetics and isotope analysis are quite literally revolutionizing our understanding of human history. Everyone carries in their genes a record of their ancestry and, in their bones and teeth, a record of where they have lived during their own lifetimes. Now that these records can be read, many long-standing assumptions have been overturned and new credibility has been given to what historians had long regarded as unreliable traditions. Even prehistoric migrations for which there are no written records at all can now be reconstructed with astonishing precision. This new science has also confirmed that migrants have always been a minority of the human race. To leave your homeland and build a new life in a foreign country has always required initiative and enterprise, and, often enough, courage. It is because of this that immigrant societies are so often dynamic societies.

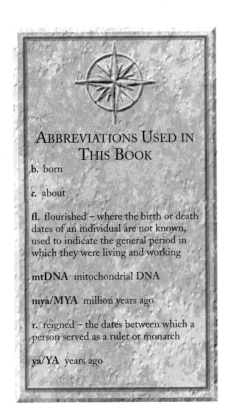

ABBREVIATIONS USED IN THIS BOOK

b. born

c. about

fl. flourished – where the birth or death dates of an individual are not known, used to indicate the general period in which they were living and working

mtDNA mitochondrial DNA

mya/MYA million years ago

r. reigned – the dates between which a person served as a ruler or monarch

ya/YA years ago

This book does not attempt a comprehensive survey of human migrations – that would require a far longer volume than this. Instead, it focuses on 51 historic migrations extending from humanity's first steps out of Africa 100,000 years ago to the present-day tide of global economic migration. The migrations are organized in roughly chronological sequence. Any selection such as this always invites criticism for what it leaves out. This is not an attempt to produce a definitive list of 'the most important migrations of all time', though all of these migrations have been chosen because they were important in their different ways. The intention is, rather, to present a wide range of different types of migration through the ages: folk movements, forced migrations, economic migrations, warrior migrations and migrations to escape political, racial or religious persecution. Many migrations, of course, combine elements of more than one of these categories. If peoples of European extraction appear to be over-represented here, it is because for most of the last 500 years Europe has been the world's main exporter of population. As a consequence, the ethnic, linguistic, cultural, economic and even the ecological character of much of the world has been transformed. Europe is now an importer of population. The political, cultural and economic consequences of this historic shift are not yet clear.

American pioneer homesteaders pictured in the late 19th century.

Migrations in History

Migration is one of the defining characteristics of the human race. No other species has ever ranged so far and colonized so many different environments. Alone among the continents, wild and icebound Antarctica has no permanent human inhabitants. Human migration has also been incessant, with the numbers of people on the move increasing constantly, keeping step with the growth of the human population. It is its ceaseless nature that makes migration one of the great driving forces of world history, spreading technology and ideas, and creating and destroying nations and empires.

The importance of migrations as agents of historical change has long been recognized. Migrations, both real and legendary, form essential components of many national identities, not least that of the United States of America. Migrations both promote diversification of human cultures and provide the means for the transfer of information and technologies between cultures. Early human migrations around the world brought about a proliferation of different cultures as humans entered and adapted to new environments. Separation in time and space led to the development of different languages and genetic drift to the modern racial characteristics. Compared to other species the genetic differences between different human populations is, however, very slight and that is also a direct consequence of migration. Few communities have ever maintained complete isolation from other communities for very long. The constant exchange of genes between populations has prevented *Homo sapiens* from evolving into separate species as it colonized the world.

Bushmen such as the Gwi people have inhabited the Kalahari Desert of southern Africa for many thousands of years. They lead a migratory existence, hunting and foraging in small, mobile groups.

Of course, migrants do not take with them only their genes, they also take with them their knowledge of technology, food, language, religions and philosophies and much else. Relatively small numbers of migrants can have a disproportionately large cultural impact on their host communities. In this way immigrants can greatly enrich the host community, but it would be foolish to pretend that migrations always have positive effects for everyone involved. The cost of migration can be high for the individuals involved. Before the modern age migration always involved a degree of hardship and physical danger. Very large numbers of migrants have died on the way to their particular promised lands. Migrations have often been accompanied by wars and the displacement, or even extermination, of indigenous peoples and cultures. Migration has always had the effect of strengthening some communities at the expense of others.

Types of migrations

Migrations can be divided into four main types: home-community migration; colonization; whole-community migration; and cross-community migration.

Home-community migration involves the movement of people from one place to another within their own community. With distances measured often in yards rather than miles, this is by far the most common type of migration; most people are likely to be affected by this form of migration at some point of their lives. In modern western societies home-community migration is taken for granted, it happens every time a young couple leave their family homes and set up an independent household together. Because of divorce, labour mobility and the desire to climb the 'housing ladder', individuals in western societies may make home-community migrations several times during their lives. In traditional agricultural societies home-community migration generally involves a child from one family moving to join another family in order to find a marriage partner. In patrilinear societies it is usually women who move from the farm of their birth to a new farm on marriage. Male children normally remain on their parents' farm because in due course they will inherit a share of the land and set up their own households on it. In matrilinear societies the pattern is reversed but such societies, where land passes through the female line, have been rare. In an attempt to preserve land holdings intact from one generation to the next, many agricultural societies practice primogeniture, in which only the eldest son inherits. Younger landless sons have poor prospects of becoming economically independent and may never be able to marry. This means also that many women will be unable to find marriage partners. Because there are fewer opportunities for unmarried daughters to be employed on a farm than unmarried sons, many young women leave to take up service in the households of the rich or migrate to towns searching for employment. This was as true in medieval Europe as it is in modern China.

A farmer teaches his son to plough, in an illumination from a 13th-century manuscript. Primogeniture in medieval Europe was a major stimulus to migration.

Though less dramatic than other forms of migration, home-community migration is biologically essential for healthy reproduction as it helps maintain a wide gene pool and prevent in-breeding within families. Because home-community migration is universal to all human societies, both present and historic, it is with the next three types of migration that this book is largely concerned.

Colonization occurs when a group of people leave one community to establish a replica of the home community in another place. This type of migration is not confined to humans; it is the main means by which animal species extend their geographical range. The earliest human migrations out of Africa are good examples of colonization of unoccupied territory. In more recent times successful colonization of territory has occurred where a technologically superior society has expelled its previous inhabitants, as was the case with the European colonization of Australia and the Americas. Colonists usually settle in environments similar to those of their home communities because this

makes it easier to preserve their accustomed way of life. This is an important advantage of colonization from the migrants' point of view because it enables them to settle into a new community without having to acclimatize themselves to an alien culture. Colonizing communities are usually ones that are already thriving and have surplus resources and population to invest in the effort.

Where migrants have tried to colonize radically different environments, they have often failed. European attempts at colonization in sub-Saharan Africa failed due to endemic tropical diseases to which Europeans had little resistance and the difficulties of adapting a lifestyle evolved for temperate climates to tropical conditions. Only in South Africa, which just reaches the southern temperate zone, and the relatively cool highlands of East Africa, was there any significant European settlement. Similarly, European colonizers of the tropical Caribbean had short life expectancy and died without issue. Their African slaves survived, despite their inhuman treatment, and it is their descendants who now form the majority populations in all Caribbean countries. In the pioneer stages of colonization, migrants tend to be mainly young adult males but the balance between the sexes is restored once the colony has been successfully established, as wives and families come to join their menfolk.

The propagandistic painting American Progress *(1872) by John Gast depicts an angel-like figure leading white settlers west to fulfil their 'manifest destiny' of colonizing the entire continent.*

Whole-community migration involves the displacement of all the members of a community. In historical times it has been relatively rare for humans to migrate en masse, but in prehistoric times, before the advent of settled agriculture, it was normal. Hunter-gatherers moved camp frequently to exploit seasonally available food sources. Other mobile communities include nomadic pastoralists who make regular seasonal migrations in search of new pastures for their flocks or herds. This way of life is known as transhumance. Whole communities may also migrate to escape natural disasters, such as famines, or they may be fleeing war or political oppression, or have been forcibly expelled from their homes by aggressors. The most famous example of this kind of migration is the biblical story of the Exodus.

Cross-community migration involves individuals or groups, most commonly of young adult men, from one community moving to join another community. Migrations of this kind can take many forms. Migrant labourers may move to work in another community with the intention of helping their home community by sending money home. Merchants may be seeking new trading opportunities. Wanderlust, flight from political or religious oppression or from justice, and expulsion are all factors. Migrants joining a new community may have to learn new languages and customs but at the same time they introduce new languages and customs.

A family of Blackfoot migrating to eastern Canada. In common with other Plains peoples, the livelihood of the Blackfoot was annihilated when white sport hunters hunted the American bison to near-extinction in the late 19th century.

Because of this, cross-community migration has always been the most important way that new ideas, skills and technologies have been spread around the world. An important type of cross-community migration is the diaspora (from Greek, meaning a 'scattering' or 'dispersal'). This term is used where migrants settle in another community but do not become fully assimilated with it and retain, to a greater or lesser degree, their original identity and culture. The term was originally used to describe the dispersal of Jews after the Babylonian and Roman conquests of Israel. It has also been used to describe the dispersal of Chinese, Gypsies, Armenians and Irish in more recent historical times.

DNA and migration

Until recently the study of migrations was the preserve of historians, archaeologists and geographers. However, in the last 20 years far the most important contributions to the study of migrations have come from geneticists, whose work has given unparalleled insights into the relationships between different populations and their likely origins. This began with the publication in 1987 of a groundbreaking study into the variation of mitochondrial DNA (mtDNA) of modern humans.

DNA is a complex self-replicating molecule that carries a cell's genetic material. The majority of a cell's DNA is

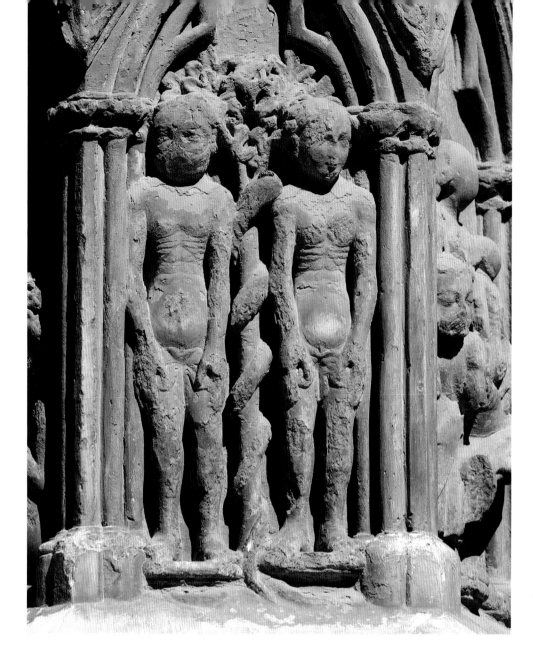

Common ancestors of us all? A carving of Adam and Eve on the exterior of Tarragona Cathedral in Spain.

carried on chromosomes in the cell's nucleus but a smaller amount is carried on thread-like membranes called mitochondria in the body of the cell outside the nucleus. MtDNA can be inherited only from the mother as the father's sperm cannot carry mtDNA. This makes it possible to use mtDNA to trace ancestry through the female line. Nuclear DNA is inherited from both parents and is subject to constant recombination. MtDNA, being inherited only from the mother, is not subject to recombination and is passed from mother to child through the generations unchanged except for random mutations. MtDNA mutates at an average rate of 2–4 percent per million years. By comparing the differences between the mtDNA of different individuals, or different species, it is possible by using this molecular clock to estimate the length of time that has elapsed since they shared a common female ancestor. For example, if there was a difference of 0.1 percent between the mtDNA of two people, it is probable that their last common female ancestor lived 50,000–100,000 years ago.

The 1987 study compared the mtDNA of several geographically widely separated populations. Analysis of the data revealed that all living humans share a common female

Bryan Sykes, Professor of Human Genetics at the University of Oxford, shown behind the autoradiograph (genetic footprint) obtained from the mitochondrial DNA (mtDNA) of the Ice Man, Otzi. Analysis of the mtDNA from the preserved 5,000 year-old body, discovered in an alpine glacier in Austria, revealed that many millions of Europeans today are genetically related to him.

ancestor who lived in Africa approximately 200,000 years ago. This female was immediately dubbed 'mitochondrial Eve'. The study also revealed that the variation in the mtDNA of African populations was twice as great as the variation in the mtDNA of populations in the rest of the world. Europeans are apparently more closely related to Australian Aborigines than western Africans are to southern Africans.

What does all this mean? About 200,000 years ago an African female – 'mitochondrial Eve' – passed on her mtDNA to her female children. As they in turn had female children, Eve's mtDNA became more and more widely spread. As generation succeeded generation, random mutations took place in the mtDNA, gradually widening the differences between her descendants. Between 100,000 and 70,000 years ago a small group of Eve's descendants, all of them closely related and therefore sharing similar mtDNA, migrated out of Africa and eventually their descendants spread out across the rest of the world. Thus Eve's African descendants have accumulated 200,000 years' worth of mtDNA mutations since sharing a common ancestor, while people in the rest of the world have had only half as long. This accounts for the greater genetic diversity of African populations as well as the relative lack of genetic variation in the rest of the world's population. It also shows that modern racial differences must have been acquired very recently in evolutionary terms, within the last 100,000 years.

Since 1987 further research into mtDNA and nuclear DNA, including the Y chromosome which is passed only through the male line, has helped further refine our understanding of the origins of different human populations. In the process it has forced a reappraisal of many long held beliefs about migrations. For instance, it was believed that Europe had experienced several major waves of inward migration, the first by the Cro-Magnons during the Ice Age, a second by farming peoples from the Middle East around 7000 years ago and a third by the Indo-Europeans, who introduced the forebears of most of the modern European languages, around 4000 years ago. It caused something of a sensation then, when, in 1997, DNA recovered from a 9000-year-old skeleton from Cheddar in England's West Country, was matched with a sample from a school teacher who lived within walking distance of the cave where the bones had been found. It has since become clear that most of the genetic diversity among modern Europeans originated as a result of population growth at the end of the Ice Age. This does not mean that there were no later migrations but it does mean that they involved much smaller numbers of people than was once thought.

Conclusions like this might make migrations seem less important as agents of change but if anything it does the opposite by showing that relatively small numbers of migrants, who may leave little genetic trace of their travels, can have disproportionately large cultural and linguistic impacts. It also demonstrates that culture and language, not genes, are the most important determinants of ethnic identity. Ethnic groups can appear to migrate by recruiting and assimilating people of different ethnic groups to their identity. This, rather than the large-scale movement of people (and their genes), may have been a major factor in the spread of the Celts in Iron Age Europe.

Isotope analysis

Further information about the movements of individuals can be gained using recently developed techniques for analysing isotopes of oxygen and strontium in bones and tooth enamel. As bones and teeth grow, they absorb oxygen and strontium from drinking water and food. Once it has formed, tooth enamel does not change through life, so its composition preserves evidence about an individual's childhood environment. Bone, on the other hand, is replaced in a seven- to ten-year cycle, so this preserves evidence about the environment where an individual lived in the last years of their life. There are three isotopes of oxygen, which vary slightly in weight. The exact ratio of heavy to light oxygen isotopes in water depends on its source (rain or snowmelt), distance from the sea and temperature: there are higher ratios of heavy isotopes in warmer climates. In 2002, this technique was applied to tooth enamel from a high-status man who was buried with archery gear near Amesbury, Wiltshire, England, around 2300 BC. Analysis revealed that he was an immigrant who had grown up far from the sea in a colder climate than England's, most likely in central Europe.

Strontium is a radioactive element that occurs in heavy and lighter isotopes. The ratio of heavy and light isotopes of strontium absorbed by bone and enamel depends upon the local geology. This provides another astonishingly precise tool for identifying the origins of human remains. Used on skeletons from a 16th-century cemetery at Campeche, Mexico, this technique was able to determine that five belonged to native Indians, three to Spanish immigrants and two to African slaves brought to Mexico by the Spanish.

As these, and other scientific methods of studying human remains, are refined and applied more widely, we can expect many more revelations about the true role and scale of migration in human history.

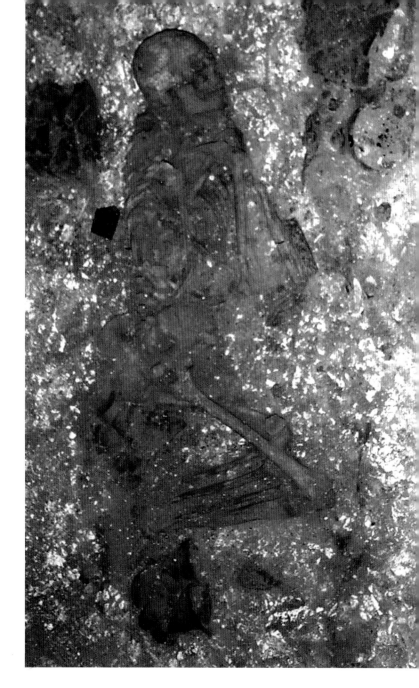

Isotope analysis of tooth enamel enabled scientists to determine that the 'Amesbury Archer' (above), whose remains were found in southern England in 2002, probably came from the Alps.

Out of Africa
1.9 MILLION—15,000 YEARS AGO

The world was first colonized by humans in distant prehistory, long before our ancestors had invented the wheel, learned to ride horses or acquired shipbuilding skills. For most of our existence as a species, humans have gone everywhere on foot. All modern apes have an innate tendency to colonize new territories, but they evolved in forests and find climbing easier than walking. More than anything else, what first opened up the world to human colonization was bipedalism – the ability to walk upright on two legs. While rare in mammals, bipedalism is an energy-efficient form of locomotion and is common animal groups, such as birds and dinosaurs.

East Africa is generally recognized as being the cradle of human evolution. Bipedalism may have evolved in early humans in response to climatic changes which led to forests being replaced by more open savannah, tropical grassland with patches of woodland. Individuals that could cross open grassland efficiently and travel from one area of woodland to another without getting eaten by a hyena on the way could greatly increase their food resources and enjoy more breeding success. The earliest human species for which there is good fossil evidence of bipedalism, *Australopithecus afarensis* ('southern ape from Afar'), lived around 3.5 to 4 million years ago and was already fully adapted to bipedalism. Later species of *Australopithecus* had become widespread on the savannahs of sub-Saharan Africa by around 3 million years ago.

The dawn of 'upright man'

The first human species known to have lived outside Africa was *Homo erectus* ('upright man'). First appearing around 1.9 million years ago in East Africa, *H. erectus* had spread as far north as Georgia and as far east as Java in little more than 100,000 years. In warm periods its range extended north into Europe and China. *Homo erectus* was the first hominin that we would recognize as being indisputably human, with fully modern body proportions. In its head and face, *H. erectus* would still have looked disconcertingly ape-like, with a projecting jaw, receding chin, flat nose, a pronounced brow ridge and a low, flat brain case, which had only about two-thirds the capacity of a modern human's. *Homo erectus* made simple tools of stone and wood and sometimes made use of fire and built simple shelters of branches. Whether *H. erectus* had any form of structured language is unknown, but there were no physical obstacles to it having some form of speech.

Savannah and mountains in Tanzania, east Africa. Open landscape such as this may have been responsible for the evolution of bipedalism in early humans, which was fundamental to their ability to migrate.

The ability of *H. erectus* to adapt to its environment was far more limited than that of modern humans but, while earlier human species lived mainly on savannah, *H. erectus* colonized tropical forests and temperate grasslands too. The appearance of *H. erectus* coincided with the beginning of the Pleistocene Ice Ages (*c.*1.8 million to 10,000 years ago), a period of climatic instability marked by cold glacial periods and warmer inter-glacial periods. Low sea levels during glacial periods would have offered *erectus* two routes out of Africa: along the Nile Valley through the Sahara to the Mediterranean or across the dry bed of the Red Sea to Arabia. The same low sea levels allowed *H. erectus* to spread through the archipelagos of Indonesia as far as Java without ever having to get its feet wet. This was the end of the line for *H. erectus*. Although low sea levels during glacial periods meant that Australia could have been reached from Indonesia by island-hopping voyages of less than 50 miles (80 km), there is no evidence that *H. erectus* did so.

Homo erectus found Southeast Asia a congenial place to live, and survived there until as recently as 50,000 years ago, possibly even 27,000 years ago. Its longevity – nearly 2 million years – makes *H. erectus* easily the most successful human species. Elsewhere *erectus* was subject to greater evolutionary pressures. In western Asia and southern Europe it evolved, via an intermediate species called *H. heidelbergensis* (Heidelberg man), into Neanderthal man (*H. neanderthalensis*) by around 200,000 years ago. The Neanderthals were physically adapted to live in a cool climate, with their stocky body shape and short arms and legs. These features helped conserve body heat by reducing the body's surface area relative to its mass. Neanderthals had brains that were slightly larger than ours but of a different shape, suggesting they had different cognitive abilities. A low forehead, bulging nose (another cold-climate adaptation, serving to warm the air before it reached the lungs), protruding jaw and receding chin would have made Neanderthals ugly to our eyes but still recognizably human. Neanderthals had the technology to clean hides, so may have worn some kind of clothing, and had mastered the use of fire. This combination of physical and technological adaptation allowed them to extend their range through Europe as far north as Britain during inter-glacial periods. Physically far stronger than modern humans, Neanderthals were tough hunters capable of tackling even a mammoth.

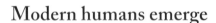

A reconstruction of Neanderthal man. Anthropologists have established that as long as 200,000 years ago, this early hominin had mastered the art of making fire.

Modern humans emerge

In Africa *H. erectus* evolved, through several intermediate species with steadily increasing brain sizes, into anatomically modern *H. sapiens* ('wise man') by around 150,000 years ago. However, there is no evidence that the first modern humans behaved any differently from their predecessors, suggesting that cognitive abilities evolved more slowly. Modern humans gradually show signs of more flexible and adaptive behaviour through the exploitation of a wider range of food sources and new, more efficient tool-making techniques. But it is only around 50,000 years ago that clear evidence emerges for the production of art, the ceremonial disposal of the dead and

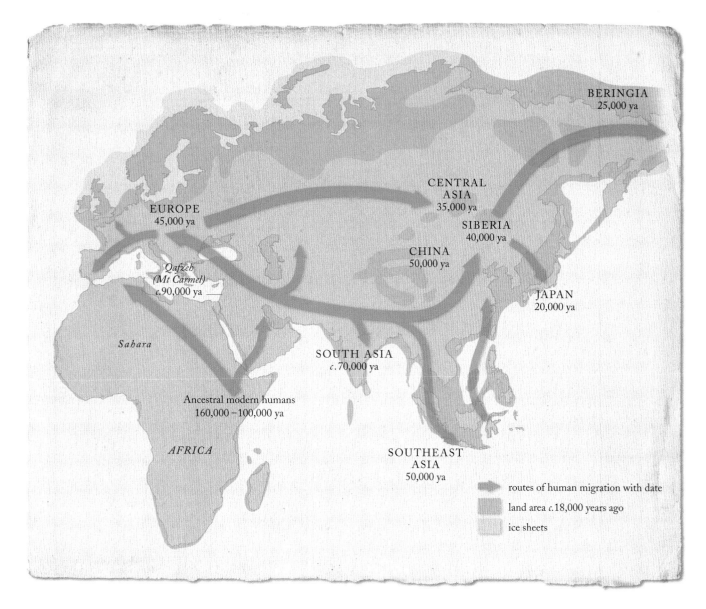

Map showing modern human (Homo sapiens) migrations in the Old World.

the use of body ornaments – all of which are indicative of a fully modern capacity for abstract and symbolic thought and structured language. Earlier human species had been confined to the environments for which they had evolved. Their new abilities made modern humans into the ultimate, infinitely adaptable generalists, freed from environmental constraints and able to make a home in every part of the globe.

Pioneering migrants

Modern humans began to migrate out of Africa during a mild inter-glacial period about 100,000 years ago. It is most likely that they followed the Nile Valley, since the oldest fossils of *H. sapiens* from outside Africa – dating to around 90,000 years ago – have been found in caves on Mount Carmel in Israel. This venture proved to be a false start: these pioneers soon died out and European Neanderthals moved into their caves. Around 70,000 years ago another group of modern humans left Africa, this time probably crossing the dry bed of the Red Sea from the Horn of Africa to Arabia. This group flourished and over the next 50,000 years its descendants would colonize every corner of the world except for Antarctica, the high Arctic and some oceanic islands. The number of humans who finally made it out of Africa was very small indeed. Studies of mitochondrial DNA have shown that, compared to Africans, there is little genetic

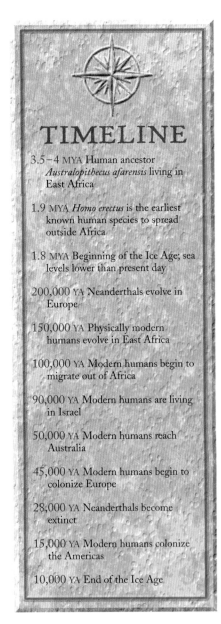

TIMELINE

3.5–4 MYA Human ancestor *Australopithecus afarensis* living in East Africa

1.9 MYA *Homo erectus* is the earliest known human species to spread outside Africa

1.8 MYA Beginning of the Ice Age; sea levels lower than present day

200,000 YA Neanderthals evolve in Europe

150,000 YA Physically modern humans evolve in East Africa

100,000 YA Modern humans begin to migrate out of Africa

90,000 YA Modern humans are living in Israel

50,000 YA Modern humans reach Australia

45,000 YA Modern humans begin to colonize Europe

28,000 YA Neanderthals become extinct

15,000 YA Modern humans colonize the Americas

10,000 YA End of the Ice Age

diversity among non-Africans, indicating that they are all descended from a single small group of common ancestors, perhaps only a few dozen strong.

Humanity's journey out of Africa was slow but steady. All early humans lived by hunting, fishing and gathering wild plant foods. As population increased in one area, putting the natural resources under strain, breakaway bands moved on a few miles further into new territory. As generation succeeded generation the area of the world colonized by humans gradually increased.

The evidence of mtDNA shows that, after reaching Arabia, the population divided into two groups. One moved east, probably following the coast of the Indian Ocean, reaching Southeast Asia and southern China by 50,000 years ago, while the other remained in the Middle East, its progress temporarily blocked by the Neanderthals. From the first group are descended the Negrito peoples of Southeast Asia, the Papuans of New Guinea and the Australian Aborigines; and from the second, Europeans, Asians and Native Americans.

Low sea levels during glacial periods aided the migrations of modern humans through Southeast Asia just as they had those of *H. erectus* so long before. Modern humans must have encountered these, by now, anachronistic humans, for they existed side by side in Southeast Asia for many thousands of years before *H. erectus* eventually became extinct. There is no genetic evidence for inter-breeding or hybridization between modern humans and *H. erectus*. The likely fate of *erectus* is that it was either exterminated by the newcomers or was pushed out of its hunting grounds. By the time they reached Java, modern humans must have acquired basic seafaring skills because the earliest evidence of human colonization of Australia and New Guinea dates to around 45,000 years ago (see The First Seafarers, pages 22–25).

Neanderthals and Cro-Magnons

It was not until about 5000 years after the colonization of Australia that modern humans finally began to migrate into Europe. It says much for the development of modern humans' adaptive abilities that this coincided with the beginning of the last, and most severe, glaciation of the Ice Age. Similarities in tool types show that these first modern Europeans, known as Cro-Magnons after a fossil site in France, originated in the Middle East. The Cro-Magnons were primarily hunters of reindeer, horses and bison. On the open plains of eastern Europe, the Cro-Magnons lived in huts of mammoth bones. In the west they favoured cave sites in sheltered valleys and it was there that they created the world's first great art. The Cro-Magnons would have been familiar with the native Neanderthals. For thousands of years the territories of both species had overlapped in the Middle East but modern humans had plainly now acquired a small but decisive advantage over the Neanderthals because they were able to displace them completely and drive them to extinction. What that advantage was is the subject of much debate.

Unlike the Neanderthals, modern humans were not physically adapted to cold climates, but they brought with them a more diverse tool kit. This included needles, so they would have been able to make warm tailored clothing to help them survive in a cold climate. Unlike modern humans, the Neanderthals did not make art, suggesting that they lacked the modern species' powers of abstract and symbolic thought. This may have manifested itself also in less developed language skills, making them less able to communicate information and co-operate as a group than the moderns. It is also clear that Neanderthals lived in isolated groups and did not stray far from their home bases. In this way they were probably at a serious disadvantage to the incomers, who maximized their food-gathering opportunities by migrating regularly with the seasons.

Modern humans also maintained contacts with other groups in order to trade tool-making stone and, no doubt, mates, thus allowing new technology and ideas to spread widely. One sign of this is the existence of Stone Age 'Venus' figurines, which can be found from the Ukraine to the Atlantic and are indications of a widespread cult that flourished around 25,000 years ago. For example, there is some evidence that Neanderthals copied Cro-Magnon tool-making techniques and even their habit of wearing necklaces of teeth or shells. However, Neanderthal culture was gradually displaced and pushed inexorably west. Their last strongholds were in Spain and Portugal, where they held out until about 28,000 years ago. Comparison of the DNA of Neanderthals and present-day Europeans suggests that inter-breeding between the two species is unlikely.

The human colonization of the Old World was finally completed around 15,000 years ago. At about the same time that modern humans from the Middle East began to move into Europe, they were also pushing north of the Himalayas into the steppes of central Asia, reaching Siberia and northern China around 35,000 years ago and, amazingly in this coldest period of the Ice Age, the shores of the Arctic Ocean only 5000 years later. Though exceptionally cold, northern Siberia at this time was largely free of glaciers thanks to its dry climate, and its vast tundra was rich in game such as mammoth and reindeer.

Low sea levels allowed the tundra to extend eastward unbroken across the Bering Strait into Alaska. Around 15,000 years ago, if not before, hunters following these herds east had crossed the Bering Straits, into Alaska (see The First Americans, pages 26–29). Further progress was blocked by the vast Laurentide ice sheet, which spanned the continent from the Pacific to the Atlantic. Exactly how and when humans overcame this obstacle to settle the New World is still disputed.

The Venus of Willendorf, a figurine believed to date from 24,000 –22,000 BC. Found in 1908 in a village in Austria, it is carved from a type of limestone that is not local to the area, indicating that it originated elsewhere in Europe.

The First Seafarers
c.50,000 YEARS AGO

Australia's Aboriginal peoples call the era of creation and the spirit ancestors the Dreamtime. Stories about the Dreamtime, passed down through countless generations, relate how their spirit ancestors came to Australia from the northwest, crossing the sea in canoes. These stories preserve distant memories of humankind's earliest maritime migration.

During the Ice Age global sea levels fell by as much as 120 metres (400 ft), causing major changes to the world's landmasses. The impact was at its most dramatic in eastern Asia and Australasia. Until about 8000 years ago, Australia, New Guinea and Tasmania formed a vast island-continent known as Sahul. The Bering Sea, which today separates Asia from North America, was dry land, Japan was joined to Korea, and Ceylon to India. In Southeast Asia the South China Sea and the Java Sea retreated so far that the Malayan Peninsula was linked to Sumatra, Java and Borneo by a vast forested lowland called Sundaland. From northern Borneo a land bridge extended north, linking the Philippines to the mainland. These low sea levels enabled both *Homo erectus* and modern humans to spread widely through Southeast Asia without seafaring skills. Beyond Java the seas are deeper. Even in the coldest glaciations, sea levels never dropped enough to link Sahul to Sundaland by a land bridge, but between them stretched a chain of islands, none of which was separated by more than 50 miles (80 km) of warm, tropical sea. Today 200 miles (320 km) of open sea separates the most southerly Indonesian islands from Australia.

The 'hobbit' of Southeast Asia

The first small steps along the chain islands east of Java were taken long before the arrival of modern humans in the area. In the 1990s stone tools dated to 800,000 years ago were found on the Indonesian island of Flores. Though even today Flores lies no more than 10 miles (16 km) from its closest neighbour, it was never at any time connected to the mainland. Therefore, whoever left these tools must have crossed the sea to get there. The only human species then known to be living in Southeast Asia at that time was *H. erectus*, but there is no evidence that it possessed the ability to make boats or rafts. The mystery deepened in 2004 when fossils of a human species only 91 centimetres (3 ft) tall were found on the same island. Named *H. floresiensis* ('man from Flores'), it was quickly dubbed 'the hobbit' by the world's press. Despite having a brain only about one-quarter the size of a modern human's, *H. floresiensis* used fire, was a skilled tool-maker and lived by hunting the island's giant rats and pygmy elephants.

The Flores 'hobbit' resembles a miniature version of *H. erectus* and may have evolved from a group of *erectus* who experienced a phenomenon known as island dwarfism after

becoming isolated on Flores. Among large mammals living in confined environments, there is an adaptive advantage in smaller body sizes because they need less food. In smaller mammals the process works in reverse because of the lack of large predators. Because it is unlikely that they could build boats, the ancestors of *H. floresiensis* were probably accidental seafarers, swept out to sea by a tsunami as they foraged along the shore, along with other terrestrial animals such as rats, monkeys and elephants.

From Sundaland to Sahul

The first humans we can say with confidence took to the sea deliberately were the ancestors of the modern Australian Aborigines and of the Papuan peoples of New Guinea. While in warm tropical seas it would have been possible for humans to survive in the water long enough to be washed accidentally a few miles from one island to another, the distances involved in a crossing from Sundaland to Sahul are such that some sort of watercraft must have been used. Because of the rise in sea level since the end of

An artist's drawing of the 'hobbit'-sized human, Homo floresiensis. *The partial skeleton of an adult female of the species was found in a cave on the Indonesian island of Flores in 2004. Its chimpanzee-sized brain is substantially different from that of a modern human.*

the Ice Age, any remains of the boats used by the settlers are submerged under several hundred feet of water and are unlikely ever to be found. In historical times, Australian Aborigines lacked advanced boat-building skills so it is probable that their ancestors arrived on simple rafts of logs or, more likely, bamboo. Whereas logs can become waterlogged and lose buoyancy, bamboo stems are coated with silica and are both highly buoyant and resistant to water. The first watercraft were probably built for fishing and short island-hopping trips along the coasts of Sundaland rather than for exploration. The experience of Aboriginal seafarers in recent historic times shows that rafting is dangerous; inevitably some of these early seafarers would have been blown out to sea. Some of the luckier ones may have discovered Sahul by accident. Once its existence was known, finding such a large landmass again would have been a simple matter.

Two routes were suitable for migration: a northern route from Borneo via Sulawesi and the Molucca islands to New Guinea, and a southern one from Java via Lombok, Flores and Timor to Arnhem Land in northwest Australia. The date of the first colonization of Sahul is uncertain since most well-dated archaeological sites are a long way from the areas where the original landfalls must have been made. The earliest evidence of occupation in New Guinea comes from the east of the island and dates to 38–45,000 years ago. A site at Lake Mungo in southeast Australia dates to 33,000 years ago and one at Bluff in Tasmania shows that humans had reached the southernmost tip of the continent by 31,000 years ago. These dates hint that humans may have been present in Australasia as long as 50,000 years ago.

Australasia's first inhabitants

Fossils of early humans from Australia show a variety of physical types, from robust to lightly built, gracile people. This suggests that the colonization of Sahul occurred in several waves and at different places. The characteristic prominent brows of Aboriginals led to speculation that their ancestors may have interbred with *H. erectus* in Southeast Asia before they reached Australia, but genetic research has ruled out this possibility. The distinctive physical features of Aboriginals evolved only after they arrived in Australia.

The early inhabitants of Australia and New Guinea lived by hunting, fishing and gathering plant foods. In New Guinea people began to practise agriculture about 5000 years ago but the Aborigines never adopted this way of life, because of a lack of native plants and animals suitable for domestication rather than any reluctance on their part. In some remote areas, the ancient Aboriginal way of life survives, making it perhaps the world's oldest continuous cultural tradition.

Map showing the migration of early humans from Southeast Asia to Australia. Because there was never a land bridge linking the landmasses, the first Australians must have used simple boats to make the voyage 50,000 years ago.

PACIFIC OCEAN

PHILIPPINES

Sunda Shelf

Niah Cave 40,000 ya

BORNEO

NEW GUINEA

JAVA

Flores

Wadjak 50,000 ya

Sahul Shelf

Bobangara 38,000 ya

INDIAN OCEAN

AUSTRALIA

Devil's Lair 34,000 ya

Lake Mungo 33,000 ya

Kow Swamp 14,000 ya

migration route

early human sites with date

ancient landmass

Bluff Rock Shelter 31,000 ya

Ubirr is one of more than 5000 recorded sites of Aboriginal rock art at Kakadu National Park in Australia's Northern Territory. This painting depicts a spirit ancestor, known as a Mimi Spirit, carrying a spear thrower and a bag.

In Australia the ancestral Aborigines found an exotic fauna dominated by giant marsupials, flightless birds and reptiles. The deadliest of these was *Megalania*, a 9-metre (30-ft) lizard that ambushed unwary prey in the undergrowth. Other monsters included *Thylacoleo* (a lion-sized carnivore) and *Procoptodon*, a 3-metre- (10-ft-) tall kangaroo. According to Aboriginal legend, the boomerang was invented to deal with this last beast.

By about 20,000 years ago Australia's exotic megafauna had become extinct. Increasingly arid conditions associated with the end of the Ice Age are sometimes blamed for this, but the megafauna had survived such climatic changes many times before the arrival of humans. Over-hunting by the Aborigines may have contributed to the mass extinction but the evidence is inconclusive. A more subtle factor may have been the way the Aborigines managed the environment by lighting bush fires. This encourages the growth of fresh grass shoots, which attracts grazing animals, such as the smaller kangaroos. Over centuries, however, burning also created a more open landscape with fewer trees – to the disadvantage of browsing animals, which most of the megafauna were. By the time Europeans began to explore Australia in the 18th century it was far from being the natural wilderness they thought it to be.

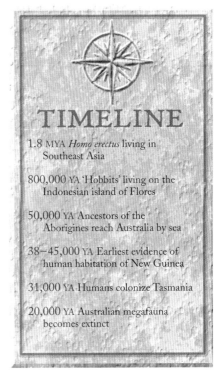

TIMELINE

1.8 MYA *Homo erectus* living in Southeast Asia

800,000 YA 'Hobbits' living on the Indonesian island of Flores

50,000 YA Ancestors of the Aborigines reach Australia by sea

38–45,000 YA Earliest evidence of human habitation of New Guinea

31,000 YA Humans colonize Tasmania

20,000 YA Australian megafauna becomes extinct

The First Americans
C.15,000 YEARS AGO

The last continents to be settled by humans were the Americas. When, by whom and how this happened are the subjects of one the most intense debates in archaeology. It has long been believed that the ancestors of the Amerindians arrived in a single overland migration at the end of the Ice Age, but a more complex picture is now emerging.

There is little doubt that the origins of modern Native North Americans lie in northeast Asia. It has long been recognized that Native North Americans and northeast Asians share a similar eye shape, similar hair type and a distinctive dental pattern. More recently comparison of DNA has confirmed the close relationship. All four main mtDNA lineages found in modern Native North Americans are linked to northeast Asia. A fifth minor lineage, X mtDNA, is also found in Europeans but, as European-type people were present in Siberia in the Ice Age, this is also likely to have arrived in the Americas from northeast Asia. Research into the Y chromosomes of Native North Americans also confirms the northeast Asian connection.

According to the most widely accepted view, ancestors of the Native North Americans, known as Palaeo-Indians, reached America by crossing the Bering Strait from Siberia to Alaska. The earliest evidence of human occupation of Alaska dates to around 15,000 years ago; it is unlikely that humans were present long before that since eastern Siberia itself was not colonized by humans much before 20,000 years ago. Reaching the Americas would have been a simple matter. Between 100,000 and 10,000 years ago so much water was locked up in ice sheets that the Bering Strait was dry land. Despite the bitter cold, the area had a dry climate and herds of mammoth, musk oxen, reindeer and other herbivores roamed freely over the tundra. Patches of woodland offered some shelter and fuel for any hunters following these herds. That hunters from Siberia did so is clear. The earliest inhabitants of northeast Siberia were the people of the Dyuktai culture (*c*.20,000 – 10,000 years ago), big-game hunters whose distinctive stone tools, including microblades and bifacially worked spearheads, have also been found at early sites in Alaska and the Yukon.

Alaska, initially, was a dead end. Further progress into the Americas was blocked by a vast ice sheet extending across the entire continent from the Pacific coast ranges east to the Atlantic and south beyond the Great Lakes. As the Ice Age drew to a close, the continental ice sheet began to retreat and by around 13,000 years ago had split into two, the Cordilleran, covering the

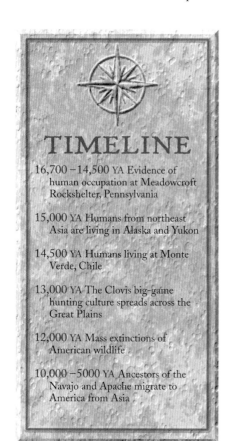

TIMELINE

16,700 – 14,500 YA Evidence of human occupation at Meadowcroft Rockshelter, Pennsylvania

15,000 YA Humans from northeast Asia are living in Alaska and Yukon

14,500 YA Humans living at Monte Verde, Chile

13,000 YA The Clovis big-game hunting culture spreads across the Great Plains

12,000 YA Mass extinctions of American wildlife

10,000 – 5000 YA Ancestors of the Navajo and Apache migrate to America from Asia

Rocky Mountains, and the Laurentide, centred on Hudson Bay. Between the two was an ice-free passage along which Palaeo-Indian hunters migrated to reach the Great Plains.

Early Plains cultures

The arrival of the Palaeo-Indians on the Great Plains is marked by finds of beautifully worked fluted spearheads (known as Clovis points after an important archaeological site in New Mexico) at sites from Alaska in the north, south almost to Panama and east to the Appalachians. The style of these spearheads strongly suggests that they are a development of the Dyuktai tradition. Clovis points were among the most effective of Stone Age weapons and have been found with the butchered remains of mammoths, showing that they were capable of inflicting a fatal wound on even the largest game. At this time, the Great Plains were a hunter's paradise, with herds of mammoth, bison,

Frozen landscape seen in Alaska today. Migration to the Americas probably began during the Ice Age, when huge ice sheets caused sea levels to drop and the Bering Strait linking Siberia to Alaska was dry land.

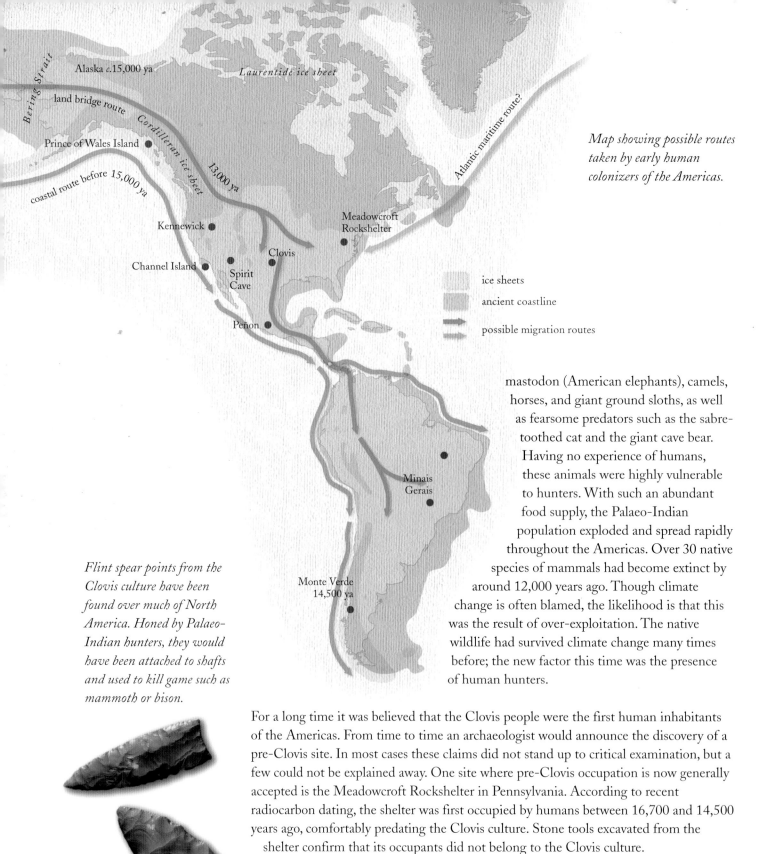

Map showing possible routes taken by early human colonizers of the Americas.

Flint spear points from the Clovis culture have been found over much of North America. Honed by Palaeo-Indian hunters, they would have been attached to shafts and used to kill game such as mammoth or bison.

mastodon (American elephants), camels, horses, and giant ground sloths, as well as fearsome predators such as the sabre-toothed cat and the giant cave bear. Having no experience of humans, these animals were highly vulnerable to hunters. With such an abundant food supply, the Palaeo-Indian population exploded and spread rapidly throughout the Americas. Over 30 native species of mammals had become extinct by around 12,000 years ago. Though climate change is often blamed, the likelihood is that this was the result of over-exploitation. The native wildlife had survived climate change many times before; the new factor this time was the presence of human hunters.

For a long time it was believed that the Clovis people were the first human inhabitants of the Americas. From time to time an archaeologist would announce the discovery of a pre-Clovis site. In most cases these claims did not stand up to critical examination, but a few could not be explained away. One site where pre-Clovis occupation is now generally accepted is the Meadowcroft Rockshelter in Pennsylvania. According to recent radiocarbon dating, the shelter was first occupied by humans between 16,700 and 14,500 years ago, comfortably predating the Clovis culture. Stone tools excavated from the shelter confirm that its occupants did not belong to the Clovis culture.

Where could these people have come from? One theory, based on a supposed similarity between the Meadowcroft tools and those of the Solutrean culture (*c.*19,000–16,000 years ago) of Ice Age western Europe, is that the occupants were Cro-Magnon Europeans who had crossed the Atlantic by following the edge of the Arctic pack ice, which at that time extended as far south as Britain and Nova Scotia. Seals that bred along the edge of the pack ice could have provided food and fuel oil. But it seems unlikely: despite being superbly adapted to Arctic life, even the modern Inuit do not spend long periods living on pack ice.

The most important pre-Clovis site so far discovered is at Monte Verde in Chile. This site has unequivocal evidence of human occupation around 14,500 years ago, including hearths, stone, wood and bone tools, and a shelter covered with mastodon hides. The only plausible explanation for the presence of humans at Monte Verde so early is that there was a pre-Clovis migration into the Americas from northeast Asia that by-passed the continental ice sheet by following the Pacific coast. Although the coastal ranges of Alaska and British Columbia were heavily glaciated, there were ice-free areas along the coast, making such a journey more likely than an Atlantic crossing. Any archaeological evidence which could confirm this hypothesis is now likely to have been submerged by post-glacial rises in sea level, but it is supported by a small amount of fossil evidence.

A Japanese connection?

The oldest human skull so far found in the Americas, a 13,000-year-old female skull from Peñon in Mexico, has a long narrow shape and a low face unlike those of modern Native Americans. A 12,500-year-old female skull from Minais Gerais in Brazil is similarly shaped, as are slightly more recent skulls from Spirit Cave, Nevada and Kennewick, Washington. Anthropological studies suggest a relationship with the Ainu, an aboriginal Japanese people whose ancestors were making open-sea voyages to offshore islands 20,000 years ago. It is possible that fishermen and seal-hunters from Japan, sailing along the Pacific coast, could have reached America long before the Clovis people. However, this skeletal evidence is not conclusive proof. Early modern human populations in other parts of the world also show considerable physical variation, as racial characteristics were still developing. Recent genetic research has discovered what may be a trace of this coastal migration. A rare pattern in DNA from a 10,000-year-old skeleton excavated in On-Your-Knees Cave on Prince of Wales Island, Alaska, has also been found in descendants of the Chumash people of California's Channel Islands and the indigenous people of Tierra del Fuego at the southern tip of South America.

If the Clovis migration was not the first, it was also not the last. MtDNA evidence shows that the ancestors of the Na-Dene Native American group, which includes the Navajo and Apache, may have arrived on the continent from northeast Asia only 5000– 10,000 years ago. And later still came the ancestors of the Aleuts and Inuit, who completed the human occupation of the Americas by settling the high Arctic.

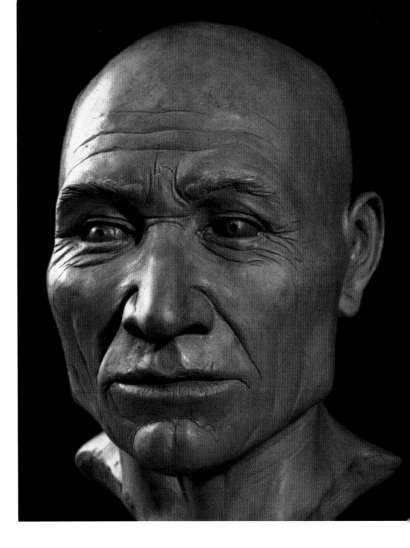

A facial reconstruction of 'Kennewick Man', whose 9000-year-old remains were found in the Columbia River in Washington State in 1996. Kennewick Man's physical features differed from those of modern Native Americans, possibly supporting the pre-Clovis migration theory.

The Indo-Europeans
c.3500–1500 BC

The Indo-Europeans were an obscure prehistoric Eurasian people. They left no written records and it is not certain exactly when and where they lived. Yet their migrations across the planet have had a global impact; today, Indo-European languages are spoken on every continent on Earth and by over half of the world's people.

The language of the Indo-Europeans, Proto-Indo-European (or PIE for short), is the ancestor of many of the world's most widely spoken languages, including English. A migratory people, the Indo-Europeans spread their language into India, the Middle East and Europe, where it began to diversify into modern language forms as different groups settled down and lost contact with one another. The family is divided into nine branches: Indo-Aryan (which includes Hindi, Farsi – or Iranian – and Urdu), Greek, Celtic, Armenian, Baltic, Slavic (including Russian and Polish), Illyrian (Albanian), Romance (including French, Italian and Spanish) and Germanic (including English, at present the most widely spoken Indo-European language).

The discovery of the Indo-Europeans was the achievement not of historians and archaeologists but of a lawyer, Sir William Jones (1746–94). Appointed chief justice of India in 1783, Jones, an accomplished amateur linguist, began a study of the ancient Indian Sanskrit language used in the Hindu scriptures. He quickly realized that its grammar and vocabulary had much in common with Latin, ancient Greek, Gothic (an extinct early Germanic language), the Celtic languages and Farsi. From this he deduced that they had all developed from a common ancestor which had been the language of a single people. In the course of the 19th century German linguists began to put flesh on the bare bones of Jones's discovery, painstakingly reconstructing a surprising amount of the grammar and vocabulary of Proto-Indo-European by comparing the common elements of the modern Indo-European languages.

The mutation of language

Linguists also attempted to date the divergence of the different branches of the Indo-European languages by comparing accumulated differences in vocabulary, grammar and pronunciation, in much the same way as geneticists date the branching out of new species by comparing the accumulation of mutations in DNA. Unfortunately, there is no linguistic equivalent of a molecular clock and no way to take account of the influences languages have on one another. Linguistic changes do not accumulate at a steady rate – some languages are conservative while others experience periods of rapid change. Ancient Greek is

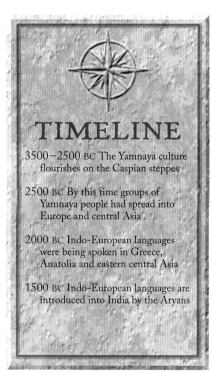

TIMELINE

3500–2500 BC The Yamnaya culture flourishes on the Caspian steppes

2500 BC By this time groups of Yamnaya people had spread into Europe and central Asia

2000 BC Indo-European languages were being spoken in Greece, Anatolia and eastern central Asia

1500 BC Indo-European languages are introduced into India by the Aryans

still intelligible to modern Greeks, for example, but Old English – the form of English spoken before the Norman Conquest of 1066 – might as well be a foreign language as far as modern English speakers are concerned.

The reconstructed vocabulary of PIE has provided many clues about the origins and way of life of the original Indo-Europeans. They had a word for snow, and the wildlife and trees they were familiar with (their vocabulary included otter, beaver, elk, red deer, bear, hare, fish, beech, ash and birch) show that they lived in a temperate area, with rivers and woodland. However, they had no word for sea, so presumably they lived inland. The foundation of the Indo-European economy was pastoralism – they had words for sheep, cow, horse, pig and goat. They must have grown some crops, as they also had words for plough, sickle and grain; they used wagons, knew about copper and bronze but not iron, and wove cloth on looms. Their society was hierarchical (they had a word for king), with three classes: warriors, priests and labourers. Cattle raiding was an important activity and bows and arrows were used in battle. They were polytheists whose chief deity was a male sky god called Dyeus-peter ('Sky-father'), best known today by the Roman name, Jupiter.

Despite these clues, we cannot identify the Indo-European homeland with any certainty. One possibility, favoured by many archaeologists, is that PIE developed in Anatolia and spread through Europe and Asia by migrating early agricultural peoples between 8000 and 6000 years ago. If true, this would help solve some thorny problems in European prehistory (such as the origins of the Celts; see pages 46–51). But the consensus among linguists is that an original Indo-European homeland somewhere in east-central Europe or west-central Asia fits the linguistic evidence best.

Many attempts have been made to locate the homeland more precisely by identifying a specific archaeological culture with the early Indo-Europeans. The most convincing

Sanskrit writing on a column of the eastern tower of the ancient temple Ta Keo, at Angkor Thom, Cambodia. It was through his studies of Sanskrit that the 18th-century linguist Sir William Jones first identified Proto-Indo-European as the common ancestor of many modern languages.

candidate so far proposed is the Yamnaya culture, which flourished *c.*3500 −2500 BC on the steppes north of the Caspian Sea. The Yamnaya people used copper and bronze, but not iron, and were the earliest to combine pastoralism with wheeled vehicles. This mobility allowed the Yamnaya people to adopt a migratory lifestyle, moving their flocks and herds long distances across the steppes in search of fresh pastures. By 2500 BC groups of Yamnaya people had spread east of the Urals onto the Asian steppes and west across the Ukrainian steppes into southeast Europe. The Yamnaya people had a hierarchical society and buried their leaders in pits under barrows known as *kurgans*. Identifying them with the Indo-Europeans also fits well with what is known about the spread of Indo-European languages to other areas. It is known that Indo-European languages were being spoken in Greece, Anatolia and east-central Asia soon after 2000 BC and in India by around 1500 BC.

If most of what we know about the Indo-Europeans comes from linguistics, it is archaeology that has given them a face. In the 1980s a number of 3000 − 4000-year-old mummies were found in the high, cold and extremely arid steppes of the Tarim Basin in Chinese Turkestan. Because they had been buried in permafrost, they are exceptionally well preserved. The Tarim Basin is inhabited today by Turkic and Mongoloid peoples but these mummies resembled neither. They were tall, had deep, round eye sockets and prominent noses, light hair and fair skin. They often had elaborate tattoos and were dressed in tartan. Their appearance is very similar to contemporary descriptions of the ancient Celts and Germans, but these people were the ancestors of the Tocharians, a nomad people who spoke a now extinct branch of Indo-European.

The tattoos on the arm and shoulder of a 2400-year-old mummy known as the 'Ice Maiden' found in the Altai Mountains on the Russian-Mongolian border are remarkably well preserved thanks to the permafrost in which the remains lay buried. The Ice Maiden is believed to have belonged to a nomadic Indo-European people known as the Scythians.

The death of indigenous languages

Although it is impossible to reconstruct the migrations of the Indo-Europeans out of their homeland, the dramatic consequences are easily understood. In both Europe and the Indian subcontinent there was an almost complete and very rapid replacement of earlier languages by Indo-European languages. Apart from a few isolated groups, such as the Brahui of Pakistan, non-Indo-European languages are now confined to the south of the subcontinent. Indo-Europeans did not enter western Europe much before 2000 BC, yet only a few hundred years later just a handful of pre-Indo-European languages were still spoken, the most important being Iberian, Etruscan and Minoan. None of these survived into the Christian era. Today, Euskara, the language of the Basques, spoken by a mere 800,000 people, is the only survivor of these ancient tongues. While they are not physically distinguishable from their neighbours, Basques are genetically distinct, having the lowest frequency of Rh-negative B and O blood groups in Europe. Is this evidence that as well as language replacement there was population replacement? Almost certainly not, because DNA lineages of other modern Europeans can also be traced back to pre-

Indo-European times. Indo-European languages were probably spread only partly by mass migrations – another means may have been the conquest of non-Indo-European speakers by a small Indo-European-speaking élite, with the conquered peoples subsequently becoming assimilated to the language and identity of their conquerors. In other cases the influence of trade and social contacts may have been important. There are no clues as to the reasons for the Indo-Europeans' success; nor is there any evidence from their language of military or technological superiority compared with other European, Middle Eastern and Indian peoples of the time.

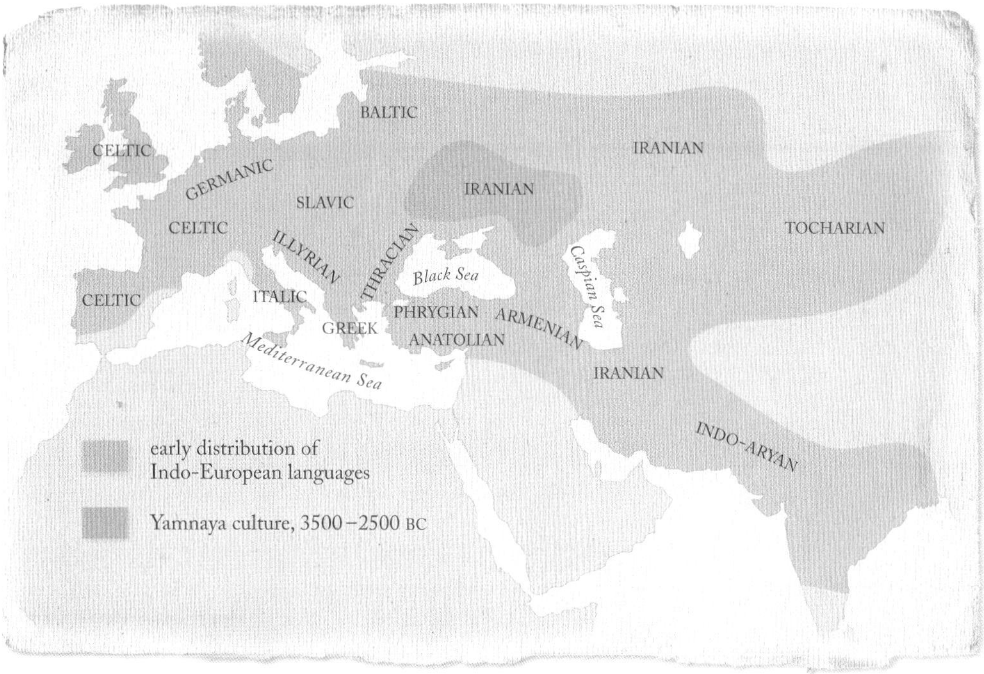

Map showing the early distribution of the major Indo-European language groups.

The influence of the Indo-European migrations was not confined to language. Only one branch of the Indo-Europeans left any record of its migrations. These were the Aryans, who crossed the Hindu Kush into northern India around 1500 BC. Around 1000 BC the legends of the Aryans' wanderings and wars were collected in the *Rig Veda*, the foundation stone of the Hindu religion. It was also migrating Indo-Europeans – the same ones whose mummies were found in the Tarim Basin – who forged the first links between China and the West. It was through them that the Chinese first learned of bronze, wheeled vehicles and domesticated horses. Preliminary studies of the DNA of one of these mummies show similarities with the DNA of modern central Europeans.

SURVIVING BRANCHES OF INDO-EUROPEAN LANGUAGES

INDO-ARYAN:
Hindi, Urdu, Bengali, Marathi, Panjabi, Nepali, Gujarati, Sinhalese, Farsi (Iranian), Kurdish, Pamir, Pashto and Ossetic. This branch also includes Sanskrit which survives as a written language only.

GREEK

ARMENIAN

BALTIC:
Lithuanian and Latvian

SLAVIC:
Russian, Polish, Ukrainian, Czech, Slovak, Serbo-Croatian and Bulgarian

ILLYRIAN:
Albanian

ITALIC OR ROMANCE:
French, Spanish, Portuguese, Italian and Romanian

CELTIC:
Welsh, Breton and Gaelic

GERMANIC:
English, German, Dutch, Frisian, Flemish, Danish, Faeroese, Icelandic, Swedish and Norwegian

EXTINCT BRANCHES OF INDO-EUROPEAN LANGUAGES:
Anatolian, Messapic, Phrygian, Thracian, Tocharian, Venetic

The Exodus
C.1200 BC

Migration is a dominant theme of the first five books of the Old Testament, which describe the foundation of the Hebrew people by the patriarchs, their slavery in Egypt and their Exodus and wanderings under Moses' leadership. This epic story forms the foundation of three great religions – Judaism, Christianity and Islam – and of the Jews' sense of identity. It also gives legitimacy to the modern state of Israel. But is it history or myth?

The biblical story of the Hebrews begins with the patriarch Abraham, a native of Ur in southern Mesopotamia who had moved with his family 600 miles (965 km) north to Haran in Syria. According to the Book of Genesis, Yahweh called Abraham to leave Haran for the land of Canaan, which Yahweh promised would be given to his descendants as a perpetual inheritance. Though he was originally a city dweller, Abraham led the life of a semi-nomadic pastoralist in Canaan, moving several times. Because of his unquestioning obedience to Yahweh, Jews, Christians and Muslims all regard Abraham as the founder of monotheism. Abraham's grandson Jacob was given the name Israel by Yahweh, and it was from his 12 sons that the 12 tribes of the Israelites were descended. Jacob's favouritism towards his 11th son, Joseph, made his brothers

envious. They faked Joseph's death and sold him into slavery in Egypt. Joseph's ability to interpret dreams won him the favour of pharaoh and he rose to high office. When his brothers came to Egypt to escape a famine, Joseph forgave them and arranged for the Israelites to settle in Goshen, probably part of the fertile Nile Delta.

The flight from Egypt

After Joseph's death an oppressive pharaoh enslaved the Israelites and put them to work rebuilding the cities of Raamses and Pithom. In the reign of this unnamed pharaoh's successor, the Israelites fled Egypt in the Exodus (literally 'going out') under the leadership of Moses. Moses was of the tribe of Levi but was brought up at the Egyptian court. He led a privileged existence until he murdered an overseer who was ill-treating an Israelite, and fled to the Midianites in Arabia. Called back to Egypt by Yahweh, Moses negotiated for the release of the Israelites but it took ten plagues to persuade pharaoh to agree. No sooner was it made than pharaoh repented his decision. But the army he sent to pursue the fleeing Israelites was overwhelmed when it tried to follow them across the miraculously parted Sea of Reeds.

The route of the Exodus and the Israelites' subsequent 40-year wanderings in the deserts of Sinai and the Negev are difficult to reconstruct because so many of the places mentioned cannot be identified with any degree of certainty. Even the location of Mount Sinai, where Moses received the law from Yahweh, is uncertain. The widely accepted identification of Jebel Musa in southern Sinai with the biblical Mount Sinai owes more to pilgrim itineraries than knowledge handed down from the time of the wanderings. Moses died on Mount Nebo in Moab before the Israelites reached Canaan. Under

This timeless landscape is the vast and barren Negev Desert in Israel, the wilderness in which the Israelites wandered following the Exodus from Egypt.

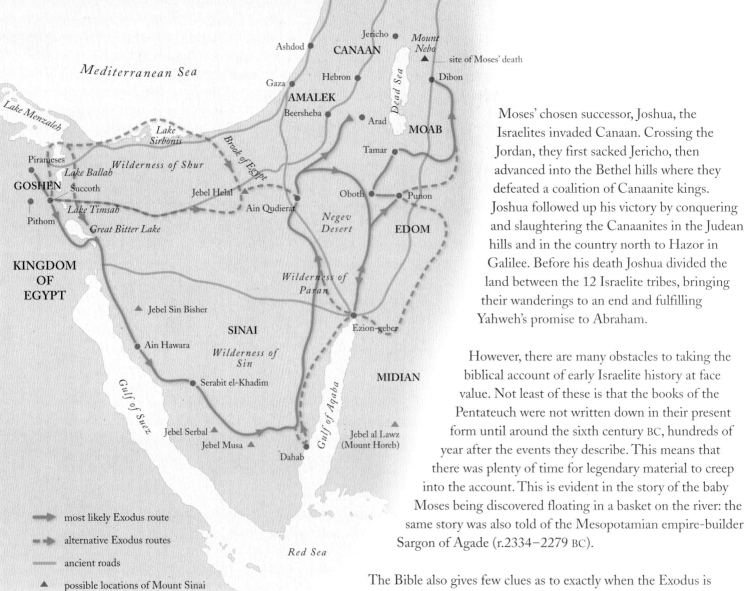

Map showing possible routes taken by the Israelites after they were driven out of Egypt.

Moses' chosen successor, Joshua, the Israelites invaded Canaan. Crossing the Jordan, they first sacked Jericho, then advanced into the Bethel hills where they defeated a coalition of Canaanite kings. Joshua followed up his victory by conquering and slaughtering the Canaanites in the Judean hills and in the country north to Hazor in Galilee. Before his death Joshua divided the land between the 12 Israelite tribes, bringing their wanderings to an end and fulfilling Yahweh's promise to Abraham.

However, there are many obstacles to taking the biblical account of early Israelite history at face value. Not least of these is that the books of the Pentateuch were not written down in their present form until around the sixth century BC, hundreds of year after the events they describe. This means that there was plenty of time for legendary material to creep into the account. This is evident in the story of the baby Moses being discovered floating in a basket on the river: the same story was also told of the Mesopotamian empire-builder Sargon of Agade (r.2334–2279 BC).

The Bible also gives few clues as to exactly when the Exodus is supposed to have taken place. The enslavement is usually dated either to the reign of Sethos I (r.1306–1290 BC) or Ramesses II (r.1290–1224 BC). If the city of Raamses, where the Israelites were put to work, can be identified with Pi-Ri'amsese, then Ramesses would be the favourite as this was his capital city. The Exodus would then have happened in the reign of his successor, Merneptah (r.1224–1214 BC). No ancient Egyptian source mentions Moses or the flight of the Israelites but this is hardly surprising. Most ancient Egyptian inscriptions are triumphal in character, and no pharaoh was going to record for posterity his humiliation by a bunch of runaway slaves.

Understanding Hebrew origins

The idea that the Hebrews were descended from a single group of people such as the sons of Jacob is contradicted by modern genetic research. Studies of the Y chromosomes of modern Jewish men show that they carry a wide variety of haplotypes (discrete sets of genes) comparable to those found among other populations of Middle Eastern origin, including the Palestinian Arabs. In fact, the variety of haplotypes is far too great for Jewish men to be descended from any common ancestor who lived in the last few thousand years. Studies of the mtDNA of Jewish women show that they are descended from an even greater range of lineages. This would suggest that the patriarchs are semi-legendary characters and that

Ramesses II is one of the likely candidates for ruler of Egypt during the Exodus. This detail from a carving, depicting running slaves, decorates one of the colossal statues of the pharaoh at the entrance to the Great Temple of Abu Simbel.

the story of Jacob's 12 sons was invented retrospectively in order to explain why there were 12 tribes of Israelites.

Archaeological evidence throws the most serious doubt on the story of the Israelite migration into Canaan. There is a marked continuity of settlement which suggests that Hebrew identity and culture developed directly from the indigenous Canaanite culture in the uplands west of the Dead Sea. That the Hebrew language is a close relative of Canaanite and the Hebrew alphabet is directly derived from the Canaanite alphabet argues for a close connection between the two peoples. The dramatic siege of Jericho, which plays such an important part in the account of Joshua's conquest of Canaan, is also unlikely to have happened. By the time it is supposed to have been captured by the Israelites, Jericho had been uninhabited for centuries and there were no standing walls to be brought down by Joshua's trumpets. Archaeology even casts doubt on the monotheistic nature of Hebrew religion at this time, as there is clear evidence for the worship of a female consort of Yahweh. It is likely that later biblical writers have obscured a degree of polytheism in early Hebrew religion.

These obstacles make it most unlikely that there ever was an Exodus involving the entire Hebrew people. However, it is probable that the story is based on real migrations involving smaller groups of Hebrews. There is abundant evidence that Semitic peoples from Canaan and the wider Middle East frequently migrated into Egypt with the blessing of the pharaohs, who had well-tried procedures for resettling them. Some Semitic peoples, such as the Hyksos who took over the Delta region between 1640 BC and 1532 BC, also came uninvited. It is entirely likely that there were Hebrews among these migrants. The period in which the Exodus is most likely to have happened – the late 13th century BC – was a difficult time in Egypt, and this provides a credible historical context for a counter-migration of Hebrews back to Canaan. It may well be that memories of these movements into and out of Egypt were later elaborated into a national epic to help the Hebrews define and affirm their separate identity and claim to the land.

The Sea Peoples
C.1200 BC

The 12th century BC was a time of great upheaval in the eastern Mediterranean world. The mighty Hittite empire of Anatolia collapsed seemingly overnight. The splendid Mycenaean civilization of Bronze Age Greece was overthrown amid great violence. Every one of its strong-walled citadels was destroyed and the art of writing died out for centuries. A dozen or more other great cities around the eastern Mediterranean were ruined. Peoples were on the move by land and sea. What role these migrations played in the upheavals of the time is simply not known; they are as likely to have been a response to the turbulent times as a cause of them.

Among the migrants were the Sea Peoples, a loose confederation of displaced peoples from around the Mediterranean who had taken to the sea. For nearly 40 years their fleets of high-prowed sailing ships wreaked havoc along the eastern Mediterranean seaboard as they searched for new lands to settle. The long-term consequences of their migration were not great, though they provided the Israelites with their most memorable enemy and the modern world with a noun to describe a boorish, uncultured person: Philistine. Theirs is also notable as the earliest documented maritime migration in history.

The term 'Sea Peoples' was actually coined in the 19th century and they are not referred to by any collective name in ancient sources. According to ancient Egyptian sources, these peoples included the Peleset, Shardana, Denyen, Lukka, Teresh, Shekelesh, Ekwesh, Tjeker and Weshesh. They were allied with the Meshwesh and Libu, two Libyan peoples who attacked Egypt by land. Though described as a confederation, the Sea Peoples were not closely related to one another: representations of them in Egyptian art show that each group had its own distinctive styles of dress, weapons and armour.

Uncertain origins

The origins of the Sea Peoples can often only be guessed at. The Shardana were most likely from Sardinia: their portrayal in Egyptian art is remarkably similar to bronze statuettes of the same period from Sardinia showing warriors wearing distinctive horned helmets. The Shekelesh may have been the Sicels of Sicily, and the Teresh the Etruscans of central Italy. The Ekwesh may have been Achaeans, the name the Mycenaean Greeks used to describe themselves, and the Old Testament records that the Peleset came from Crete. The Lukka were from Lycia in western Anatolia. The Weshesh were probably from Wilusa (known to the Greeks as Ilios, or Troy, which was sacked around this time).

What caused the Sea Peoples to migrate is also very unclear, as it is unlikely that any single factor can explain the motives of such a diverse group. Women and children are shown accompanying warriors in Egyptian depictions of the Sea Peoples, so some at least must have been refugees looking for a new place to settle. Those who came from Anatolia may have been displaced by the Phrygians, an Indo-European-speaking people whose own migration into Anatolia around this time is the most likely cause of the fall of the Hittite empire. Similarly, the Peleset and Ekwesh may have been refugees created by the fall of the Mycenaean civilization. Those from the western Mediterranean may simply have been opportunists, seeking to take advantage of the general disorder in the region. What is clear is that many of these peoples were already known in the eastern Mediterranean, either as pirates or as mercenaries in the Egyptian army.

Whatever their origins, the Sea Peoples began their migration towards the end of the 13th century BC, moving around the eastern Mediterranean, attacking the coasts of

The Sea Peoples were active during the time of the ancient Egyptians, as evidenced by this relief of a naval battle from the mortuary chapel of Ramesses III. In fact, they proved to be a thorn in Egypt's side for many years.

Anatolia, Cyprus, Syria and Canaan and leaving a trail of ruined cities in their wake. Documents from Ugarit, an ancient port on the Syrian coast, refer to their ceaseless pirate raids and their practice of kidnapping people for ransom.

Attacks on Egypt

The Sea Peoples are said to have lived in their ships. Soon after these documents were written, Ugarit itself was destroyed. Moving rapidly on, the marauders invaded Egypt in the fifth year of the reign of Pharaoh Merneptah (r. *c.*1224–1214 BC). The Egyptians were taken completely by surprise and the Sea Peoples ravaged unchecked for a month before Merneptah could organize resistance. After 6000 of them were killed and 9000 taken prisoner, the Sea Peoples withdrew to lick their wounds at a camp on the coast of Syria. They did not return to Egypt until the reign of Ramesses III (r. *c.*1194–1163 BC), one of the last great warrior pharaohs. An inscription from Ramesses III's mortuary temple at Medinet Habu records how, in 1186 BC:

'The foreigners made a conspiracy in their islands. All at once the lands were shattered in the fray. No land could stand before their arms, Hatti, Kode, Carchemish, Arzawa and Alashiya were destroyed one after the other. On they came towards Egypt … Their confederation included the Peleset, Tjeker, Shekelesh, Denyen and Meshwesh. They laid their hands upon the lands to the very limits of the earth. Their hearts were confident, they said "our plans will succeed".'

They did not. Defeating them first in a land battle, then in a great naval battle fought somewhere in the Nile Delta, Ramesses shattered their coalition beyond repair. Most of the survivors – 100,000 of them, according to a boastful letter written by Ramesses – were settled on land in Egypt, where they soon became assimilated with the native population. The Tjeker, Shardana and Peleset had a different fate. The Egyptians decided to employ them as mercenaries, settling them in garrisons in Canaanite territory.

A group of bronze statuettes found in Sardinia, from the seventh century BC, shows the Shardana to have been a warrior people, with distinctive horned helmets and circular shields.

TIMELINE

1224–1214 BC The Sea Peoples attack Egypt during reign of Pharaoh Merneptah

*c.***1200 BC** The Greek Mycenaean civilization is destroyed by invaders

*c.***1186 BC** Pharaoh Ramesses III defeats the Sea Peoples

1184 BC Traditional date for the sack of Troy

*c.***1180 BC** Peleset (Philistines) settle around Gaza (in Canaan)

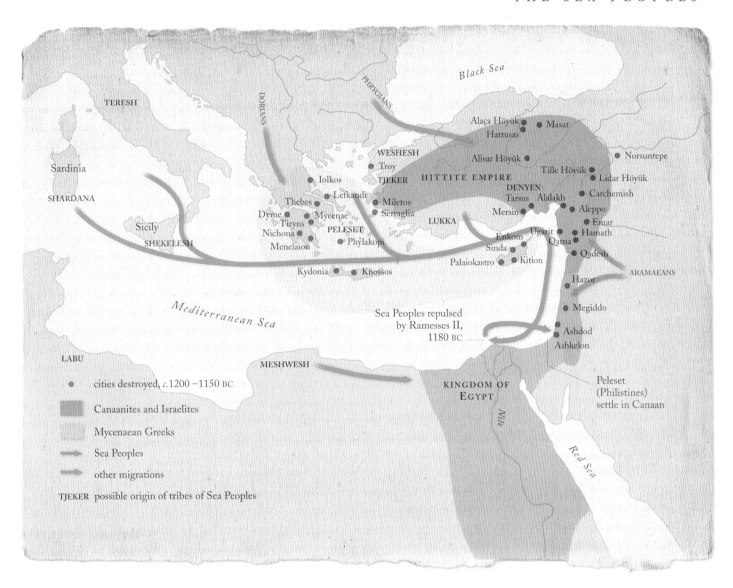

Map showing the possible origins and migrations of the tribes of the Sea Peoples.

Egyptian power in Canaan quickly withered away after Ramesses' death. The isolated garrisons seized power and set up independent city-states at Ashdod, Ashkelon, Ekron, Gaza and Gath, so emerging as the Philistines (from Peleset) of the Old Testament. From this base, roughly corresponding to today's Gaza Strip, the Philistines began to expand north along the coast and inland towards Beer Sheba. The Philistines' settlements are easily recognized from their distinctively decorated pottery which is derived from Mycenaean pottery styles.

In some cases new Philistine settlements were built on unoccupied land but excavations have shown that many were built on the sites of destroyed Canaanite settlements, suggesting that they increased their territory by expelling the native inhabitants. Philistine expansion was halted by the Israelites, who were also increasing their territory at the expense of the Canaanites. Despite frequent wars with the Israelite kingdoms, the Philistines survived until the seventh century BC, when they were conquered by the Assyrians and subjected to mass deportations and resettlement in Mesopotamia. A lingering memory of the migrations of the Sea Peoples survives in the Middle East in the name of Palestine which derives, ultimately, from the Peleset.

The Phoenicians
9TH–7TH CENTURIES BC

One of the great seafaring peoples of history, the Phoenicians pioneered trade routes across the Mediterranean, creating the first links between western Europe and the ancient civilizations of Egypt and Mesopotamia. Their voyages of exploration took them as far as the British Isles and tropical West Africa. They may even have been the first to circumnavigate the African continent. To support their merchant ventures, the Phoenicians planted colonies at strategic points along the trade routes. The most successful of these, Carthage, became a great imperial power that vied with Rome for the mastery of the western Mediterranean.

The homeland of the Phoenicians lay along the coast of modern Lebanon and Syria, where there are the best natural harbours in the eastern Mediterranean. Small ports began to develop here in the third millennium BC, trading cedar wood from the Lebanon Mountains with treeless Egypt and Mesopotamia. Other local specialities were glass, wine, ivory carvings and an intense purple dye obtained from the murex shellfish that was literally worth more than its weight in gold. This became such an important export that it probably gave the Phoenicians their name, from *phoinix*, derived from the Greek word for red. The Phoenicians were closely related to the Canaanites, speaking a similar language and sharing many beliefs. By around 1000 BC the main Phoenician ports – Tyre, Sidon, Berytus (Beirut), Byblos, Arvad and Ugarit – had developed into prosperous independent city-states ruled by hereditary kings. The most famous of these was King Hiram of Tyre (r.969–936 BC), who sent timber and craftsmen to help his friend King Solomon (r.971–931 BC) with building projects in Israel. Kings ruled with the advice of a senate of city elders and a larger people's assembly.

Until the end of the ninth century BC Phoenician trading activity was restricted mainly to the eastern Mediterranean and the Aegean. In the eighth century BC booming demand in the fast-growing Assyrian empire for iron, copper, tin and exotic products stimulated Phoenician merchants to travel further afield; and by around 700 BC their trade routes extended throughout the western Mediterranean and through the Pillars of Hercules into the Atlantic. Pushing the limits of the known world, Phoenician traders reached the Cassiterides (the 'Islands of Tin'), which was probably southwest Britain, and at least as far as Mogador on the Moroccan coast. According to the ancient Greek historian Herodotus, Pharaoh Necho (r.610–595 BC) sent a Phoenician fleet to circumnavigate Africa. Setting off down the Red Sea, the Phoenicians returned to Egypt via the Mediterranean three years later. The sailors reported that for much of the voyage the sun was seen in the north, suggesting that they must have sailed south of the equator.

Far-reaching influence

Most early seafarers preferred to sail within sight of land, navigating by onshore landmarks and anchoring in a sheltered bay or harbour each night. The Phoenicians were renowned for their ability to make long voyages on the open sea, navigating at night using their knowledge of the stars, especially the Pole Star, which was known in ancient times as the Phoenician Star. Handbooks containing sailing directions and distances, known as *periploi*, were widely used. By way of insurance, Phoenician mariners made sacrifices to the storm god Baal both before and during their voyages. The Phoenicians used a variety of ships. For war they had biremes (galleys with two banks of oarsmen on each side). On shorter trading voyages merchant galleys were used. These ships had a single rectangular sail and a crew of oarsmen. Their long-distance traders relied solely on a single, broad, rectangular sail for propulsion. Up to 30 metres (100 ft) long, these had deep, rounded hulls to maximize their capacity to carry cargo. Appropriately, they were known as *gaulos*, meaning 'tubs'.

Along their trade routes the Phoenicians founded trading posts and colonies. These required considerable resources of manpower, shipping and provisions to set up but were expected to benefit the parent city in the long run by increasing trade opportunities, paying taxes and providing safe havens where ships could take on water and

The Phoenicians are generally thought to have been the greatest navigators of their time. This heavily romanticized 19th-century engraving shows the Phoenician fleet heading out to sea in biremes and sailing galleys.

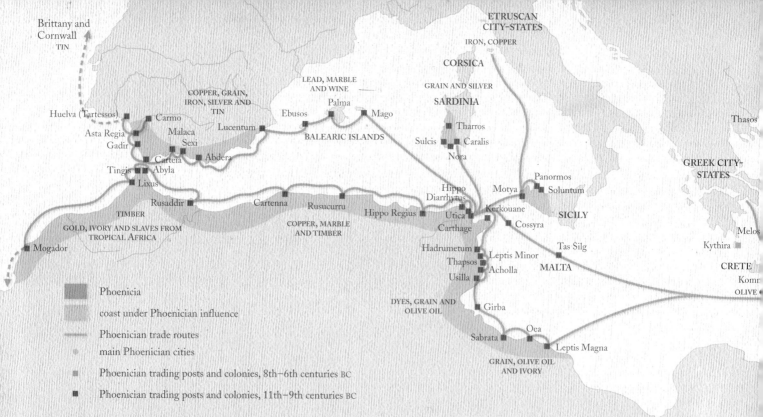

Brittany and Cornwall **TIN**

COPPER, GRAIN, IRON, SILVER AND TIN

Huelva (Tartessos)
Carmo
Asta Regia
Gadir
Malaca
Sexi
Lucentum
Carteia
Tingis
Abyla
Lixus
Rusaddir
Abdera
Cartenna
Rusucurru
Hippo Regius

LEAD, MARBLE AND WINE
Ebusos
Palma
Mago

BALEARIC ISLANDS

TIMBER

GOLD, IVORY AND SLAVES FROM TROPICAL AFRICA

Mogador

COPPER, MARBLE AND TIMBER

ETRUSCAN CITY-STATES
IRON, COPPER

CORSICA

GRAIN AND SILVER
SARDINIA
Tharros
Sulcis
Caralis
Nora

Panormos
Motya
Soluntum
Hippo Diarrhytus
Kerkouane
Utica
Carthage
Cossyra
SICILY

GREEK CITY-STATES

Thasos

Melos
Kythira

Hadrumetum
Thapsos
Acholla
Usilla
Leptis Minor
Tas Silg
MALTA

CRETE
Komr
OLIVE

DYES, GRAIN AND OLIVE OIL
Girba

Sabrata
Oea
Leptis Magna

GRAIN, OLIVE OIL AND IVORY

- **Phoenicia**
- coast under Phoenician influence
- Phoenician trade routes
- main Phoenician cities
- Phoenician trading posts and colonies, 8th–6th centuries BC
- Phoenician trading posts and colonies, 11th–9th centuries BC

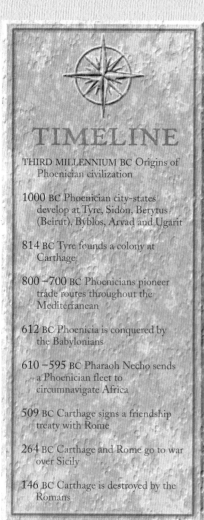

TIMELINE

THIRD MILLENNIUM BC Origins of Phoenician civilization

1000 BC Phoenician city-states develop at Tyre, Sidon, Berytus (Beirut), Byblos, Arvad and Ugarit

814 BC Tyre founds a colony at Carthage

800–700 BC Phoenicians pioneer trade routes throughout the Mediterranean

612 BC Phoenicia is conquered by the Babylonians

610–595 BC Pharaoh Necho sends a Phoenician fleet to circumnavigate Africa

509 BC Carthage signs a friendship treaty with Rome

264 BC Carthage and Rome go to war over Sicily

146 BC Carthage is destroyed by the Romans

provisions. The earliest colonies were founded on Crete, Cyprus, Rhodes and other islands in the Aegean Sea. As their trading network snaked out into the western Mediterranean in the eighth century, dozens more colonies were founded on Malta, Sicily, Sardinia, the Balearic Islands, the south coast of Spain and along the length of the North African coast from Libya to Morocco. Tyre, which by the ninth century had come to dominate the other Phoenician cities, was by far the leading colonizer. Colonies remained subject to their founding cities and were ruled by royally appointed governors. As a reminder of its dependency, each colony had a temple dedicated to its parent city's patron deity. In the case of Tyre's colonies, this was a temple to the national god Melqart.

Phoenicians tried to avoid conflict with native peoples by allowing them to benefit from the commercial opportunities they brought. Although the Phoenicians did not come as conquerors, their colonies had a far-reaching impact on their neighbours, stimulating the growth of towns and kingdoms. One of their most important achievements was the introduction of the alphabet (a Canaanite invention) to Greece, North Africa, Italy and Spain. Alphabetic writing systems were much easier to learn than earlier writing systems, such as hieroglyphs and cuneiform, and promoted the widespread literacy which is the basis of Western civilization. The Tyrian colony of Gadir (Cadiz) became the first outpost of Mediterranean civilization in Atlantic Europe. Founded as a market for metals, Gadir's main trading partner was the silver-rich Iberian kingdom of Tartessos, the biblical Tarshish. Phoenician engineers helped expand the kingdom's mining industry, supervising ore processing at its silver mines.

The Assyrian empire stimulated trade but it also eventually curtailed the Phoenicians' independence. The temptation to take control of Phoenicia's trade proved too much for the aggressive king Tiglath-pileser III (r.745–727 BC),

Map showing Phoenician colonies, trading posts and major trade routes.

The carving on this Phoenician sarcophagus from the first century AD depicts a trading ship.

and in 734 BC he conquered the region. After the fall of the Assyrian empire in 612 BC, Phoenicia came under the control of the Babylonians and then, in 539 BC, of the Persians, before being conquered by Alexander the Great (r.336–323 BC) of Macedon in 332 BC. While the Phoenicians retained considerable autonomy under this succession of foreign overlords, and remained prosperous, they were unable to maintain control of their overseas colonies, which became independent. They also began to lose their distinctive cultural identity. The Phoenician language had largely given way to Aramaic by the time of Alexander's conquest, after which their culture became increasingly Hellenized.

The rise of Carthage

Phoenician language and culture lived on its western Mediterranean colonies, which by now were united into a loose empire under the leadership of the former Tyrian colony of Carthage. Sited on an easily defended peninsula in northern Tunisia with a fine natural harbour, Carthage was ideally placed to dominate the main east–west trade route through the Mediterranean. Founded in 814 BC, Carthage had prospered from the start. After Phoenicia was conquered by Babylon, Carthage took upon itself the role of protector of the other Phoenician colonies. Independent Carthage adopted a republican constitution. The government was headed by two suffetes ('judges') who were elected annually. Below the suffetes was an aristocratic senate of around 30 members which oversaw foreign policy and prepared legislation for presentation to the elected people's assembly.

Perhaps it was because their forms of government had so much in common that Carthage signed a treaty of friendship with the Roman Republic within a year of its foundation in 509 BC. The treaty was renewed at least three times and the two states co-operated to curb Greek expansion in the western Mediterranean. Rome's growing power put the friendship under strain and a dispute over spheres of influence in Sicily led to the outbreak of war in 264 BC. In the three hard-fought Punic Wars (from *Poeni*, the Roman name for 'Phoenicians') – 264–241 BC, 218–201 BC and 149–146 – Rome first stripped Carthage of its empire and finally razed the city to the ground and sold its people into slavery. Roman, not Phoenician, civilization would henceforth shape the West.

The Celts
c.600 BC–279 BC

Now commonly thought of as a people of Europe's Atlantic fringe, the migrations of the ancient Celts resulted in one of Europe's most widespread peoples, inhabiting a territory which, at its height in the early third century BC, stretched from the Atlantic Ocean in the west to the shores of the Black Sea in the east.

The term 'Celt' was first used by ancient Greek writers to describe the tribal peoples of central and western Europe. The Romans named these same people Gauls. Today, the term is used generally to describe all the peoples of Europe, past and present, who speak Celtic languages. These languages are a branch of the great Indo-European family of languages (see pages 30–33). At the time of their first appearance in the historical record around 500 BC, Celtic-speaking peoples were already spread over a wide area of central and western Europe, including much of the Iberian Peninsula and the British Isles.

Disputed origins

How they got there is the subject of academic dispute. Many historians believe the origin of the Celts is closely associated with the emergence of the central European Hallstatt culture in the late Bronze Age (c.1200 – 800 BC). Named for an archaeological site in the Austrian Alps, this culture is defined by its distinctive decorative style based on animal and vegetation motifs, and high-quality metalworking. The spread of the Hallstatt culture west to France and into the Iberian Peninsula and Britain in the early Iron Age (c.800 – 450 BC) is seen as evidence for prehistoric migrations of Celtic-speaking peoples out of their central European homeland. These emigrants conquered the native peoples and either displaced them or assimilated them to Celtic culture, language and identity.

An alternative view, influenced by new archaeological and genetic research in Britain, sees migrations as playing less of a role in Celtic origins. Britain and Ireland are home to the majority of Europe's surviving Celtic speakers so it came as something of a surprise when genetic research failed to find any evidence of a Celtic migration to Britain. It is now clear that there were no major migrations into Britain in the 8000 years between the initial colonization of the island after the end of the Ice Age and the arrival of the Anglo-Saxons in the early Middle Ages. This agrees with what the ancient Britons themselves believed; they had no traditions of migration and regarded themselves as the aboriginal inhabitants of Britain.

But if there were no migrations, how did the British Isles become Celtic speaking? There is no easy answer to this, but the Bronze Age was a time in European history when ideas, cultures and languages could have spread very easily through trade and social

Mousa broch, Shetland. Hundreds of brochs were built by the Celts in Scotland between 200 BC and 1 BC, as homes and fortresses for petty chieftains and their families. This is the best preserved and the only one which survives to its original height of 13 metres (43 ft).

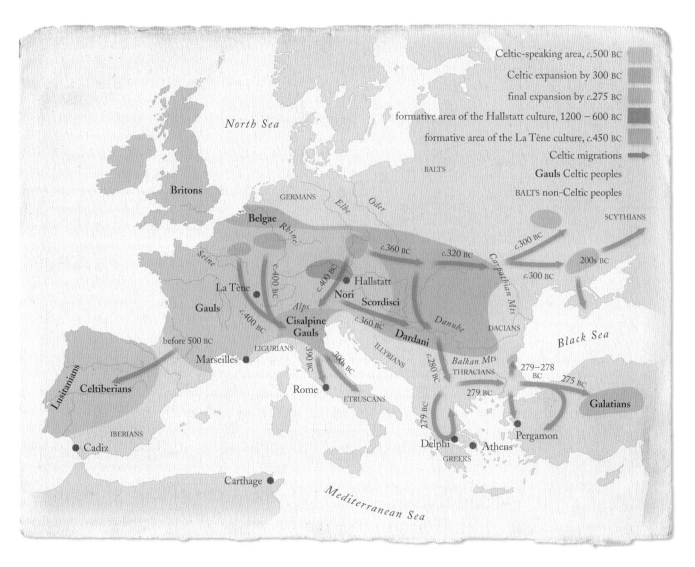

Map showing Celtic migrations in Europe, c.500 – 275 BC.

contacts. During the Bronze Age European societies were becoming more hierarchical, and rising social élites were trying to bolster their new-found status by acquiring prestige goods unaffordable to the common people. Because gold and silver, and copper and tin (the ingredients of bronze) are unevenly distributed and scarce, prestige metalwork such as weapons and jewellery was widely traded in Bronze Age Europe. This promoted a high degree of cultural homogeneity in the region, so it is not really necessary to invoke migration to explain the spread of the Hallstatt style or of Celtic languages. (Future archaeologists will find abundant evidence – countless millions of discarded Coca-Cola bottles, for example – for the spread of American material culture in the 20th century, but if they interpreted these as evidence of migrating Americans they would be very wide of the mark.)

Celts in Italy and Greece

If the jury is still out on the question of Celtic migrations in prehistoric times, Celtic migrations in historical times are well documented and were dramatic in scale and impact. Between the fifth and third centuries BC, migrations carried the Celts from central Europe across the Alps into Italy and, following the River Danube, east to the Carpathian Mountains and beyond onto the Ukrainian steppes; they also went southeast into the Balkans and Greece and across the Bosphorus into Anatolia. Small groups even finished up in Syria and Egypt.

The earliest historically attested Celtic migrations took place around 600 BC. According to a much later account by the Roman historian Livy (59 BC–AD 17), Ambigatus, chief of the Bituriges tribe, realized his territory was overpopulated and decided to send his nephews Bellovesus and Segovesus out with as many followers as they could muster to find new homelands. Segovesus was dispatched to southern Germany, Bellovesus to Italy. It appears that Italy's wine, olive oil and warm climate made it irresistible to the Celts. Bellovesus attracted thousands of followers from many different tribes who crossed the Alps with him and settled on the plains north of the River Po.

Another wave of migrations into Italy began around 450 BC. First came the Cenomani, followed by the Libui, the Saluvii, the Boii, the Lingones and finally, around 400 BC, the Senones. Soon there was no more space for settlement north of the Po so the Celts poured south, seizing land from the Etruscans, who were then the dominant people of peninsular Italy. Some traces of this migration are still evident in Italian place names: Bologna is named for the Boii and Senigallia for the Senones, for example. The weakening of the Etruscans by the Celtic migrations created a long-term opportunity for the small Italian city-state of Rome to start expanding its own territory. In the short term the Celts were just as much of a problem to the Romans as the Etruscans. In July 390 BC (or possibly 386 BC) the Senones captured Rome and were only persuaded to leave when the Romans offered to pay a huge ransom in gold.

This gold coin, copied from a Greek original and depicting the god Apollo, was made by the Celtic Ambiani tribe of northern Gaul (France). It dates from the second century BC.

The sack of Rome proved to be the limit of Celtic expansion in Italy. As Rome's power grew it avenged its humiliation by first conquering the Italian Celts (between 283 and 191 BC), and then most of the rest of the Celtic world by the mid-first century AD. But even as the Romans were beginning to roll back the Celts in Italy, new migrations were taking them across eastern Europe. The beginnings of these migrations are probably marked by the spread of the Celtic La Tène culture (c.450 – 50 BC) into the Carpathians and the middle Danube region around the middle of the fourth century BC. In 336 BC the Celts caught the attention of the Greek world when they sent an embassy to Alexander the Great (r.336–323 BC), who was campaigning on the northern borders of his kingdom of Macedonia. Alexander asked the envoys what they were most afraid of, expecting they would say it was him. When they told him that they were most afraid the sky would fall on them, Alexander was heard to mutter that these Celts had far too high an opinion of themselves. At around the same time, other groups of Celts had crossed the Carpathians into the Ukraine. Settling along the River Dnepr, they began raiding the Greek colonies around the shores of the Black Sea. These Celtic settlements were exposed to attack by the steppe nomads and do not seem to have survived for very long.

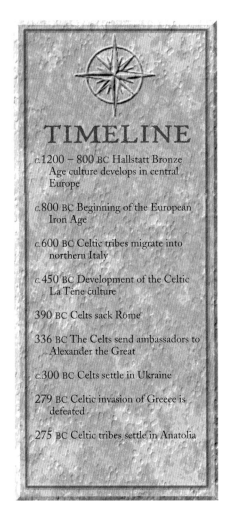

Alexander's empire fell apart soon after he died, and the Greek world was thrown into decades of instability and war. The Celts exploited this weakness to extend their territory further into the Balkans and in 298 BC they even raided Macedonia. Though they were quickly chased out, they returned in 281 BC, when they defeated and killed the Macedonian king Ptolemy Keraunos (the 'Thunderbolt'; r.281–279 BC). The Celts were head hunters and as they returned home loaded with booty they proudly paraded Ptolemy's severed head on the end of a spear. The success of this raid encouraged a large coalition of Celtic tribes to try to move into Greece in force in 279 BC.

Breakaway tribes

Unity never came easily to the Celts, and even before they got to Greece three tribes, the Tectosages, the Tolistobogii and the Trocmi, numbering 20,000, broke away; a further group remained behind to plunder Macedonia. Outflanking a Greek army which tried to stop them at the narrow pass of Thermopylae, the main Celtic force headed for the rich sacred city of Delphi, home to the oracle of the sun god Apollo. The city was saved, the Greeks believed, only by the intervention of Apollo himself, who sent snow storms and avalanches to block the mountain passes, forcing the Celts to retreat.

The breakaway tribes were invited to settle on the Black Sea coast of Anatolia by King Nicomedes of Bithynia (r.279–255 BC) who thought they would make useful mercenaries. Once there, they exploited the rivalries between the different Greek kingdoms vying for control of the region to carve out an independent kingdom for themselves. Known as Galatia, the kingdom remained independent until 25 BC, when it was peacefully annexed by Rome. Many Galatians signed on as mercenaries with the Seleucid rulers of Syria and the Ptolemies of Egypt, and settled in these desert lands, which could hardly have been more different from the pine forests of their central European homelands. Within a few generations, these isolated Celtic colonies were assimilated into the native populations.

These forays to the east brought the great age of Celtic migrations to an end. As a result of their migrations, the Celts were probably the most widespread peoples of Europe around 250 BC. Within 50 years they were in retreat, squeezed between the expanding Roman empire and the Germanic peoples; and by the first century AD only in northern Britain and Ireland did any Celts still retain their independence.

For the Celts, migrations were primarily a means to relieve the social tensions caused by rising population or shortage of resources. Julius Caesar tells us that when the Helvetii, a Celtic tribe from the Swiss Alps, decided to migrate in the first century BC they did so because they felt that their own territory was too small for their population and had too few opportunities for plundering raids on other peoples. Celtic society was dominated by a warrior élite. For them, warfare was essential, both as an opportunity to perform status-enhancing acts of valour, and for the spoils, which when distributed enhanced the status

Ancient Celts were a warlike people, frequently engaged in plundering raids on other peoples and competing for status with other tribes. This early 20th-century engraving reconstructs the appearance of a Celtic warrior.

The ancient Celts were skilled in the art of metalwork, producing high-quality items such as this gold torque found in Ireland.

of a chief, attracted more warriors to join his retinue and so made even more successful raids possible. Ambitious chiefs also had to compete with one another for status and followers, reinforcing the warlike tendency of Celtic society. If the opportunities for raiding were restricted for some reason, the competitive nature of warrior society might turn inwards, causing civil war.

In these circumstances, migration offered a safety valve. Celtic migrations could involve part of a tribe, a whole tribe or even a coalition of tribes. Migrations were not spontaneous affairs. The Helvetii spent two years preparing for their migration, conducting a population census, stocking up on provisions, acquiring draught animals and wagons and negotiating with tribes whose territories they needed to travel through to reach their intended new homeland 400 miles (640 km) to the west in Aquitaine. When they were finally ready to leave, they burned their settlements so that return would not be an option. Caesar claimed that there were 368,000 migrants altogether, including 92,000 warriors – a very formidable force by ancient standards.

Greek Colonization of the Mediterranean
c.1450 BC–500 BC

The civilization of ancient Greece was, and continues to be, one of the most influential in world history. Western science, philosophy, architecture, art, literature and political institutions have all been shaped by the achievements of the ancient Greeks. Greek civilization had a formative impact on the development of Roman civilization and was a significant influence on the Celts, Persians, Jews and even the Indians. The main means by which Greek civilization was spread was by the foundation of colonies around the Mediterranean, Black Sea and even further afield in Asia. As with the Celts, the main stimulus for this colonizing effort was over-population at home.

The Greeks were not the aboriginal inhabitants of Greece but an Indo-European people who had migrated into the peninsula from the north sometime around 2000 BC. These earliest Greeks probably called themselves Achaeans but they are better known to history as the Mycenaeans, after Mycenae, the citadel of the legendary king Agamemnon, who led the Greeks in the Trojan war. In the 15th century BC the Mycenaeans began an expansion overseas, conquering Crete in about 1450 BC and founding colonies on Rhodes, Cyprus and the Anatolian coast. It may have been in this period that the Trojan War took place. Greeks continued to form the majority population of the Anatolian coast until the 1920s, when they were expelled by Turkish nationalists. The Mycenaeans were also active as traders around the eastern Mediterranean, and as far west as Malta, Sicily and Italy. The legend of the Golden Fleece may be derived from a Mycenaean trading voyage to the gold-rich kingdom of Colchis east of the Black Sea. These trade links were abandoned after the fall of the Mycenaean civilization around 1200 BC, and Greece entered a 'dark age'.

Independent city-states

The growth of the Assyrian empire in the ninth century promoted a revival of trade in the eastern Mediterranean. The Phoenicians were the first to seize the new opportunities but the Greeks soon followed suit and re-established their old trade routes. As prosperity returned, the population of Greece rapidly began to increase. The basic political unit in ancient Greece was the *polis*, or city-state. City governments promoted colonization overseas as a means to defuse the social tensions caused by population pressure. There was nothing voluntary about becoming a migrant. In many cities, colonists were chosen by lot and anyone who refused to go faced severe penalties. While whole families often emigrated together, many cities sent only young men, who were expected to find wives from among the native populations. Generally, the numbers involved were only a few hundred, sometimes only a few dozen, but more would follow if the settlers managed to establish themselves securely. In one exceptional case, the whole population of Phocaea in Anatolia migrated to Corsica after the city was destroyed by the Persians in 545 BC.

The Greek colonies were intended to be complete replicas of their home societies in every way. Unlike the Phoenician colonies, which remained subject to their parent cities, Greek colonies were meant to be independent city-states from the outset. Successful colonies could also found colonies of their own. Relations between colonies and their parent cities generally remained close and friendly. The most active colonizers were the Ionians, who were descendants of the Mycenaeans, and the Dorians, Greek-speakers from the Balkans who had only arrived in Greece during the 'dark age'.

When founding a colony, the Greeks chose sites that could be defended easily, such as a peninsula, a steep-sided hill or an offshore island. A harbour to attract traders, and fertile farmland nearby so that the colonists could feed themselves, were also essential. Not surprisingly, such desirable real estate was often already occupied by indigenous peoples, who had to be dealt with either by diplomacy or force. There was also competition from the Phoenicians and the Carthaginians, who wanted to protect their established dominance of western Mediterranean trade routes.

The Temple of Zeus in Cyrene (modern Shahat). Cyrene was established as a colony of the Aegean island of Thera in the seventh century BC.

Greek colonization was at its peak in the eighth and seventh centuries BC. One of the earliest colonies was Al Mina in Syria, but the powerful empires of Assyria and Babylon limited opportunities to found independent colonies in the eastern Mediterranean. For most of the eighth century BC the Greeks preferred to sail west to Sicily and southern Italy, where there were good harbours, fertile farmland and no big empires to restrict their freedom. So many Greeks emigrated there that the area became known as 'Greater Greece'. In spite of frequent wars with the indigenous peoples, the Greek colonies in Italy had an enormous cultural influence, especially on the Etruscans and the Romans. Attempts to found colonies further west in the Mediterranean were strongly resisted by the Phoenicians. However, the colony of Massalia (modern Marseilles), founded *c.*600 BC to tap into the trade route from northern Europe along the Rhône Valley, was highly successful and introduced the Celts to the influence of Mediterranean civilization.

In the seventh century BC the Greek colonizing effort shifted to the Bosphorus and the rich grain-growing lands around the shores of the Black Sea. Greek colonies here imported wine and other luxuries from the homeland and exchanged them with the indigenous peoples for grain, which they sent back to Greece to feed its rapidly growing cities. This period also saw the foundation of colonies in Cyrenaica and Egypt. The pharaohs welcomed Greek settlers for the trade they brought and their military skills, but did not allow them full independence. Through these colonies, Greece felt the influence of Egyptian art and architecture. By 500 BC there were few opportunities left for colonization but there would be one more burst of Greek migration in the wake of the conquests of Alexander the Great (r.336–323 BC) in the fourth century.

A relief carving from Cyrenaica showing the sun god Apollo and the nymph Cyrene, after whom the Greeks named their colony.

Thera and Cyrene

What was the experience of founding a colony like? Around 630 BC the government of the Aegean island of Thera (now Santorini) decided to found a colony because a prolonged drought was having a severe impact on the island's agriculture. The Thereans sought the advice of the sun god Apollo through his oracle at Delphi and were directed to Cyrenaica in Libya. Knowing little of Cyrenaica, the Thereans hired an experienced pilot and sent a scouting mission which identified a small island called Platea off the coast of Cyrenaica as a suitable location for a colony.

Lots were drawn to choose one young unmarried man from each family on Thera to join a colonizing expedition under Battus, a son of the island's king, who was to rule the new colony. The death penalty would be imposed on anyone who refused to go. If after five years, however, they had failed to establish a viable colony, the colonists would be

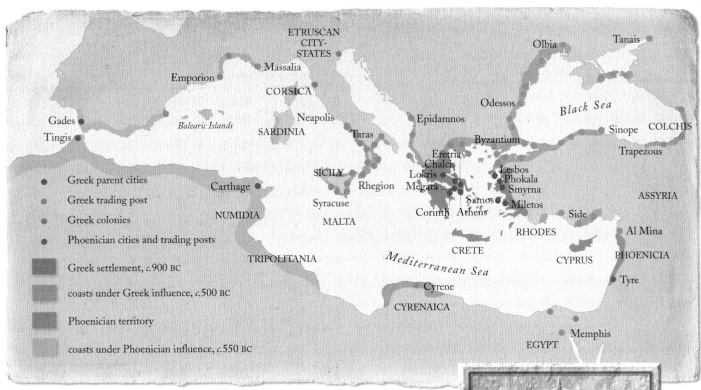

Map showing Greek colonies and parent cities in the Aegean region, c.900–500 BC.

allowed to return home without punishment. The colonists were guaranteed equal rights and a fair share of land, whatever their family's status at home. Any Thereans who went voluntarily to join the colony within the first five years would have the right to be admitted on equal terms to the original pioneers. Two 50-oared galleys were all that was needed to transport the colonists, making it unlikely that there were many more than 100 of them (galleys did not have much room for passengers).

On reaching Platea, the colonists despaired of turning the barren island into a successful colony and went home. On their return to Thera they were prevented from landing and ordered back to Platea, where they struggled for two years before moving to a more fertile site on the mainland opposite. They stayed there for six years without any great success, until the native Libyans offered them a new site about 7 miles (11 km) inland on a fertile plateau with a good spring and reliable rainfall. The new colony, Cyrene, began to prosper by exporting grain and olive oil, and soon outgrew its parent state. Cyrene kept a close relationship with Thera and granted automatic citizenship to all Thereans who came to live there. But the friendly attitude of the Libyans did not last. Cyrene's success attracted a flood of Greek settlers who demanded more and more land. In 570 BC the Libyans allied with the Egyptians and tried to expel the Greeks: they failed and Cyrenaica remained part of the Greek-speaking world until the Arab conquest in the seventh century AD.

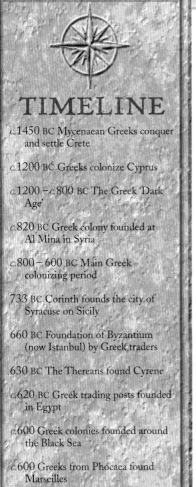

TIMELINE

*c.*1450 BC Mycenaean Greeks conquer and settle Crete

*c.*1200 BC Greeks colonize Cyprus

*c.*1200 – *c.*800 BC The Greek 'Dark Age'

*c.*820 BC Greek colony founded at Al Mina in Syria

*c.*800 – 600 BC Main Greek colonizing period

733 BC Corinth founds the city of Syracuse on Sicily

660 BC Foundation of Byzantium (now Istanbul) by Greek traders

630 BC The Thereans found Cyrene

*c.*620 BC Greek trading posts founded in Egypt

*c.*600 Greek colonies founded around the Black Sea

*c.*600 Greeks from Phocaea found Marseilles

The Bantu Migrations
c.2500 BC—AD 1000

The greatest migration of African prehistory was unquestionably that of the Bantu. From their original homeland, around 3000 BC, in a small region of West Africa near the present-day border between Nigeria and Cameroon, Bantu-speaking farmers spread south and east to occupy fully one-third of the African continent by AD 1000.

By 100,000 years ago, Africans had begun to separate into three distinct populations. These were the ancestors of the main ethnic groups of modern sub-Saharan Africa: the Khoi (or 'Bushmen'), the 'Pygmies' (Mbuti, Twa, and Mbenga) and other Africans (including the groups classified by anthropologists as Negroes and Nilo-Saharans). The first two groups were once far more widespread in Africa than they are today. Around 5000 years ago the Khoi, whose DNA includes the most ancient lineages of any modern human population, inhabited the savannah of eastern and southern Africa but today are confined to a few areas around the Kalahari Desert in southwest Africa. In the same period, the 'Pygmies' inhabited the vast equatorial forest of the Congo River Basin: their small stature is probably an adaptation to forest living. 'Pygmies' are now confined to isolated pockets within their former range. The huge reduction in the territories of the Khoi and the 'Pygmies' was the result of the Bantu migrations.

Settled farming and migration

Bantu is a linguistic classification rather than the name of a distinct ethnic group (the word means simply 'people'). Because of the large area they inhabit, the Bantu-speaking peoples are very diverse in physical appearance, beliefs and ways of life. The Bantu languages are a sub-group of the major Niger-Congo family of languages, to which most languages of West Africa belong. The Bantu languages originated in the rainforest of southern Nigeria and Cameroon sometime before 3000 BC. Soon after this, Bantu-speaking peoples split into eastern and western groups. Beginning around 2500 BC the Eastern Bantu peoples began to migrate east following the northern edge of the rainforests of the Congo River Basin into southern Sudan. They moved south to reach the Great Lakes region of East Africa by around the time of Christ. At about the same time the Western Bantu began migrating south, reaching the lower Congo River Basin area by 400 BC. All the time the Bantu were expanding, the number of languages and dialects kept multiplying. Today there are some 500 Bantu languages, spoken by over 60 million people.

The exact cause of the Bantu migration is unknown but it may well be connected in some way to the adoption of settled farming in sub-Saharan Africa. Surprisingly, the first

farmers in Africa lived in the Sahara about 8000 years ago. The climate was much wetter than it is today and the Sahara was a game-rich savannah, with good grazing for herds of cattle, sheep and goats, and sufficient rainfall for growing millet, sorghum and African rice. Around 6000 years ago, the Sahara began to dry out, forcing farmers out to North Africa, the Nile Valley and south onto the Sahel, the savannah belt that lies between the Sahara and the equatorial forest to the south. Most of the crops and livestock were not suited to the equatorial forests. It was only following the domestication of the yam, a high-yielding starchy root vegetable, in the West African forest around 2750 BC that farming really got established – though only at the price of arduous labour felling trees with polished stone axes to create fields. In most of West Africa the forest is limited to a narrow coastal strip but in the east, in the Bantu homeland in southern Nigeria and Cameroon, it merges seamlessly with the vast forested Congo River Basin. Bantu farmers therefore had enormous opportunities for expansion into an area then inhabited only sparsely by 'Pygmy' hunter-gatherers. And the Bantu would have needed these opportunities as their population began to grow thanks to the increased food supply.

Prehistoric rock paintings found in caves in Tassili N'Ajjer National Park in Algeria, which show grazing animals, are thought to have been made by hunters thousands of years ago, indicating that the Sahara was once a land of lush savannah.

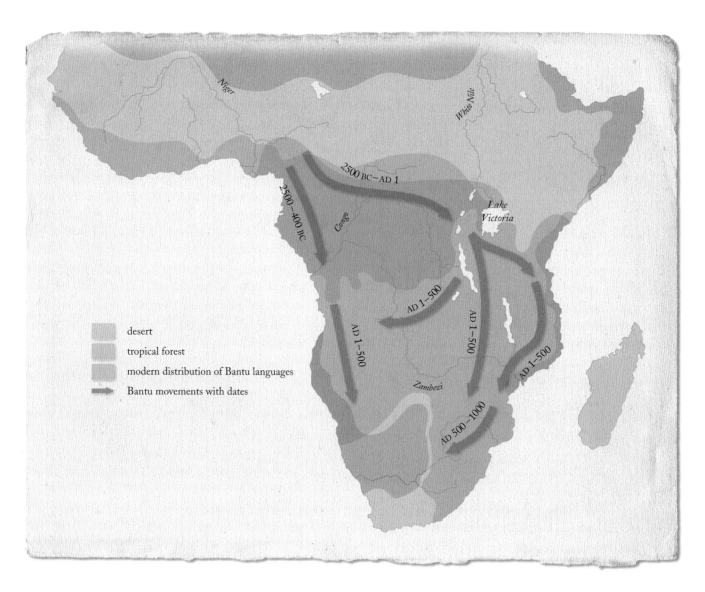

Niger

White Nile

2500 BC–AD 1

2500–400 BC

Congo

Lake Victoria

AD 1–500

AD 1–500

AD 1–500

AD 1–500

AD 500–1000

Zambezi

desert

tropical forest

modern distribution of Bantu languages

Bantu movements with dates

A map showing the spread of early Bantu people from their origins in West Africa to eastern and southern parts of the continent.

Simply because of their greater numbers, Bantu farmers would have had an advantage over the neighbouring hunter-gatherers whose territory they were encroaching on. Rainforest soils are relatively infertile and are quickly exhausted by agriculture. This required farmers to adopt swidden agriculture (also known as slash-and-burn). Fields would be cleared, cultivated for a few years only and then abandoned for the forest to reclaim. Left to itself, the soil would eventually recover its fertility, but meanwhile the farmers moved on. As their numbers increased, the agricultural frontier would have advanced more and more rapidly. Hunter-gatherers in the way, seeing their hunting grounds vanishing under the iron axes and hoes of the Bantu would have faced stark choices. They could resist, but numbers were against them and they would invite extermination or enslavement. They could migrate, but that would mean fighting another hunter-gatherer band for its territory. Or they could adopt farming too and eventually be assimilated, by intermarriage or conquest, by the more numerous incomers. It is likely that different groups tried one or all of these options. The small communities of 'Pygmies' who survive in the Congo Basin are all now Bantu speakers and are largely acculturated with their Bantu neighbours.

The Bantu experienced more complex interactions in East Africa, where the Khoi peoples had already abandoned hunting and gathering in favour of semi-nomadic pastoralism based on breeding sheep and cattle on the savannah, which had probably been introduced to the region from the Sahel. Hunting and gathering was still the way of life of the Khoi peoples of southern Africa but there was a pastoralist front moving south, ahead of the Bantu farmers. By the time of Christ, pastoralism had been adopted by Khoi even in southern Africa, but they continued to practise hunting and gathering in arid areas like the Kalahari Desert and in low-lying areas where tsetse-fly infestation made pastoralism uneconomic (tsetse flies carry a virus which causes a sleeping sickness in humans and animals).

The savannah was a different environment from the forests they were used to, so the Bantu adopted many aspects of the Khoi's way of life, including a greater reliance on stock rearing. Many southern Bantu words associated with pastoralism, such as those for 'cow', 'milk' and 'sheep' are of Khoi origin, indicating direct interaction between the two groups. Some southern Bantu groups also adopted the unique 'click' sounds of Khoi language, suggesting a high degree of intermarriage between the two groups. In historic times there was also frequent violence between the southern Bantu and the Khoi. Cattle raids were common and Bantu often captured and enslaved Khoi.

TIMELINE

3000 BC Origins of the Bantu languages in West Africa

*c.***2750 BC** Yam cultivation is adopted in West Africa; the population begins to increase

2500 BC Bantu migrations begin; they split into eastern and western groups

*c.***500 – 400 BC** The Bantu peoples adopt ironworking

400 BC Bantu-speaking peoples reach the Congo River

AD 1 Bantu-speaking peoples reach the East African Great Lakes region

AD 1000 Migrating Bantu herders reach South Africa

Technological innovations

The pace of the Bantu migrations was maintained by the adoption of iron-making technology in the last two or three centuries BC. Although the earliest ironworking sites in sub-Saharan Africa (around 800 BC), are all in West Africa, it was the eastern branch of the Bantu who first acquired iron-making skills. This suggests they acquired the skill from contacts with the Egyptianate kingdom of Meroë in Sudan. Metalworking spread quickly among the Bantu peoples. African smiths were highly skilled and, using an innovative furnace designed to increase air flow and create higher temperatures, they could produce iron of a higher quality than that produced by Mediterranean civilizations of the time. Iron tools increased agricultural productivity by making it easier to fell forests and work fields. Iron weapons also gave them a military advantage over the Khoi and 'Pygmy' peoples, who never acquired metalworking skills.

By about AD 1000 the Bantu migrations were coming to an end. The Eastern Bantu had reached as far south as the Kalahari and almost fully occupied the Congo Basin. The western branch had continued south from the Great Lakes and by AD 1000 had reached the Drakensberg Mountains in South Africa. However, the Bantu were still encroaching slowly on Khoi territory when European settlers arrived at the Cape of Good Hope in the 17th century and began to take territory from both the Khoi and the Bantu.

Masters of the Steppes
1200 BC—AD 370

Many times in history, the fortunes of the civilizations of the Old World were decided by the conflicts and migrations of distant nomad peoples on the Eurasian steppes. In the Christian era these nomads were Turk and Mongol peoples but the first, and largely forgotten, masters of the steppes – the Cimmerians, Scythians and Sarmatians – were all descendants of the Indo-Europeans.

The steppes are a vast expanse of grassland extending 6000 miles (9600 km) from eastern Europe through central Asia to Manchuria in East Asia. To the north, the steppes merge with the taiga, the equally vast boreal pine forest which stretches across Eurasia from Scandinavia to the Pacific Ocean. To the south, the steppes are bordered by the Tibetan Plateau and the deserts of the Middle East. The steppes have a harsh climate, with only light, and sometimes unreliable, rainfall in the warm summers, and extremely cold, dry winters.

Farmers from western Eurasia began moving onto the steppes as early as the fifth millennium BC. The harsh climate was not ideal for arable farming, so they relied mainly on herds of sheep, goats, cattle and horses. Because of the distances involved, settlement remained sparse until the invention of wheeled vehicles around 3500 BC. Pulled at first by bullocks bred for meat and milk rather than transport, these wagons allowed farmers to move their herds between summer and winter pastures, significantly increasing their grazing resources and allowing them to keep more livestock. The Indo-Europeans (see pages 30–33) were among the earliest peoples to pursue this way of life. They began to split up around 2500 BC , with groups heading into Europe and the Middle East, where they adopted settled lifestyles. One major branch, the Iranians, remained on the steppes, spreading as far east as the Gobi Desert. The invention of bits and bridles in around 1000 BC made riding on horseback possible, allowing the Iranians to manage herds efficiently over vast ranges, and led to the adoption of a fully nomadic lifestyle by about 900 BC.

The Iranian nomads were divided into several distinct peoples, sub-divided into independent clans with their own chiefs. Many chieftain burials have been discovered on the steppes – underground chambers with offerings of weapons, jewellery, horses, wagons and human sacrifices, covered with a *kurgan*, or barrow. Because permafrost underlies much of the steppes, the bodies in these burials are often in an excellent state of preservation. Efficient use of grazing dictated that the clans of any nomad people were usually widely dispersed over the steppes but if the need arose they could unite and

A Mongolian landscape, part of the vast steppes which stretch from eastern Europe to Manchuria.

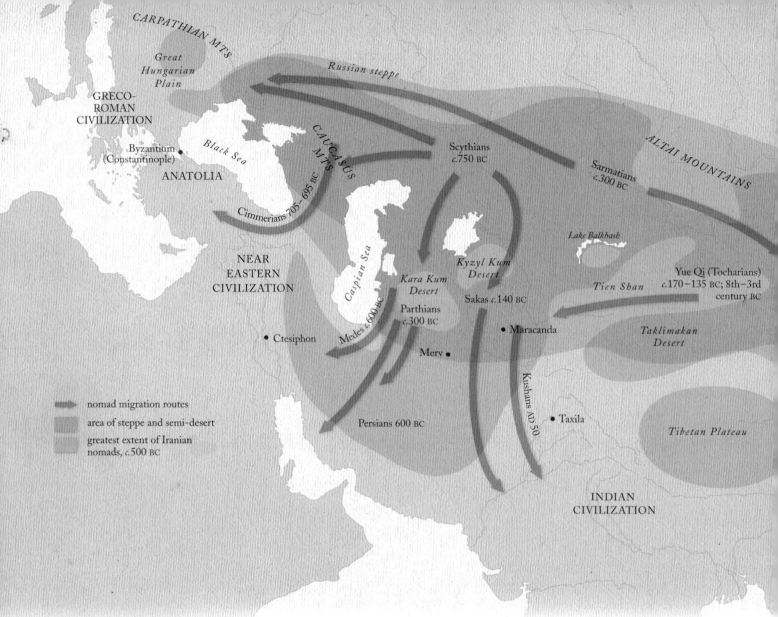

Map showing the movement of Iranian nomads, c.900 BC–AD 400.

migrate en masse. Skilled horsemen, they were engaged in near permanent low-intensity warfare, clan against clan, people against people, fighting over grazing rights or access to water, or raiding for livestock and, sometimes, women.

Nomadism was a hard life and it bred hard people. People who might have to abandon their own parents, leaving them to starve to death on the steppes when they became too old to travel, did not shrink from acts of cruelty to their enemies. Most Iranian nomads preferred to fight as light cavalry, using bows and arrows to attack from long range and relying on speed and mobility rather than armour for protection. These tactics made it hard for the urban civilizations around the edges of the steppes to protect themselves from nomad raids and invasions. Nomads were often able to conquer their settled, urbanized neighbours and found substantial kingdoms. However, once they had left the steppes, nomads gradually adopted the lifestyle and culture of their settled subjects.

The Cimmerians

The earliest of the Iranian nomads to appear in recorded history were the Cimmerians. The Cimmerians dominated the steppes north of the Black Sea from around 1200 BC to about 800 BC, when they came under pressure from the Scythians, another Iranian

Mongolian steppe

Gobi Desert

Ordos Desert

● Luoyang

● Hao

CHINESE CIVILIZATION

nomad people from the Altai Mountains in central Asia. To escape, they migrated south across the Caucasus Mountains and tried to establish themselves in Armenia in 705 BC. Driven off by the Assyrians, they invaded and overthrew the Phrygian kingdom on the Anatolian Plateau. This was to be the first of many occasions when conflicts on the steppes set off migrations that had a destructive impact on distant urban civilizations.

The Cimmerians continued to live as nomads on the lands they had conquered. In 652 BC they invaded the wealthy western Anatolian kingdom of Lydia and sacked its capital. Lydia survived, however, and in 637 or 626 BC inflicted a decisive defeat on the Cimmerians. After this the Cimmerians settled permanently in Cappadocia (whose name in Armenian, 'Gamir', is derived from the Cimmerians) and soon lost their identity.

Other nomads who may have been displaced from central Asia by the migrating Scythians were three closely related peoples: the Medes, the Iranians and the Parthians. The Parthians finished up in what is now Turkmenistan, while the Medes occupied the Iranian Plateau. The Iranians travelled furthest, to Parsa (now called Fars) in the southern Zagros Mountains. From the name of their new homeland, the Iranians became known to the rest of the world, but never to themselves, as Persians. After they allied with the Babylonians to overthrow the Assyrian empire in 612 BC, the Medes became one of the great powers of the Middle East. The Persians were tributaries of the Medes

A felt wall hanging dating to c.300 BC from a burial at Pazyryk in the Altai Mountains in Siberia, depicting a Scythian or Sarmatian chief on horseback.

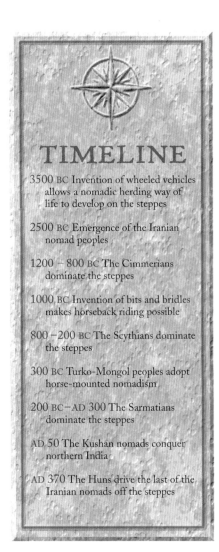

TIMELINE

3500 BC Invention of wheeled vehicles allows a nomadic herding way of life to develop on the steppes

2500 BC Emergence of the Iranian nomad peoples

1200 – 800 BC The Cimmerians dominate the steppes

1000 BC Invention of bits and bridles makes horseback riding possible

800 – 200 BC The Scythians dominate the steppes

300 BC Turko-Mongol peoples adopt horse-mounted nomadism

200 BC – AD 300 The Sarmatians dominate the steppes

AD 50 The Kushan nomads conquer northern India

AD 370 The Huns drive the last of the Iranian nomads off the steppes

until their king, Cyrus (r.550 – 530 BC), rebelled in 550 BC and seized the Median throne. Cyrus went on to conquer the Babylonian empire and the Anatolian kingdom of Lydia, so founding the Persian empire, the largest the world had yet seen.

Cyrus's empire survived for 200 years, until it was conquered by Alexander the Great of Macedon (356–323 BC) in 334–329 BC. No sooner had Alexander died than squabbling generals ripped his empire apart. In the ensuing chaos, the Parthians began to seize former Persian territory and by 140 BC they had built an empire that stretched from the Indus to Mesopotamia. They were prevented from completely recreating the Persian empire by the Romans. For nearly 300 years Rome and Parthia vied for supremacy of the Middle East, with neither side gaining a permanent advantage over the other. When the Parthian kingdom finally came to an end in AD 224–6 it was because it was overthrown by its Persian subjects.

The Scythians

The Scythians who pushed the Persians on their road to empire raided far and wide across the Middle East, even reaching the borders of Egypt, but they never seem to have attempted permanent conquests away from the steppes. Unusually for nomads, the Scythians were superb craftsmen in bronze and gold. Their vigorous art style, based on animal motifs, was adopted by other nomad peoples as far east as the borders of China and also had a significant influence on the development of Celtic art. The Scythians were unusual in allowing women to fight as warriors alongside the men. This custom probably gave rise to the Greek legend of the Amazons, the fierce women warriors who cut off their right breasts so that they would not get in the way of their javelin throwing and archery.

The arrival of Greek settlers on the northern coasts of the Black Sea in the sixth century BC introduced the Scythians to new cultural influences. Many abandoned nomadism to farm wheat to trade with the Greeks for wine and other luxuries. Around 400 BC a fortified city was founded at Kamenskoye Gorodishche, which was probably the capital of a Scythian kingdom. With vague, undefined and indefensible borders no kingdom on the steppes could ever be secure. In the third century BC it was the Scythians' turn to be displaced by another migrating Iranian people, the Sarmatians, who forced them off the steppes and into the Crimea. They finally vanished from history in the third century AD.

The Sarmatians

By the first century AD the Sarmatians controlled a territory stretching from the River Volga west to the frontier of the Roman empire on the River Danube. The Sarmatians were divided into two main branches: the Iazyges in the west and the Roxolani in the east. A closely related group, the Alans, occupied the steppes between the Black Sea and the Caucasus. In the second and third centuries the Sarmatians often allied with the Germanic tribes to raid the Roman empire. At the same time the Alans crossed the

Caucasus to raid the empire's eastern provinces. Perhaps in response to fighting the armoured and well-disciplined Roman infantry, whose formations were not easily broken by archery alone, the Sarmatians fought as heavy-armoured cavalry, using the lance and long sword as their main weapons. The loss of mobility did not serve them well in the long run. In the fourth century the foot-plodding Goths spread onto the steppes, conquering and assimilating the Sarmatians.

The Sarmatians were the last great Iranian nomad power. Around 300 BC the Turk and Mongol peoples on the eastern steppes adopted horse-mounted nomadism and began to spread west at the Iranians' expense. The likely advantage possessed by the Turko-Mongol nomads was that their bows were more powerful than those used by the Iranian nomads.

The first to suffer were the Yue Qi, or Tocharians, who lived in the Turfan Depression close to the borders of the Chinese empire (which they often raided). In 170 BC they suffered a crushing defeat by a Turk confederation called the Xiongnu. Though some Yue Qi stayed behind, surviving into the Middle Ages, most took flight west to the steppes around the Tien Shan Mountains. Here they clashed with the Sakas, a branch of the Scythians who had remained in central Asia, in turn forcing them to flee to northern India. Around AD 50 India suffered its last influx of Iranian nomads when it was invaded by the Kushans, a branch of the Yue Qi.

The Kushans built an empire which, at its peak under Kanishka (r. c.AD 100 – 30), extended from the Aral Sea to the River Ganges and the Indian Ocean and controlled the main trans-Asian trade routes. Always wealthy, the Kushans developed a remarkably eclectic civilization combining elements of Hindu, Buddhist, nomad and Greco-Roman cultures. After Kanishka's reign the Kushans gradually lost control of their central Asian territories to the Turkic nomads, while their Indian territories were re-conquered by the Indians in the fourth century. Both the Kushans and the earlier Saka immigrants were fully assimilated into Indian culture by this time. The displacement of the Iranian nomads from the steppes by the Turko-Mongols was finally completed around AD 370 when one of these peoples, the Huns, arrived on the Black Sea steppes and collided with the Alans. By now the last significant Iranian nomad people, the Alans, fled west and, in alliance with the Vandals, a Germanic people, they invaded the western Roman empire in AD 409, helping to set it on course for its final collapse 70 years later. Not that the Alans survived to see that momentous event: they were all but wiped out by the Germanic Visigoths in Spain in AD 415, bringing the history of the Iranian nomads to an end.

This gold pectoral (neck ornament) from the fourth century BC is an example of the fine craftsmanship of the Scythians, which was unusual among nomad peoples of the time.

65

In the Wake of Alexander the Great
336 BC–323 BC

In only eight years Alexander the Great of Macedon (r.336–323 BC) forged an empire stretching east from Greece to the Indus River in India. Throughout his empire Alexander founded cities, most of which he named Alexandria after himself, populating them with Macedonian and Greek soldiers and emigrants. Though his empire quickly fell apart after his death, his cities ensured that Hellenism would be the dominant cultural influence across the Middle East into the Christian era.

Alexander was only 20 when he inherited the throne of Macedon from his father Philip II (r.359–336 BC). Handsome and charismatic, Alexander was imaginative, bold – even reckless – and violent. He had already shown an aptitude for war fighting while serving in his father's army and had received an excellent education from his personal tutor, the philosopher Aristotle (384–322 BC). Alexander was always conscious of his illustrious forebears – his father claimed descent from Heracles (Hercules), his mother from the Trojan War hero Achilles – and he was driven by the urge to live up to this noble lineage and achieve divinity. By the time he died in 323 BC, still aged only 33, he had fully realized his ambition, having been recognized as a god in his own lifetime.

Lightning campaigns in Persia and India

Alexander invaded the Persian empire in 334 with an army of just 47,000 men. This was a large army by Greek standards but pitifully small according to the norms of the Persian empire. However, Alexander enjoyed many advantages over his adversary. Because of their empire's vast size, it took months for the Persians to assemble an army for a major campaign. Persian armies could be hundreds of thousands strong but sheer numbers were not the advantage they seemed. Such large armies created huge problems of provisioning and, in an age of primitive communications, were impossible to control effectively in battle. Most soldiers in the Persian army were poorly equipped and unenthusiastic levies from the empire's subject peoples. In contrast, Alexander's soldiers were well trained and were all equipped with body armour. And unlike Alexander, the Persian king Darius III (r.336–330 BC) was an indecisive and uninspiring general.

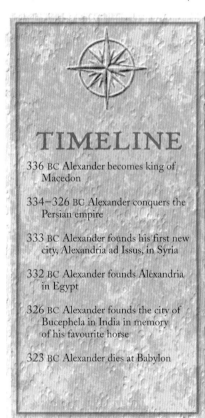

TIMELINE

336 BC Alexander becomes king of Macedon

334–326 BC Alexander conquers the Persian empire

333 BC Alexander founds his first new city, Alexandria ad Issus, in Syria

332 BC Alexander founds Alexandria in Egypt

326 BC Alexander founds the city of Bucephela in India in memory of his favourite horse

323 BC Alexander dies at Babylon

Within weeks of his arrival, Alexander won his first battle against the Persians, at the Granicus River, near the shores of the Sea of Marmara. Encountering little opposition, Alexander swept triumphantly through Anatolia. Reinforced by more troops from Greece, Alexander crushed an army led by Darius in person at the Issus River in southern Turkey in 333. To commemorate his victory, Alexander founded the first of his cities, Alexandria ad Issus, now known as Iskenderun. The following year, Egypt was surrendered to Alexander by its Persian government. After being crowned king of Upper and Lower Egypt at Memphis, the ancient capital of the pharaohs, Alexander sailed down the Nile and on a spit of land between Lake Mareotis and the Mediterranean he oversaw the laying out of another Alexandria.

After Alexander defeated Darius a second time, at Gaugamela near Nineveh in Mesopotamia in 331, Persian resistance began to crumble. A year later, Alexander captured and sacked the empire's capital at Persepolis. Darius fled and was murdered soon after. Three more years of tough campaigning ensued as Alexander pacified the eastern Persian provinces of Drangiana, Sogdiana and Bactria (roughly modern Turkmenistan, Uzbekistan and Afghanistan), founding other Alexandrias as he went, including Alexandria (Ghazni) and Alexandria Areion (Herat).

From Afghanistan Alexander turned south and conquered the Indus Valley in northern India in 326. Even here he founded cities, one of which he named Bucephela after his favourite horse, which had been fatally wounded in battle with the Indians. The last major engagement of Alexander's campaign was his victory at the Hydaspes River, but his army was now war-weary and refused to follow him any further. His conquests at an end, Alexander died three years later at Babylon, an overweight alcoholic.

Detail from a famous mosaic uncovered in the ruined Italian city of Pompeii, showing Alexander defeating Darius III of Persia at the Battle of Issus in 333 BC.

Alexander's cultural legacy

On his death, Alexander left as heirs only a mad brother and a posthumous son, neither of whom were able to rule. Power in the provinces was seized by Alexander's generals and the empire broke up in a complex series of conflicts known as the Wars of the Diadochi ('the successors'). The big winners were Ptolemy (r.323–283 BC), who seized Egypt, and Seleucos (r.312–281 BC), who took Syria, Mesopotamia and Persia. The most remote of the successor kingdoms was Bactria, which comprised much of Afghanistan and Turkmenistan. The Diadochi were just as enthusiastic about founding cities as Alexander had been and emigrants continued to leave Greece and Macedon for the east for a generation after his death. The loss of manpower for Macedon was so severe that it was unable to maintain its great power status. The widely scattered cities founded by Alexander and his successors became agents for an enormous expansion of Greek cultural influence. Greek became the common language for traders and travellers from the Mediterranean and the Indus Valley. Alexander had created a vast melting pot in which aspects of Greek civilization were borrowed and adapted by the Egyptians, Persians and Indians to create a new international Hellenistic civilization. It was this, rather than his ephemeral empire, that was Alexander's lasting achievement.

At first, Alexander's cities were simply garrisons left behind to police conquered areas, reinforced by veteran soldiers and resettled prisoners of war. The cities enjoyed mixed fortunes. Bucephala did not last a year: it was badly sited and was washed away by the first wet season's monsoon rains. Alexander's other foundations in the Indus Valley also did not last because the area was returned to Indian control after his death. However, when they were founded on strategic routes they often flourished because they attracted merchants and other civilian settlers. For example, many of Afghanistan's most important cities, including Ghazni, Kandhahar, Farah and Herat were once Alexandrias. Far and away the most successful Alexandria was in Egypt. Its position on the Mediterranean close to the mouths of the Nile made it a natural entrepôt for trade between Egypt and the rest of the Mediterranean. The city's original military settlers were soon joined by Greek and Jewish merchants and craftsmen and it began to grow explosively. Under Ptolemy and his successors (there were 16 of them, 14 of whom were also named Ptolemy), Alexandria became the capital of Egypt and a rival to Athens as the leading cultural centre of the Greek world. The city's most famous monument was its lighthouse, the Pharos. Completed in 275 BC it was regarded as one of the Seven Wonders of the Ancient World. Alexandria was notorious for the bloody riots that took place between its Greek

- ● city founded by Alexander
- ● other major cities
- — borders of Alexander's empire
- empire of Alexander 323 BC
- — campaign of Alexander 334–324 BC
- ✘ major battle site

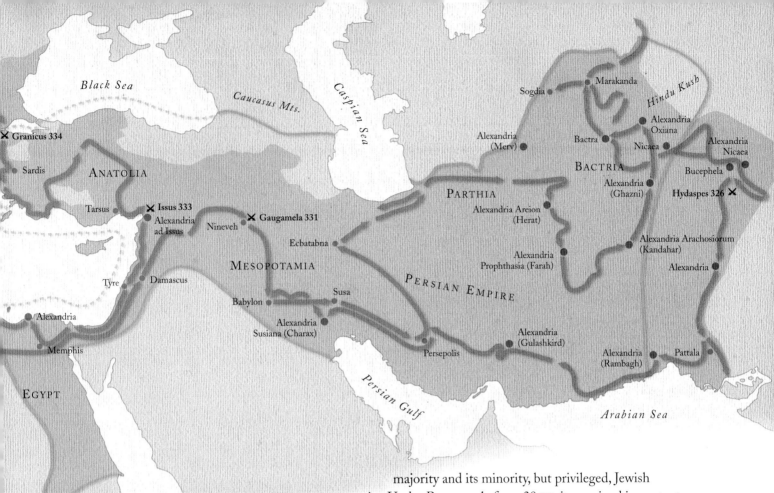

Map showing the area
conquered by Alexander the
Great from 334 to 324 BC.

The Greek architect
Dinocrates, who laid out
Alexandria in Egypt for
Alexander the Great, also
drew up plans for a city in
his honour on Mount Athos
in Macedonia, including a
colossal sculpture of the
warrior hero. These plans
were never realized.

majority and its minority, but privileged, Jewish
community. Under Roman rule from 30 BC, it remained important
as the port through which most of the city of Rome's grain supplies flowed,
and, later, as a leading centre of early Christianity. After the Arab conquest in
AD 641 the population gradually became Arab and Muslim but the Greek and Jewish
communities remained important until the Second World War. However, growing
nationalistic hostility to non-Muslims forced the remaining Greeks and Jews to
emigrate in the late 1940s.

If Alexandria in Egypt was the most successful of Alexander's Alexandrias, one of the
most remote was Alexandria Oxiana, now called Ay Khanoum, a major centre of the
Bactrian kingdom. Alexandria Oxiana was a perfect re-creation of a typical Greek city
of the age, with a theatre, library, gymnasium, palace, fortified acropolis and city walls.
Remote it may have been, but Alexandria Oxiana was not isolated from the Greek
cultural mainstream. It was visited by the philosopher Klearchos of Soli (fl. 320 BC), one
of Aristotle's students, and it contained a stele inscribed with 150 moral maxims copied
from a column at the Greek sacred city of Delphi over 3000 miles (4800 km) away. In
the middle of the second century BC, Bactria was cut off from the rest of the Greek
world by the expanding Parthian kingdom, but this outpost of Greek civilization held
out for another hundred years before it was overrun by nomads. Folk memories of
Alexander remain strong in this region and many ethnic groups, such as the Burusho,
Nuristanis and Kalash have a strikingly European appearance that gives credence to their
claims to be descendants of Alexander's soldiers. Alexander's settlers were mainly men,
and would have taken local wives, but there were tens of thousands of them, so their Y-
chromosomes should still be present in local populations. Only more peaceful conditions
in Afghanistan will allow scientists to test the truth of these traditions, however.

The Cimbri and the Teutones

c.120 BC–101 BC

In 1891, farm workers digging in a peat bog at Gundestrup in the far north of Jutland, Denmark, discovered a large silver cauldron. The cauldron was decorated with spectacular scenes of Celtic gods, warriors, mythological animals and human sacrifice. The workmanship shows that the cauldron was made in Bulgaria in the second century BC by a Thracian craftsman, probably for a Celtic patron. This remarkable artefact is the only surviving legacy of the amazing migration of two early German peoples, the Cimbri and the Teutones.

The Germans were another offshoot of the well-travelled and far-spreading Indo-Europeans (see pages 30–33). The Germans are thought to have emerged in northern Germany between 2500 and 1000 BC, well beyond the horizons of literate observers in the Mediterranean world, who remained blissfully unaware of their existence until the Cimbri and the Teutones burst rudely onto the scene in 113 BC. The original homeland of the Cimbri and the Teutones was the same part of Jutland where the Gundestrup cauldron was found. In ancient times Jutland was known as Cimbria, and the present-day names of the districts of Himmerland and Thy are thought to be derived from the names of the two peoples.

The Cimbri and the Teutones began their migration around 120 BC. According to ancient writers they were looking for new farmlands. Some Cimbri and Teutones remained behind in Jutland, so it is unlikely that they were driven out by an invader. The tribal territories of both peoples were not large, so over-population is the most likely cause of their migration. How the emigrants were chosen is not known. Women and children, as well as men, were involved and they took wagon loads of possessions with them in their search for a new homeland. The seemingly aimless course of their migration, which would take them the length and breadth of western Europe, makes it clear that they set out without any clear idea of where they were going to finish up. Roman sources claim that there were hundreds of thousands of migrating Germans. This seems improbable, but there is no way to tell for certain whether or not the numbers are exaggerated.

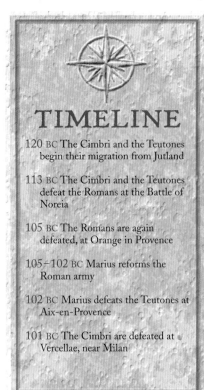

TIMELINE

120 BC The Cimbri and the Teutones begin their migration from Jutland

113 BC The Cimbri and the Teutones defeat the Romans at the Battle of Noreia

105 BC The Romans are again defeated, at Orange in Provence

105–102 BC Marius reforms the Roman army

102 BC Marius defeats the Teutones at Aix-en-Provence

101 BC The Cimbri are defeated at Vercellae, near Milan

A run-in with the Romans

Five years after leaving Jutland, the Cimbri and Teutones passed through the territory of the Celtic Boii in Bohemia; on reaching the Danube, they followed it south into the territory of another Celtic tribe, the Scordisci, who lived in Serbia. The Scordisci were near neighbours of the Thracians, so it was probably from them that the Gundestrup cauldron was looted and returned home to be placed in a sacred bog as an offering to the tribal gods. The Scordisci put up stiff resistance and forced the migrants to turn west into the territory of the Taurisci, a Celtic tribe of the eastern Alps which was allied to Rome. Responding to their appeals for help, the Romans despatched an army to protect them but it was crushed by the Germans at the Battle of Noreia in 113 BC. Fortunately for the Romans, the Germans did not try to follow up their victory by invading Italy but instead headed northwest around the Alps into the territory of the Gauls, the major group of Celtic tribes inhabiting what is now France and Switzerland. On the way they were joined by three Gaulish tribes: the Helvetii, the Tigurini and the Ambrones.

Detail of the Gundestrup cauldron, a richly decorated silver vessel. The cauldron's 13 panels recount a Celtic foundation myth, in which numerous deities and rituals are featured. Found in northern Denmark, the cauldron is thought to be loot from the migration of the Cimbri and Teutones.

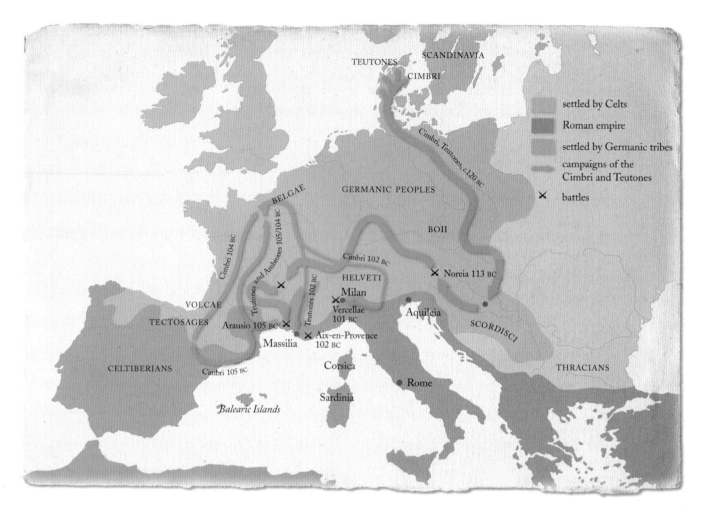

Map showing the migration of the Cimbri and the Teutones, with sites of major battles.

Alarmed by this development, the Romans sent another army against the Germans and their allies but this was defeated when it tried to stop them crossing the River Rhône in 109 BC. This success encouraged two more Gaulish tribes, the Volcae and the Tectosages from the region around Toulouse, to join the Germans. The Romans quickly conquered the Volcae and the Tectosages in 107–106 BC, plundering 100 tons of gold and silver from their temple at Toulouse in the process, but if they thought the crisis was over, they were to be disappointed.

After a request for lands to settle was rebuffed, the Germans annihilated another Roman army at Arausio (Orange, Provence) in 105 BC and rampaged through Roman settlements in the area. Up to 120,000 Roman soldiers and civilians may have been killed. News of the disaster caused panic in Rome. The road to Italy was wide open but the Germans did not take it. Instead they split up: the Cimbri migrated west, crossing the Pyrenees into Spain, while the Teutones headed north into the territory of the Belgae, a large group of warlike Celtic tribes living in what is today northern France and Belgium (which is named for them). The Romans were given a breathing space and made good use of it.

The apparently irresistible advance of the Germans revived uncomfortable memories for the Romans of the sack of their city by the Celts in 390 BC (see pages 46–51). Since that awful event, the Romans had become accustomed to winning. Not even mighty

Carthage and Macedon had stood before their legions, so the experience of defeat by a barbarian rabble was deeply shocking. In the aftermath of Arausio, Gaius Marius, a popular and capable general, was given command of the war against the Germans. Marius saw that nothing less than radical army reform would save Rome from another sack. The army of the Roman Republic was a citizen army that served only in wartime. Service in the army was open exclusively to property owners because it was believed that the only people who could be relied upon to fight for the state were those who owned a stake in its survival.

Radical Roman reforms

The most important source of recruits was the peasant freeholder class, but this class was in decline. Freeholders were finding it hard to compete with the great estates of the aristocracy, which were run using cheap slave labour. This was in plentiful supply because of the mass enslavement of conquered peoples. Falling into debt, freeholders were dispossessed by aristocratic landowners and they drifted to Rome to join the ranks of the landless urban poor. To head off the looming recruitment crisis, Marius abolished the connection between military service and property ownership, allowing Rome to fully mobilize its considerable reserves of manpower, and opened the way for the creation of a professional standing army. The structure of the legions was reorganized to make them more flexible, and drill, weapons training and equipment were standardized.

Marius's reforms were completed in the nick of time because by 102 BC the Cimbri and the Teutones were heading back towards Italy. Defeated in their separate ventures, the Cimbri and Teutones planned a two-pronged invasion of Italy. The Teutones would invade from the west, while the Cimbri would cross the Alps and invade Italy from the north. Marius first led his new army against the Teutones, defeating them at Aix-en-Provence. Those Teutones who were not slaughtered were captured and sold into slavery. Around midsummer the following year, Marius won a similarly total victory over the Cimbri at Vercellae, near Milan. Thousands of the defeated Cimbri committed suicide rather than be taken captive; the survivors went to the slave markets.

The migration of the Cimbri and the Teutones was a disaster. All 20 years of wandering had brought them was death or enslavement. But this was just the beginning of five centuries of German expansion resulting from population growth and social change. The north was stirring. Though victorious over the Cimbri and the Teutones, the Roman Republic did not escape unscathed. Marius's reformed legionary army became the backbone of Roman power for the next 400 years. However, it also enabled ambitious generals to dominate political life. The representative institutions of the republic were sidelined, and Rome slid into military dictatorship and civil war. Finally in 30 BC, Octavian, the victor of the civil war that followed the murder of Julius Caesar, abolished the republic and ruled as emperor under the name Augustus.

This somewhat fanciful later interpretation shows Teutone soldiers gathered on shore. Having defeated the Romans in southern France, the Teutones headed north to modern-day Belgium, sparing Rome.

73

Roman Colonialism
499 BC—AD 14

Although the Roman empire was established through the imposition of military might, its longevity was due to the Romans' skill in assimilating conquered peoples and turning them into loyal Roman citizens. A major element in this process of Romanization was the foundation of colonies for poor Roman citizens and discharged veteran soldiers.

In 509 BC the Romans overthrew their king, Tarquin the Proud (r. *c.*535–509 BC) and founded a republic. Though its territory was only about ten miles (16 km) across, with a population of up to 40,000 people Rome was already beginning to outstrip its neighbours. Situated at an intersection of major travel routes at the lowest bridging point over the River Tiber, Rome was a natural trade centre. Rome was almost uniquely welcoming to immigrants; since citizenship, and the privileges that went with it, depended on residency rather than birth, it was easy for immigrants to assume a Roman identity. Even a freed slave could aspire to citizenship. It is significant in this context that the Romans believed themselves to be the descendants of immigrants – Trojans, who under their leader Aeneas had escaped from the sack of Troy and made their way to Italy.

A diverse mix of peoples

Ancient Italy was a land of great ethnic diversity. The north was dominated by the Etruscans, whose heartland lay in Tuscany. Most of the rest of peninsular Italy was inhabited by Italic peoples, including the Sabines, Samnites, Umbrians, Lucanians and the Latins, the latter of whom included the Romans. In the foothills of the Alps were Celts and Ligurians, while the 'heel' of Italy was inhabited by the Messapians, distant relatives of the modern Albanians. Around the coasts, there were also many Greek colonies. In the centuries that followed, the Romans would assimilate these diverse peoples into a single identity and citizenship.

The immediate effect of the foundation of the republic was to deprive Rome of the strong military leadership the kings had provided. Rome's Latin neighbours sensed an opportunity and combined against it but were narrowly defeated at the Battle of Lake Regillus in 499 BC. In retaliation, the Romans seized Latin territory and planted it with colonies of Roman citizens. This policy of colonizing newly conquered land continued into imperial times. It served the double purpose of consolidating Roman control and relieving social problems by providing opportunities for the city's poor.

Soon after the end of the war with the Latins, the Sabines and other hill tribes began to move into Latium. In 494 BC the Romans patched up their differences with their fellow

Latins and organized a defensive league. It was a century before Rome could renew its expansion. In 396 BC the Romans captured the Etruscan city of Veii, almost doubling their territory. Even so, Rome's furthest borders were still no more than a long day's walk from the city centre. Rome suffered a brief setback in 390 BC when it was sacked by the Gauls, Celtic invaders from north of the Alps. However, the Gauls did far more damage to the Etruscans, driving them out of the fertile Po River Valley, permanently weakening them and so creating new opportunities for Roman expansion in the long term.

In 340 BC Rome's domination of Latium caused its Latin allies to rebel in a war that the Romans won after two years of hard fighting. The settlement provided the pattern for future Roman expansion in Italy. Some defeated Latin cities were incorporated into the Roman state and their inhabitants received Roman citizenship. Other Latin cities kept their status as self-governing municipalities but lost territory and were forced to provide Rome with military support in wartime. Their citizens had the right to marry Roman citizens and trade freely with Rome. Non-Latin peoples who had joined the revolt were incorporated into the Roman state but only gained half-citizenship, giving them all the military and tax obligations of a full citizen without the voting rights. These settlements greatly increased the manpower available to Rome and fuelled further conquests.

The lands confiscated from the defeated rebels initially became the property of the Roman state. In return for giving up their Roman citizenship members of the Roman poor were offered farms and the same rights enjoyed by the Latin cities. Because of this, these settlements became known as Latin colonies (*coloniae*). These colonies could be

Detail from an ancient Etruscan funerary urn, showing a battle scene. The Etruscans of Tuscany were just one of many Italian peoples to be eclipsed by the inexorable rise of Rome.

75

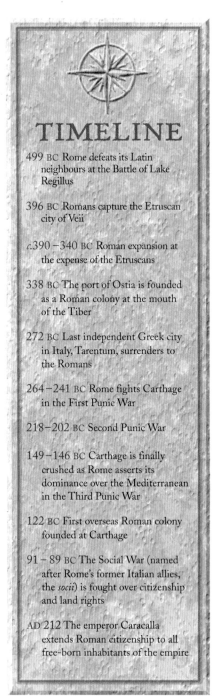

large: Alba Fucens in 303 BC was founded by 6000 Roman families. For defence against pirates, the Roman state also founded small colonies along the coast of Latium, where the settlers were allowed to retain full Roman citizenship. The most important of these was Ostia, at the mouth of the River Tiber, where 300 families were settled in 338. As the growth of Rome outstripped the ability of the surrounding countryside to feed its people, Ostia became Italy's key port, where imported grain, oil and wine were transferred to barges to be sent upriver to Rome.

Masters of the Mediterranean

In the third century BC Roman expansion gathered pace. In a series of wars the peoples of peninsular Italy were conquered one by one and given similar rights and obligations to the conquered Latins. Roman control was complete after Tarentum (Taranto), the last independent Greek city in Italy, fell in 272 BC. Roman control of the Po Valley was secured by the conquest of the Gauls later that century. Rome was transformed from an Italian power to an empire by its victory over Carthage in the three Punic Wars (264–241 BC, 218–202 BC, 149–146 BC), which brought Corsica, Sardinia, Sicily and much of North Africa and Spain under its control. The same period saw the beginning of Roman expansion into the eastern Mediterranean and by 31 BC the entire Mediterranean world was under their control.

Because Romans were increasingly reluctant to give up their citizenship, no more Latin colonies were founded after 177 BC. The Romans now began to found large citizen colonies of 2000–5000 families in strategic locations. Colonization was particularly important in consolidating Roman control over the former Gaulish lands in the north. A few colonies, such as Ariminum (Rimini), founded in 268 BC, were consciously modelled on Rome, with their own capitals and seven administrative districts. This was unusual, however. Colonies were usually laid out on a grid pattern and were generally fortified. The outlines of this original street plan can still be seen in many Italian cities, such as Florence, which were originally founded as Roman colonies.

The distribution of land to Roman colonists was based on a process of surveying and division known as 'centuriation'. The land was marked out in large squares of 200 *iugera* (one *iugera* was 28,000 square feet or around 0.64 acres [0.26 hectares]), which was then divided into 100 plots of two *iugera* for distribution to settler families. These divisions laid out by the Romans have in many cases survived to the present day. Though not large, these plots were sufficient to support a family and provide a surplus for sale.

GALLIA
LUGDUNEN

TARRACONENSIS

LUSITANIA

BAETICA
Corduba

Tingis

MAURETANIA

The citizen colonies were a source of friction with the native population, who resented their privileges. In 91 BC the Italians rebelled and were only pacified after they were promised full Roman citizenship in 89 BC. This concession removed the last obstacle to the total Romanization of Italy; local ethnic identities and languages quickly vanished.

The first Roman colony to be founded outside Italy was at Carthage in 122 BC. A second was founded at Narbo (Narbonne) in Provence in 118 BC to guard the main road from Italy to Spain. Further colonies in Corsica, North Africa and Provence were founded in the early first century BC, but it was not until the heyday of Julius Caesar (49–44 BC) that overseas colonization became normal. During the first century, real power in the Roman republic had passed into the hands of ambitious generals. At the end of the second century BC, the general Gaius Marius (157–86 BC) had reformed the Roman army. Formerly only landowners had been eligible to serve in the legions (it was thought that only men with a stake in the state could be trusted to defend it). However,

Map showing principal Roman settlements by c.AD 100 in the Mediterranean region, North Africa and the Middle East.

Rome's constant wars meant that around 13 percent of adult male citizens were on military service at any one time. This was a heavy burden on the peasant smallholder class. At the same time, slaves, captured in war, were flooding into Italy and being put to work on the large estates of the aristocracy. Peasant freeholders could not compete with this free labour force and many were forced to sell up and join the ranks of the landless Roman poor. Faced with a looming recruitment crisis, Marius had relieved citizens of their military obligations and allowed landless citizens to join the legions as professional full-time soldiers. Because there were no formal arrangements for resettling discharged veterans, soldiers looked to their commanders to provide for them. This led them to support their commanders' political ambitions, in effect turning the legions into private armies. Civil wars fatally destabilized the republican government.

Colonization under the emperors

Finally, in 49 BC Julius Caesar overthrew the republic and declared himself dictator for life. The restoration of peace left tens of thousands of soldiers unemployed and landless. To defuse this potentially explosive situation, Caesar founded colonies of veteran soldiers, with small numbers of Roman poor, in Italy, North Africa, Greece, Anatolia and Spain. After Caesar was murdered in 44 BC another round of civil wars broke out, which were eventually won by Octavian in 31 BC. Octavian restored political stability to Rome by introducing the imperial constitution in 27 BC, after which he ruled as the emperor Augustus (r.27 BC–AD 14). Octavian followed Caesar in resettling large numbers of discharged soldiers in colonies. Though some veterans were given land in Italy, most of the 400 or so colonies founded by Octavian were in the provinces, especially around the coasts of Greece and Anatolia. Although the colonies attracted small numbers of merchants, craftsmen and landless poor, there was no great flow of civilian emigrants from Roman Italy to the provinces.

The ruins of the amphitheatre at Timgad (Thamugas) in Algeria. This settlement was founded in around AD 100 by the emperor Trajan as a colony for veterans of the Third Legion. As in Italy, Roman colonies were planned on a grid pattern, with each settlement having its central forum (town square) and basilica (town hall), temples to Jupiter and other Roman state gods, markets, bath-houses, theatres and amphitheatres.

In many cases, for example Beirut in Lebanon and Cologne in Germany, Roman colonies were founded next to existing native communities. These colonies acted as exemplars of the Roman way of life and eventually absorbed the older community, whose inhabitants were granted Roman citizenship once they were deemed to be sufficiently Romanized. Most colonists were unmarried men, who took local wives. The children inherited Roman citizenship from their father, becoming the first of generations of Romans born in the provinces. Most would never in their lives set foot in Rome or Italy.

To try to ensure that soldiers could not be manipulated by ambitious generals again, Octavian formalized the resettlement of discharged veterans. When his 20-year term of service expired, a legionary soldier received a pension and a grant of land. It became usual for soldiers to be settled in the provinces in which they served. Serving soldiers were not allowed to marry, but most acquired unofficial wives and families in the native civilian settlements that grew up outside most forts. As a result most veterans were happy to settle in the same area. Veterans' colonies continued to be founded until around AD 300, but in much smaller numbers than in Octavian's reign. Increasingly existing communities were granted the title of colony as a way of raising their status, by extending citizenship to their inhabitants, rather than to find homes for discharged veterans. All legal distinctions between Romans and provincials were finally removed when the emperor Caracalla (r.211–17) extended Roman citizenship to all free inhabitants of the empire in 212.

Despite the importance of colonization, the main impetus for Romanization came from the provincials themselves. Except at provincial level, local government in the empire was always left in the hands of local élites. This encouraged them to adopt the Latin language and Roman culture and those who held public office were rewarded with citizenship. Provincials were not allowed to serve in the legions but they could join the auxiliaries, which had less favourable terms of service than the legions but still assured ex-soldiers Roman citizenship on discharge. Adopting Roman ways was also commercially advantageous. Moreover, the Romans did not actively try to suppress local identities; in a pattern familiar in modern times from the USA, provincials became Gallo-Romans in Gaul, Hispano-Romans in Spain, Romano-Britons in Britain, and so on. In the Greek east, this adopted Roman identity lasted long after the fall of Rome itself. Though they were Greeks to western Europeans, the inhabitants of the Byzantine empire continued to regard themselves as Romans right up to the empire's fall in 1453.

Julius Caesar initiated the practice of resettling demobilized Roman legionaries in overseas colonies in times of peace, both as a reward for military service and as a way of forestalling rebellion.

The Jewish Diaspora
721 BC—AD 1948

Most migrations may be over in a few generations or, exceptionally, they may take the form of a directional drift of population spread over centuries, as with the Bantu in Africa. The Jews are unique in that they have been in a state of near permanent migration for 2000 years. Known as the Diaspora, from the Greek word for 'dispersal', their migrations had made the Jews arguably the most widespread people in the world by the early 20th century, with communities on every continent and in almost every country.

The pattern of Jewish settlement has been ever shifting as Jews have responded to the push of persecution and the pull of new opportunities. The survival of the Jewish identity throughout 2000 years of migration and persecution is remarkable. Though it is their religion that has usually led to their persecution, it has also been the key to their survival as a people, for it has prevented them from becoming assimilated into their host communities. Their belief that they have a special covenant with God and in the coming of a Messiah who will restore the kingdom of Israel has helped Jews sustain their faith through all the vicissitudes of history. Because Judaism is essentially a tribal religion, a Jew could not convert to another religion without losing his or her identity and, as Judaism does not seek converts, it has remained a virtually closed society. (In practice, however, small numbers of converts have been accepted, usually by marriage into Jewish families, while some Jews have converted to Islam or Christianity and been assimilated into their host communities.)

Flight to Mesopotamia

The Jewish Diaspora began after the Assyrian king Sargon II (r.722–705 BC) conquered the kingdom of Israel in 721 BC and deported thousands of Jews to Mesopotamia. Deportation to Mesopotamia on a much larger scale followed in 587 BC when the Babylonian king Nebuchadnezzar II (r.605–562 BC) captured Jerusalem and destroyed the temple. Thousands more Jews fled to Egypt to escape Babylonian domination.

The Babylonian exile became a formative period in Jewish history. The experience of defeat caused much religious reflection. Many elements from Mesopotamian religion and mythology were incorporated into Judaism and this was the time, too, that much of the Old Testament was written down in something close to its present form. In 539 BC the Persian king Cyrus the Great (r.550–530 BC) conquered Babylon and gave the Jews permission to return home and rebuild the temple at Jerusalem. However, thousands of Jews decided to stay in Mesopotamia.

A 19th-century painting by the Italian artist Francesco Hayez tells the story of the destruction of the temple in Jerusalem by the Babylonians in 587 BC.

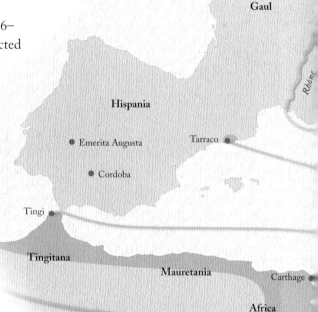

Britannia

Gaul

Hispania

Emerita Augusta

Tarraco

Cordoba

Tingi

Tingitana

Mauretania

Carthage

Africa

Rhône

Jews in the Hellenistic and Roman world

The next phase of the Diaspora began after Alexander the Great (r.336–323 BC) conquered the Persian empire in the fourth century BC. Attracted by the commercial opportunities and grants of privileged status, large numbers of Jews migrated to Alexandria in Egypt, turning it into a third major centre of Judaism after Judea and Mesopotamia. By 100 BC Jews had settled in most of the major Greek cities around the Mediterranean, and also in the up-and-coming city of Rome. In Greek cities, Jewish settlers were organized in officially recognised corporations, with their own leaders, councils and law courts. Jews were exempted from worshipping pagan gods, paying divine honours to rulers and from working on the Sabbath. These privileges were resented by their Greek neighbours and inter-communal rioting was not uncommon: Alexandria was notorious for it. In this period Jews also began to settle in towns, such as Medina, along the caravan routes in Arabia. These large Jewish communities were later to be the major influence on the development of Muhammad's religious ideas.

In 63 BC Judea became a Roman protectorate. High taxes made Roman rule unpopular, while the Jews' belief in the coming of a Messiah led to the formation of the radical Zealots, who were dedicated to regaining independence. In AD 66 the Zealots led an uprising against Roman rule. The revolt was crushed by 74, and large numbers of Jews were sold into slavery and dispersed throughout the empire. After another revolt in 132, Jews were banned from Jerusalem and Judaism was briefly proscribed. In 212 Jews were granted full Roman citizenship but, after Christianity became the empire's official religion in the fourth century, repression resumed. Large numbers of Jews emigrated to Mesopotamia and Judea itself ceased to be the major centre of Judaism. The Jews were now also an overwhelmingly urban people.

Anti-Semitism emerged in early medieval Europe and appeared overtly in religious and secular writing, such as this manuscript illumination from 1023. It illustrates 'heretics and Jews unable to hear the word of God'.

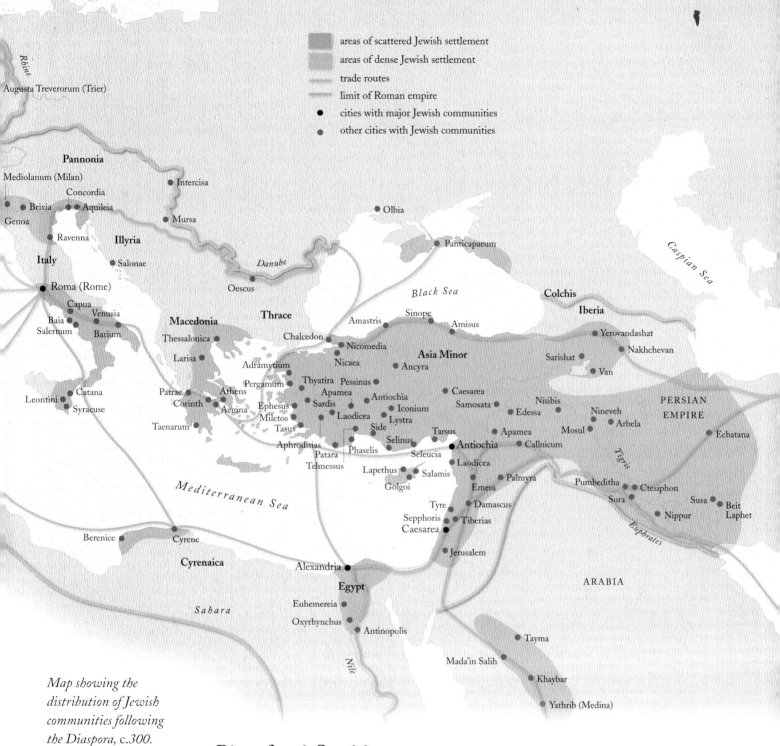

areas of scattered Jewish settlement
areas of dense Jewish settlement
trade routes
limit of Roman empire
● cities with major Jewish communities
● other cities with Jewish communities

Map showing the distribution of Jewish communities following the Diaspora, c.300.

Rise of anti-Semitism

The fall of the Roman empire did not improve things for Jews living in Europe. The Greek Byzantine empire and the Visigothic kingdom of Spain were only the first medieval European states to introduce repressive anti-Semitic legislation. The position of Jews in medieval Europe was never secure. Christians justified anti-Semitism by casting the Jews as the murderers of Christ. Wild superstitions flourished, such as the belief that Jews sacrificed children (known to Jews as the 'blood libel'). The church always condemned such views but to little effect. Jews were frequently required to wear distinctive clothes or badges and faced restrictions on where they could live, on property ownership and on which occupations they could follow. This forced Jews towards

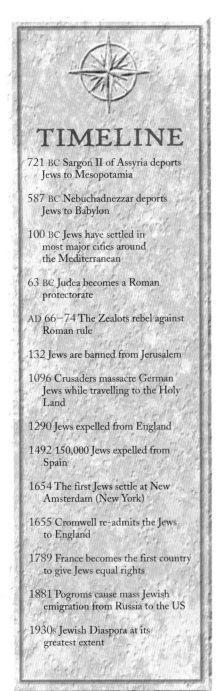

TIMELINE

721 BC Sargon II of Assyria deports Jews to Mesopotamia

587 BC Nebuchadnezzar deports Jews to Babylon

100 BC Jews have settled in most major cities around the Mediterranean

63 BC Judea becomes a Roman protectorate

AD 66–74 The Zealots rebel against Roman rule

132 Jews are banned from Jerusalem

1096 Crusaders massacre German Jews while travelling to the Holy Land

1290 Jews expelled from England

1492 150,000 Jews expelled from Spain

1654 The first Jews settle at New Amsterdam (New York)

1655 Cromwell re-admits the Jews to England

1789 France becomes the first country to give Jews equal rights

1881 Pogroms cause mass Jewish emigration from Russia to the US

1930s Jewish Diaspora at its greatest extent

commerce and moneylending (which was forbidden to Christians and to Muslims). Jewish moneylenders were often killed by anti-Semitic rioters, who also burned their accounts, showing that whatever religious justification they might claim, they often had more practical motives.

Because their financial and commercial skills were in short supply in medieval Europe, Jewish settlers were often welcomed by Christian rulers, who offered them protection and privileges. But Jews could also be cynically milked of their wealth by kings, who exploited popular anti-Semitism to demand increasing amounts of protection money. In the early Middle Ages most European Jews lived in western Europe, mainly in Spain, France, Italy and the German Rhineland. It was in Germany that the Ashkenazi branch of Judaism developed, to which around 80 percent of modern Jews belong.

In response to increased persecution in the west from around 1100 onwards, Jews began to migrate to eastern Europe. In 1254 Jews were expelled from France, and in 1290 from England. The worst persecutions were in Spain in the 15th century. As the Christian reconquest of Muslim Spain gathered pace, many Jews were forcibly converted to Christianity; and in 1492 the rest, some 150,000 of them, were expelled. Known as Marranos, many of the forced converts continued to practise Judaism in secret.

Numbering around 150,000, the largest Jewish community in Europe by the end of the Middle Ages was in Poland, where Jews had enjoyed strong royal protection from the 13th century onwards. Many served the nobility as estate managers and tax collectors. With the co-operation of the crown, Polish Jews gained the right of communal self-government with the setting up of the 'Council of the Four Lands'. This privilege, however, aggravated popular anti-Semitism and Jews were always required to wear distinctive clothes by which they could be easily identified.

Jews under Islamic rule

The Arab conquests of the Middle East and North Africa in the seventh century brought around 90 percent of Jews under Islamic rule. Arab rule gave relief from Christian persecution, but Jews were still treated as second-class citizens and subject to discriminatory legislation. As 'People of the Book', they enjoyed the right to physical protection and freedom of worship subject to payment of the *jizya* (tribute) tax which was imposed on unbelievers. Jewish life and culture at first flourished under Islamic rule, especially in Spain, where the Sephardic branch of Judaism developed under the influence of the peninsula's Christian and Muslim intellectual traditions.

Heavy land taxes forced most Jews in the Arab world into commerce and moneylending. Jewish merchants, known as Radanites, were active as middle men in long-distance trade

This undated engraving illustrates the expulsion of the Jews from Spain in 1492 at the order of the Catholic Inquisition.

between Asia and Europe. Small colonies of Jews became established in India and Ceylon, and even in China as a result of these activities. It may have been through contacts with merchants that the Khazar nomads of the Caspian steppes converted to Judaism around 740. Many east European Jews are thought to be of Khazar descent.

Attacks on the Islamic world by Christian Crusaders in the 12th century led to an increase in religious intolerance and anti-Semitic violence. In spite of this, there was a final influx of Jews into the Islamic world at the end of the 15th century, following their expulsion from Spain: most went to Morocco or the Ottoman empire. The 16th century was a prosperous time for Jewish communities in the Ottoman empire, but from the 17th century they went into a steady decline. New trade routes opened by European explorers had created an economic depression in the Islamic world, while western Europe was being re-opened to Jewish settlement. By the middle of the 18th century, the majority of Jews lived in Europe.

One of the more remarkable branches of the Diaspora are the Falasha, the so-called 'Black Jews' of Ethiopia. The Falasha claim they came to Africa in the time of King Solomon but it is generally thought that they were converted to Judaism by missionaries from Arabia around the time of Christ. Most Falasha were resettled in Israel in 1985–92. Another African people claiming Jewish descent are the Lemba, a Bantu-speaking people of southern Africa, who claim their ancestors were Jews from San'a in Yemen. The Lemba are monotheists, they practise male circumcision and have similar dietary laws to the Jews. Because the Lemba have a typically Bantu appearance, their claims to Jewish ancestry were not taken seriously until 1997 when it was discovered that two-thirds of Lemba men have Y chromosomes that can be traced to Middle Eastern lineages. Moreover, a majority of those carry the Cohen Modal Haplotype. This is associated specifically with the *kohanim* (priests), Jewish men who claim to be direct descendants of Moses' brother Aaron. The mtDNA of Lemba women is, however, entirely of African origin. The Jewish ancestors of the Lemba were all men, perhaps merchants, who settled and took local wives.

A contemporary engraving shows a mob assaulting Jews during a pogrom in the Russian city of Kiev in the 1880s, while police do nothing to intervene. Many such attacks were sanctioned or even encouraged by the Tsarist government.

Dispersal to new lands

From the 17th century, eastern European Jews faced increasing persecution. Many Polish Jews were massacred in Cossack revolts in the 1650s. The situation became worse after Poland was partitioned among Prussia, Russia and Austria in the 18th century. Most of the country's Jews found themselves under hostile Russian rule. Jews were confined to a pale of settlement in Poland, Lithuania, Belorussia and Ukraine and faced frequent pogroms. At the same time, attitudes to Jews were becoming more tolerant in western Europe. Official religious toleration made the Netherlands a popular destination for Jewish refugees from Poland and Marranos from Spain in the 17th century. Once they arrived in the Netherlands, Marranos openly reverted to Judaism. England was re-opened to Jewish settlement by the Lord Protector Oliver Cromwell in 1655. Following the revolution in 1789, Jews were granted full citizenship in France. Other European countries gradually followed suit in the 19th century so that, by 1900, the only countries where Jews had no rights were Spain, Romania and Russia. Russian Jews were in full flight by this time. Large numbers went to Britain and France, but far the most popular destination was the United States. A few went to Palestine.

The British, Dutch and French colonial empires facilitated the further spread of Jews around the world. The Portuguese and Spanish empires were officially closed to Jews and it was only after the fall of these empires in the 19th century that Latin America became fully open to Jewish settlement: Uruguay and Argentina saw the most Jewish immigration. The first Jews to live openly in the Americas were 600 Amsterdam Jews who settled in the Dutch colony of Pernambuco in Brazil in 1642. Only 12 years later the Portuguese expelled the Dutch settlers. Most of the Jews returned to Amsterdam but 23 sailed to the Dutch North American colony of New Amsterdam, renamed New York when it came under English rule in 1664. The few limitations Jews suffered in colonial America were completely removed after independence by the separation of church and state in the Constitution of the United States.

From around 3000 at the time of independence, the number of Jews in the US gradually increased to around 250,000 by 1880, mainly as a result of immigration from Germany and eastern Europe. The escalation of anti-Semitic violence in eastern Europe in the 1880s led to a flood of immigration which more than quadrupled the Jewish population by 1900: by the 1920s, when the Soviet Union restricted Jewish emigration, it was over 4 million. Most of these eastern European Jews were poor and uneducated. They were forced to accept unskilled, low-paid jobs in the factories and on construction sites in the major industrial cities, such as New York, Chicago and St Louis. There remains a strong concentration of Jews in the northeastern US states. Through education and hard work, Jewish immigrants dramatically improved their status so that by the middle of the 20th century they had graduated to white collar jobs and the professions.

By the 1930s Jews were at their most numerous – there were around 18 million worldwide – and most widespread. However, the Holocaust, the foundation of the state of Israel and increasingly violent anti-Semitism in Muslim countries would lead to further dramatic changes in the pattern of Jewish settlement in the 1940s and 1950s.

Jewish immigrants stand on the quayside at Ellis Island, looking towards Manhattan and New York Bay, as they wait to be admitted as residents of the United States, 1912.

The Huns
AD 48–454

Spreading terror before them, the Huns burst from the vast spaces of the Eurasian steppes around AD 370. Less than a century later they had vanished almost without trace. By that time they had completely altered the course of European history, having indirectly brought about the fall of the Roman empire.

The Huns were a Turkic nomadic pastoralist people. They were probably one of the peoples who made up the Xiongnu, a powerful nomad confederation that dominated the eastern Asian steppes in the last centuries BC. When the Xiongnu broke up in AD 48 after suffering several defeats at the hands of the Chinese, the Huns migrated westwards, finding a homeland on the lush rolling steppes north of the Altai Mountains in Siberia. By the middle of the fourth century the Huns were moving west again. This may have had something to do with the emergence of Balamber, a successful war leader about whom little else is known.

The Indo-Iranian nomad peoples who lived on the western steppes, such as the Alans and the Sarmatians, either took flight as the Huns approached or were assimilated by them. Around 370 the Huns ran into the Ostrogoths, a Germanic people who were expanding east across the Ukrainian steppes. Generally acknowledged to be the mightiest of the Germanic peoples, they proved no match for Balamber and the Huns. Within a few years the Huns had advanced to the Danube and settled in the Carpathian basin. This was the most westerly area of steppe grassland where the Huns could pasture their vast herds of horses. The defeat of the Ostrogoths spread panic among the Germans. Some, like the Visigoths, Vandals and Burgundians, escaped into the Roman empire but by the 430s most of the Germanic peoples had been forced to acknowledge Hun overlordship.

Fearsome warriors

The secret of the Huns' success was their style of fighting. Like all the steppe nomads, the Huns spent much of their lives on horseback, tending their flocks of sheep and herds of cattle and horses. They built no dwellings but lived in their wagons. Conflict with other nomadic groups over grazing rights was common. The Huns were skilled and disciplined horse archers. They rarely wore armour and relied on speed and manoeuvrability to keep them out of harm's way, while raining arrows on the enemy from a safe distance with their powerful composite bows. Made by gluing together layers of wood, horn and

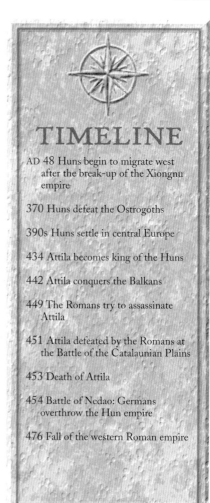

TIMELINE

AD 48 Huns begin to migrate west after the break-up of the Xiongnu empire

370 Huns defeat the Ostrogoths

390s Huns settle in central Europe

434 Attila becomes king of the Huns

442 Attila conquers the Balkans

449 The Romans try to assassinate Attila

451 Attila defeated by the Romans at the Battle of the Catalaunian Plains

453 Death of Attila

454 Battle of Nedao: Germans overthrow the Hun empire

476 Fall of the western Roman empire

sinew, the composite bow's compactness made it ideal for use on horseback and it was widely used by the steppe nomads. What gave the Huns a special advantage was a unique asymmetrical design that almost doubled the power of their bows, so that they could pierce armour at a range of up to 100 metres (300 ft).

The effectiveness of the Huns' cavalry was enhanced by their terrifyingly outlandish appearance, which led Roman writers to compare them to grotesque beasts. Stories spread that they were the offspring of the mating of witches with evil spirits. Huns practised deformation of the skull. Infants' skulls were tightly bound above the eyebrows so that as they grew they would be deformed into a long flat shape with no forehead. The Huns also practised scarification of the face, which left them with little facial hair.

At the time of their arrival in Europe, the Huns did not acknowledge a single leader. Several power-sharing kings operated within a ranking system, with one of their number recognized as senior king. Balamber was probably such a figure. To avoid overgrazing, the Huns needed to be dispersed over a wide area, and this lent itself naturally to the formation of a devolved power structure. In the fifth century, the Huns came to rely less on pastoralism and more on tribute from subject peoples and subsidies for mercenary

Fast and manoeuvrable Hun horsemen overwhelm an army of Alans – Iranian tribesmen from the western steppes. Forced westward by the Hun invasion, the Alans and other displaced peoples attacked already weakened outposts of the Roman empire such as Gaul.

service with the Roman armies. This made possible a process of political centralization which led eventually to the Huns being united under the rule of their greatest warlord Attila (r.434–453). Even within his own lifetime Attila attained semi-legendary status as the self-appointed 'scourge of God'.

Attila's campaign of conquest

The trail of destruction that his forces left across Europe earned Attila, king of the Huns, the nickname 'scourge of God'.

Attila first appears in history in the late 430s, at which time he was joint ruler of the Huns with his brother Bleda (r.434–45). Attila's terrifying reputation rests mainly on his effectiveness as a war leader; in his dealings with his subjects he was not outstandingly tyrannical. Attila relied primarily on his personal charisma, rather than terror, to maintain power. Up to this point, relations between the Huns and the Romans had generally been good. Attila's adoption of a hostile stance towards the empire was probably determined by internal politics – success in war would help consolidate the unity of the Huns – but he was also fully aware of its weakness.

Using a contrived border incident as a justification for war, Attila conquered the northern Balkans in 442. The Romans enjoyed a brief respite in 444–5 after Attila and Bleda fell out. After Attila murdered Bleda, becoming sole king of the Huns, he advanced as far as the east Roman capital at Constantinople in 447 but found its walls impregnable. In 449 the eastern Roman government tried to assassinate Attila using a diplomatic embassy as cover. The plot was betrayed and Attila exploited Roman embarrassment over this treacherous act to extract a huge payment of tribute.

His southern flank secured, Attila turned his attention to the western Roman empire. Since 433, the Roman master general, and effective ruler, of the west had been Flavius Aetius (c.396–454). Aetius knew the Huns well. As a young man he had spent three years as a hostage with them and he frequently employed Hun mercenaries in the 430s, in genocidal campaigns against the Visigoths, Burgundians, Alamanni and Franks who were threatening Roman control of Gaul. Fear that Aetius would let the Huns loose on them again if they rebelled kept the German settlers in Gaul obedient throughout the 440s. Fear of the Huns also left the Visigoths, Burgundians and Franks no choice but to support Aetius when Attila invaded Gaul in 451.

Attila had been so confident of victory that he briefly contemplated burning himself alive on a funeral pyre after Aetius, commanding a coalition of Romans, Visigoths, Burgundians and Franks, fought him to a standstill at

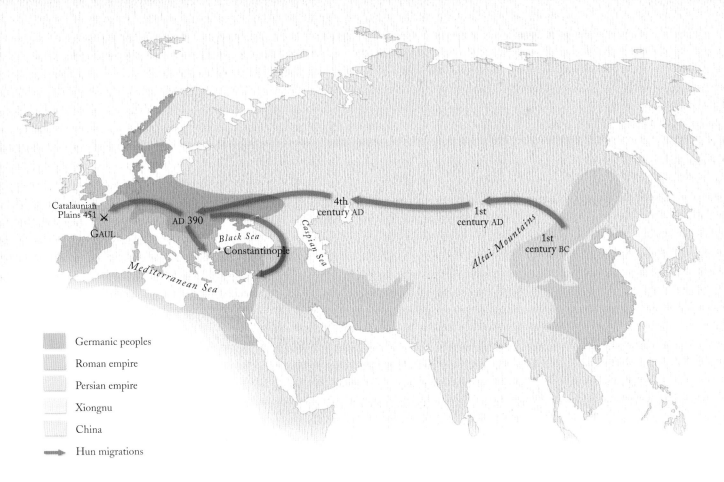

Catalaunian
Plains 451 ✕
GAUL

AD 390

4th
century AD

1st
century AD

1st
century BC

Altai Mountains

Black Sea
• Constantinople

Caspian Sea

Mediterranean Sea

■ Germanic peoples

■ Roman empire

■ Persian empire

■ Xiongnu

■ China

➤ Hun migrations

the Battle of the Catalaunian Plains, near Troyes, in June 451. However, Aetius did not follow up his victory – the Huns had been too useful to him for him to want to destroy them – leaving Attila strong enough to invade Italy in 452. The cities of the Po Valley were devastated but supply problems and disease forced Attila to withdraw. A year later Attila got drunk at a wedding feast, suffered a haemorrhage and choked to death on his own blood. While Attila's sons fought over the throne, his Germanic subjects rebelled and overthrew the Hun empire at the battle of Nedao in the Balkans in 454. Hun unity was shattered and the survivors retreated to the steppes where they disappeared without trace.

Europe continued to struggle with the consequences of the Huns' migration long after they had disappeared. For two centuries before the Huns arrived in Europe, the Roman empire had fought successfully to secure its borders against unrelenting German pressure. The Huns completely destabilized the Germanic world, beginning the *Völkerwanderung* ('the migration of peoples'), as terrified tribes fled to seek refuge in the Roman empire. Some, like the Visigoths, entered by arrangement, most just fought their way in. Few of these refugees wanted to destroy the empire but the problems of controlling and resettling them strained the Romans' already limited resources. When Attila turned hostile, the Romans were fatally distracted from their efforts to recover territory that the Germans had seized by force. Fear of the Huns had at least kept some of the Germanic settlers obedient some of the time. Once Attila died, even this restraint was gone. By 476 the western Roman empire had vanished, replaced by a patchwork of Germanic kingdoms. The eastern Roman empire survived for another 1000 years, becoming known as the Byzantine empire, but its fate too would be sealed by nomads from the steppes.

Map showing the migratory route taken by the Huns from their origins in the steppes of eastern Asia.

The Goths
376–493

Comprising two groups – the Visigoths of Dacia (now Romania) and the Ostrogoths of the Ukraine – the Goths are remembered first and foremost for their sack of Rome in 409. However, far from being marauders bent on destruction, they were refugees seeking a new home after fleeing from the terrifying Huns.

Around 370 the Ostrogoths ('Eastern Goths') were crushingly defeated by the Huns. In despair their king, Ermanaric (d.376), killed himself, probably as part of a ritual sacrifice for the safety of his people. After Ermanaric's successor, Vithimer, was killed in battle, the demoralized Ostrogoths submitted to the Huns. News of the Goths' troubles at first delighted the Romans but they were soon faced with a refugee crisis they could not control. Alarmed by the defeat of the Ostrogoths, the Visigoths ('Western Goths') abandoned their lands and sought asylum in the Roman empire. Some groups of Ostrogoths which had escaped from the Huns decided to do likewise. In the late summer of 376 around 200,000 Goths set up camp on the north bank of the Danube while their leaders negotiated terms for entry with the Romans.

The Roman emperor Valens (r.364–78) had committed the bulk of his army to a war against Persia and he knew that he could not prevent the Goths entering by force if they chose to try. He decided on a compromise: to allow the entry of the Visigoths and use the available troops to oppose the entry of the Ostrogoths. Valens tried to put a positive gloss on the situation. Population decline was having a severe economic impact on the Roman empire in the late fourth century and there were serious problems recruiting enough soldiers for the army. This allowed Valens to present the admission of the Visigoths as an opportunity for strengthening the empire. They would be settled on vacant land in the Balkans, bring uncultivated land back into production, provide recruits for the army and pay taxes. Thousands of German prisoners of war had been successfully settled in the empire over the previous 200 years but the Romans had always been in complete control. Valens's decision was fraught with danger: the Visigoths had not been defeated by Roman arms, their leadership was intact and Valens did not have the troops to control the Visigoths if things went wrong. Which they soon did.

Balkan rebellion

The settlement was catastrophically mismanaged by corrupt officials and in 377 the Visigoths went on the rampage. In the general disorder, bands of Ostrogoths crossed the Danube illegally and joined the Visigoths. In 378 Valens made peace with Persia, so freeing his troops to deal with the Visigoths. On 9 August Valens launched a poorly planned attack on the Visigothic camp near Adrianople and was defeated and killed.

For four years the Visigoths ravaged the Balkans until they were pacified by Valens's successor, Theodosius I (r.379–95). The price of peace was high. Unable to inflict a decisive defeat on them, or expel them from the empire, Theodosius allowed them to settle as semi-autonomous *foederati* (allies) under their own leaders in 382.

After Theodosius' death in 395, the Visigoths rebelled again under their ambitious new king, Alaric (r.395–410). The Visigoths had suffered heavy casualties fighting for Theodosius in a civil war. Alaric believed that Theodosius had been happy to see them weakened in this way and he wanted a new settlement that would give his people greater security. He demanded that he should be given the rank of a Roman master general, and that his people should have control of a province and subsidies of grain and gold. In 397 the Visigoths were settled on new lands in Macedonia but negotiations on Alaric's key demands stalled.

The collapse of the Rhine frontier in 406 strengthened Alaric's hand. The Romans now needed Visigothic support against a new wave of Germanic invaders. The effective ruler of the western Roman empire was the master general Stilicho, who was regent for the young emperor Honorius (r.395–423). Desperate to secure his support, Stilicho offered Alaric everything he wanted. It was too much for most Romans to swallow, however, and Honorius ordered Stilicho's execution for treason. Alaric's attempts at negotiation had collapsed again so, in November 408, he invaded Italy and camped outside Rome. More

A 19th-century engraving depicting Alaric's entrance into Rome in 410, an event that heralded the fall of the western Roman empire.

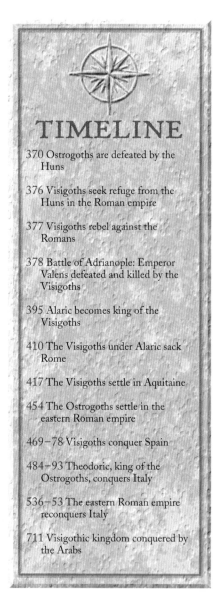

than a year of fruitless negotiations followed. Fighting was not an option for Honorius, as he needed to save his troops to defend Gaul. Despite his strong position, Alaric's terms were modest. He dropped his demands for a generalship and gold and asked only for a province and a grain subsidy.

Alaric's patience ran out in August 410 and, after a short siege, Rome opened its gates to him. After three days sacking the city, Alaric withdrew. Rome was no longer the administrative capital of the empire (the emperors now ruled from Ravenna and Constantinople) but its sacking exposed the decline of Roman power to the whole world. Not since the sack of Rome by the Celts exactly 800 years before had the Romans been so humiliated. Honorius, safe in Ravenna, still refused Alaric's demands. Frustrated, Alaric led the Visigoths into southern Italy, intending to invade Africa, but he died before the year was out. His successor, Athaulf (r.412–15), turned around and took the Visigoths to Gaul.

Doomed to decline

Athaulf had married a Roman princess and wanted a major role in imperial politics for himself. The Visigoths began to see his ambitions as an obstacle to a peace deal with the Romans, and in 415 he was murdered. His successor Wallia (r.415–19) agreed to help the Romans recover control of Spain from the Vandals and Alans. In 417 the Visigoths were rewarded with a settlement on rich lands in the Garonne Valley in Aquitaine. This remained the Visigothic homeland until the 470s, when their king Euric (r.466–84), recognizing the final collapse of Roman power, conquered Spain.

Despite being a minority group among the native population, the Visigoths successfully retained their Germanic identity. To prevent their assimilation, the Visigoths used traditional Germanic law for themselves and Roman law for their subjects. Intermarriage between Visigoths and natives was forbidden. Religion was also an obstacle to assimilation. Before entering the Roman empire, the Goths had converted to Arian Christianity. Catholic Romans regarded Arianism as heretical, so the Visigoths clung to it as a badge of Germanic identity. Though the Visigoths preserved their cultural and religious heritage, they were unable to win the positive allegiance of their subjects and when the Arabs invaded Spain in 711, their kingdom quickly collapsed.

Ceiling mosaic in the Arian Baptistry at Ravenna, northern Italy, which was erected by Theodoric the Great (d.526) at the end of the fifth century.

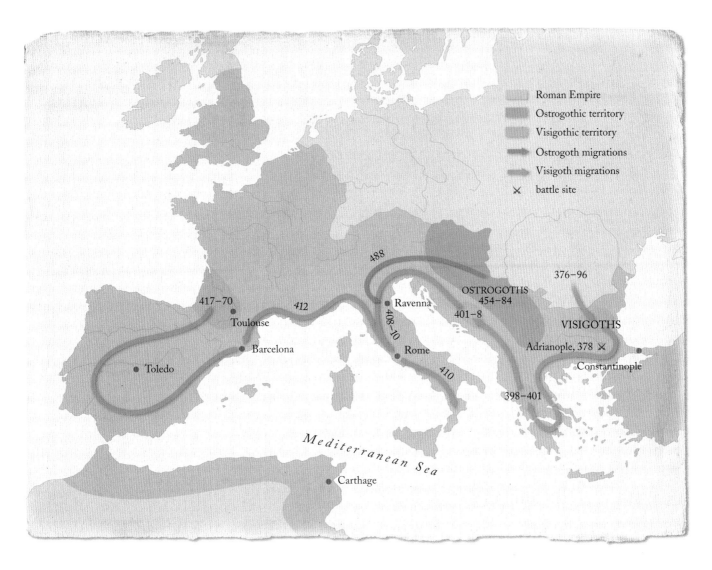

Those Ostrogoths who had not made it into the Roman empire in 376 lived under the domination of the Huns until the fall of their empire in 454. Freed, the Ostrogoths settled in the province of Pannonia (Hungary) and were reluctantly recognized as *foederati* by the eastern Roman empire. Never happy with the Ostrogoths living in his backyard, the eastern emperor Zeno (r.476–91) commissioned their king Theodoric (d.526) to go to Italy in 484 and overthrow Odoacer, the barbarian king who had seized power there after the deposition of the last western Roman emperor in 476. By 493 Odoacer was dead and Theodoric was ruler of Italy. The Ostrogoths settled mostly in the fertile Po River Valley in northern Italy.

Even here, the Ostrogoths were a small minority among the Italians and they were just as concerned about preserving their identity as the Visigoths. The same legal segregation was practised and there was the same religious divide. There was also the same fatal failure to win the allegiance of the native population. When the eastern emperor Justinian (r.527–65) sent an army to take back control of Italy in 536, the Ostrogoths got little support from the Italians. After 17 years of hard fighting the Ostrogoths were crushed. Some went into exile in other Germanic kingdoms, while those who remained were soon assimilated into the Italian population.

Map showing the migration of the Visigoths and the Ostrogoths during the late fourth and early fifth centuries.

The Vandal Migration
c.390–439

Of all the Germanic peoples displaced by the Huns none migrated further in search of a new homeland than the Vandals. From their origins in central Europe the Vandals made an epic journey of over 3000 miles (5000 km) through western Europe, across the Straits of Gibraltar to North Africa, eventually to found a new kingdom in Tunisia.

Few peoples in history have a worse reputation than the Vandals. Certainly no other barbarian people played a greater role in the fall of the western Roman empire. Yet the Vandals were as much the victims of circumstance as the Romans, and their migration was, at times, little more than a headlong flight from stronger enemies.

According to semi-legendary early Germanic historical traditions, the Vandals originated in the region of far-northern Denmark still known as Vendsyssel. When the Vandals left Vendsyssel is not known but by the first century BC they were living on the Baltic coast of Poland. In the following two centuries, the Vandals gradually drifted south and split into two groups, the Silings, who settled in what became known as Silesia, and the Asdings, who settled further south on the Hungarian plain. Here they remained until the arrival of the Huns in the 370s threw the entire Germanic world into panic and chaos.

Flight from the Huns

The Asdings were the first to take flight from the advancing Huns. By the 390s harassment by the Huns had become so severe that they decided to flee west along the north bank of the River Danube. Along the way the Asdings linked up with the Silings, who had also decided to abandon their homes rather than submit to the Huns. They were joined by a group of Alans, Indo-Iranian nomads who had been driven from the trans-Caspian steppes by the Huns. Unfortunately, the Vandals' planned migration took them into territory that was already fully occupied by other German peoples, who, naturally, were unwilling to make room for them.

By the winter of 401–2 the Vandals had reached the upper Danube but their progress was blocked by the Alamanni. They tried moving north onto the Rhine in 405 but that brought them into conflict with the Franks. The Vandals' king Godegisel was killed and only the support of the Alan cavalry saved them from annihilation. In 406 another wandering German people, the Sueves, joined the Vandal–Alan confederation but, with the Huns behind them, the Franks and Alamanni pressing on them from either side and the Romans facing them across the Rhine, their position remained desperately insecure. The unusually severe weather which set in during November 406 offered the Vandals an

unexpected escape route from their perilous situation. By December the Rhine was frozen hard enough to carry wagons. The galleys of the Roman fleet, which normally patrolled the river, were immobilized and the frontier garrisons had been weakened to fend off a Gothic attack on Italy. The Vandals saw their chance and on New Year's Eve they and their allies crossed the Rhine near Mainz and invaded the Roman empire.

After years of hardship the invaders' first instinct was to loot. They sacked Mainz before spreading out across the rich and defenceless countryside. Constantine, commander of the Roman garrison in Britain, hurried to the rescue. The Vandals, Sueves and Alans regrouped and headed south, crossing the Pyrenees into Spain. Long one of the most peaceful provinces of the Roman empire, Spain had only a small garrison and it was quickly overrun by the invaders. The Asdings and Sueves settled in the mountainous northwest, the Alans on the high *meseta* of central Spain and the Silings in the far south.

Wagon train

Little is known about the organization of the Vandal migration. The migrants were accompanied by thousands of creaking ox wagons, loaded with personal possessions,

A Roman mosaic portraying a Vandal on horseback. During the Vandal migration, only the elderly and infirm travelled in wagons. The more fortunate, higher-status men rode horses while everyone else – men, women and children – walked. Best estimates suggest the vast wagon train covered only an average of 4.5 miles (7 km) a day.

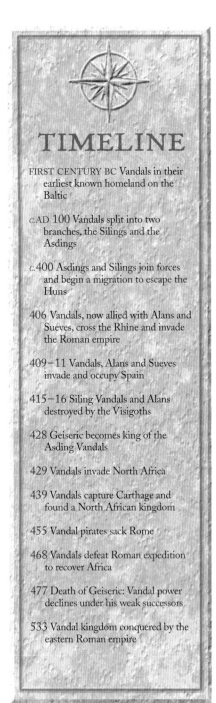

TIMELINE

FIRST CENTURY BC Vandals in their earliest known homeland on the Baltic

c.AD 100 Vandals split into two branches, the Silings and the Asdings

c.400 Asdings and Silings join forces and begin a migration to escape the Huns

406 Vandals, now allied with Alans and Sueves, cross the Rhine and invade the Roman empire

409–11 Vandals, Alans and Sueves invade and occupy Spain

415–16 Siling Vandals and Alans destroyed by the Visigoths

428 Geiseric becomes king of the Asding Vandals

429 Vandals invade North Africa

439 Vandals capture Carthage and found a North African kingdom

455 Vandal pirates sack Rome

468 Vandals defeat Roman expedition to recover Africa

477 Death of Geiseric: Vandal power declines under his weak successors

533 Vandal kingdom conquered by the eastern Roman empire

tents and supplies. For the people whose homes and farms lay in their path, the Vandals must have seemed like a plague of locusts. Foraging parties stripped the countryside of everything edible and looted anything of value.

If the Vandals hoped to find a safe haven in Spain, they were disappointed. In 415 the Romans reached a deal with the Visigoths. In return for lands in Aquitaine, the Visigoths launched a genocidal campaign against the Vandals. The Asdings and Sueves held out but the Silings and the Alans were all but exterminated – the survivors fled to join the Asdings. The Romans and Visigoths launched another campaign against the Vandals in 422. It failed but the Vandal's new king Geiseric (c.389–477) knew it was only a matter of time before they were attacked again and decided to move on, this time to North Africa. The Sueves, who had fallen out with the Vandals, stayed behind.

Escape to Africa

In May 429 Geiseric gathered the Vandals at Tarifa, near Gibraltar, from where they were ferried across the narrow sea to Tangier. They were about 80,000 in number, including some 15,000 warriors. Roman naval power had withered away during the centuries of the Pax Romana in the Mediterranean, and no attempt was made to interfere with the crossing. Geiseric's objective was the rich agricultural provinces of Byzacena and Numidia and the port city of Carthage – the major source of tax revenue for the western Roman government as well as the main supplier of grain to Italy.

After their landing, the Vandals travelled east, meeting no serious opposition until they reached the city of Hippo in June 430. The fall of Hippo after a year-long siege finally provoked a reaction from the Romans. A major force was sent to Africa and Geiseric was driven back into Mauretania. With Geiseric still in easy striking distance of Carthage the Romans could not afford to relax their guard, but a rebellion by the Goths left them no choice. Geiseric broke out and seized Carthage in October 439. Recognizing the seriousness of the situation, Aetius (c.396–454), the master general of the west, gathered a massive expeditionary force in Sicily in 442 but had to withdraw his troops to face an invasion by the Huns. To maintain grain supplies to Italy, the Romans had to agree a humiliating treaty acknowledging Vandal possession of Carthage, Byzacena and Numidia. Roman landowners were expelled and the Vandals settled into their comfortable country villas.

The Vandals and the fall of the Roman empire

Of all the disasters to befall the ailing Roman empire this was by far the most serious yet. Without the revenues of Africa, the west was not fiscally viable. To make matters worse, Geiseric used Carthage as a base to launch pirate raids on Italy and Sicily. In 455 Geiseric even sacked Rome itself, so making the Vandal name synonymous with wanton destruction. In 468 the Romans made a last-ditch effort to recapture Africa. It failed.

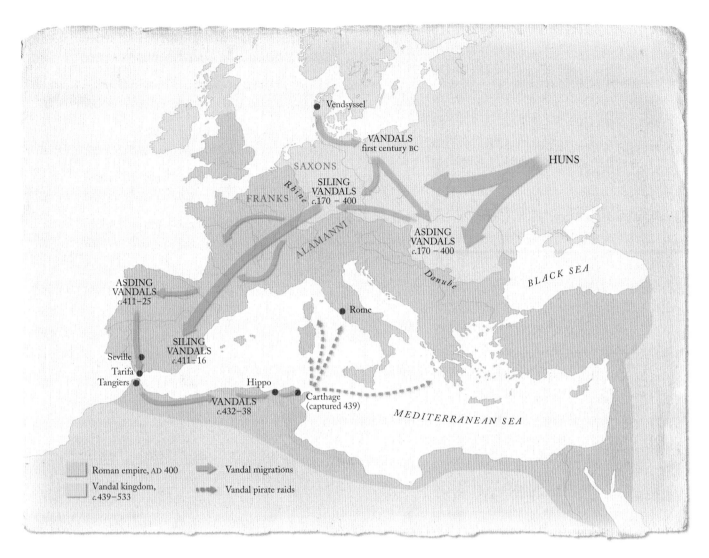

Geiseric played for time by pretending to negotiate surrender while he prepared a fire-ship attack which destroyed the Roman invasion fleet as it lay at anchor off Carthage. Just eight years later the western Roman empire was history.

Geiseric died in 477, having apparently brought his people's long migration to a triumphant conclusion. The immediate danger was that the Vandals would lose their identity by assimilation with the more numerous native population. However, the Vandals' extreme hostility to all things Roman was an effective barrier, as was their adherence to Arianism, a form of Christianity which their Catholic Roman subjects regarded as heretical. Unfortunately, while it helped preserve their identity, Arianism also guaranteed that the eastern emperors would remain hostile to the Vandals. The Vandals were also unfortunate that Geiseric's successors lacked any of his military and political skills. When the eastern emperor Justinian (*c*.482–565) sent an expedition to recover Africa in 533, the Vandal kingdom quickly collapsed. The last Vandal king, Gelimer (r.530 – 4), was allowed a comfortable retirement in Anatolia but his people were enslaved and dispersed. The Vandals' former allies, the Sueves, survived only a little longer. In 585 their kingdom in northwest Spain was conquered by the Goths, and the Sueves soon lost their separate identity.

Map showing the progress of the Vandals across Europe, having been driven from their homeland in central Europe by the Huns. Their crossing from Spain to North Africa went unchallenged by the Romans, and their eventual successful settlement in Carthage contributed to the downfall of the western Roman empire.

The Anglo-Saxon Migrations to Britain
5TH CENTURY AD

The Anglo-Saxon migrations were not as dramatic as those of the Goths and Vandals which were taking place at the same time, but their consequences were far more significant in the long term. The conquest and settlement of much of Britain by the Anglo-Saxons was the first step in the creation of the English nation and the English language.

The Anglo-Saxons were Germanic peoples who migrated to Britain in the fifth century. Following the end of Roman rule in Britain in 409, the newly independent Britons came under attack from their fellow Celts, the Picts (from Scotland) and the Scots (from Ireland). According to the Anglo-Saxon monk Bede (672/3–735), who wrote one of the earliest accounts of the migration, the British king Vortigern invited a band of Saxon mercenaries, led by Hengist and Horsa, to settle in Kent in 449 in return for their help fighting the Picts and Scots. Vortigern was probably following the Roman practice of settling Germanic tribes as *foederati* (allies) in return for military service. The Saxons defeated the Picts and Scots but then rebelled, brought reinforcements from across the sea and began to conquer Britain for themselves. The Saxons, whose homeland was on the North Sea coast of Germany, were joined in the conquest by two other Germanic peoples: the Angles, from the neck of the Jutland Peninsula, and the Jutes, from northern Jutland. Bede records that the Angles settled in East Anglia, the Midlands and Northumbria; the Saxons in Sussex ('South Saxons'), Essex ('East Saxons') and Wessex ('West Saxons'); the Jutes in Kent and the Isle of Wight.

Though the Jutes were clearly junior partners, it is not obvious whether it was the Angles or the Saxons who were the predominant group. Archaeology is little help because all the immigrants shared a similar Germanic material culture. The English take their name from the Angles, suggesting they may have predominated, but the British Celts take their names for the English from the Saxons (Saesneg in Welsh, Sassenach in Gaelic), suggesting the opposite. The term 'Anglo-Saxon' was first coined in France in the sixth century and was not used by the Anglo-Saxons themselves until much later.

The Church of St Mary in Sompting, Sussex, noted for its characteristically Anglo-Saxon spire, known as a 'Rhenish Helm'.

Invited guests?

The location of the earliest identified Anglo-Saxon settlements supports the idea that they were invited to Britain: there is a concentration of early settlements in Kent and many others are inland, which would not be expected if they were uninvited immigrants.

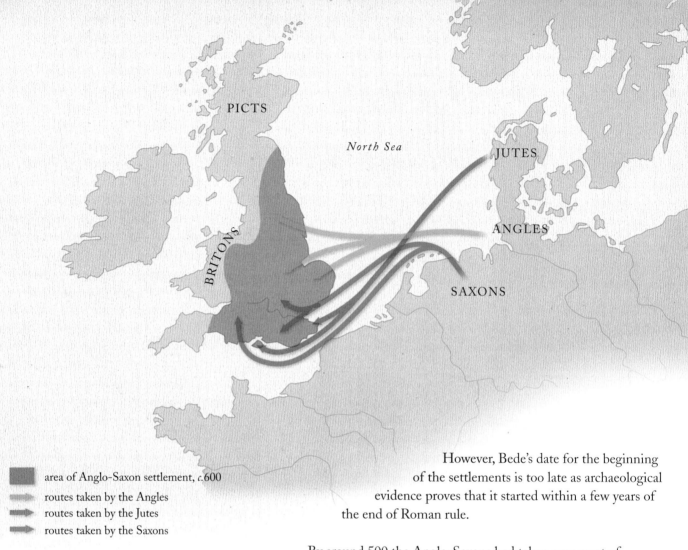

area of Anglo-Saxon settlement, c.600
routes taken by the Angles
routes taken by the Jutes
routes taken by the Saxons

Map showing the sea routes taken to Britain by migrating Germanic peoples in the fifth and sixth centuries, and the area of settlement by 600.

However, Bede's date for the beginning of the settlements is too late as archaeological evidence proves that it started within a few years of the end of Roman rule.

By around 500 the Anglo-Saxons had taken over most of southeast Britain, and in the next century several small kingdoms emerged. The Britons' victory under the Romano-British warlord Ambrosius Aurelianus (the probable prototype of the legendary king Arthur) at Mount Badon *c.*500 stopped the Anglo-Saxon advance for decades and there is some evidence of Anglo-Saxons even returning to the continent. In 577 the West Saxons resumed the advance, reaching the Bristol Channel after they defeated a coalition of British kings at the Battle of Dyrham. A last-ditch effort by the Gododdin, a British tribe from the district of modern Edinburgh, to hold the line in the north was crushed at the Battle of Catterick (*c.*600), and in 616 the Northumbrian king Aethelfrith pushed Anglo-Saxon control to the shores of the Irish Sea when he defeated the Britons at Chester. By the middle of the seventh century almost all of England, and much of southern Scotland, was under Anglo-Saxon rule. The creation of a united English nation was, however, still a long time in the future.

The exact nature of the Anglo-Saxon migrations has been debated by historians for decades. One view was that it was a mass folk movement from northern Germany, involving whole families and villages, who came to Britain and largely displaced the native Celtic Britons from that part of the island which is now known, after the settlers, as England ('Angle-land'). The opposing view was that élite groups of warriors had come to Britain, displaced the rulers of native British kingdoms and set themselves up as a new ruling class over the ordinary Britons, who in time adopted the language, culture and identity of their rulers.

The arguments in favour of the first view were probably always the stronger. Though Bede's and other early accounts describe the earliest settlers as mercenary warriors, they also describe the large-scale displacement or massacre of the native population. Archaeological evidence shows that there was a complete disruption of settlement patterns and material culture in eastern England in the fifth century AD. Germanic types of houses, pottery, weapons and jewellery almost completely replace earlier Romano-British styles. New burial customs were introduced. The Anglo-Saxons were pagans until the seventh century so their burials contain grave offerings, making them quite distinct from those of the Christian Britons. There is also persuasive evidence of depopulation in the Anglo-Saxon homelands: dozens of villages in this area were abandoned in the fifth century.

Language clues

The linguistic evidence for a folk movement is also strong. The near complete absence of Celtic place names in most of eastern England argues for a rapid and complete replacement of the native population in this area. The English language itself also supports the folk-movement theory. Old English, the form of English spoken by the Anglo-Saxons, contains less than a dozen Celtic words, suggesting that there was little social or economic interaction between natives and invaders, such as would have been unavoidable if the Anglo-Saxons were only a tiny ruling minority. Following the Norman conquest of England in 1066, which certainly was accomplished by an élite group of warriors, the subject English adopted hundreds of words from the French language but they did not finish up speaking French. Instead, it was the descendants of the Norman conquerors who finished up speaking English.

An Anglo-Saxon coin dating from the tenth or 11th century.

Support for the second view was based on a more critical reading of the primary sources. Apart from a few brief references in Roman sources, no accounts of the Anglo-Saxon migration were written until at least a century after the events they describe. Bede's account was written over 200 years later. This has left plenty of time for legendary material, invented to explain and bolster emerging ethnic identities, to have crept into the sources, making them possibly unreliable or even misleading. There was also the well-founded reluctance automatically to interpret a correlation between the spread of material culture and the movement of ethnic groups. In this case, the spread of Anglo-Saxon material culture could have resulted from its adoption by conquered native Britons rather than by migrating Anglo-Saxon peasant families.

Research into the genetic make-up of the modern population of England has now settled the argument; the Anglo-Saxon migration was the first major influx of new populations into Britain since the original settlement of the country at the end of the Ice Age. The ancestors of the vast majority of the population of eastern England, both male and female lineages, originated in northern Germany and Denmark, the countries described by Bede as the original homelands of the Anglo-Saxons. The massacres and

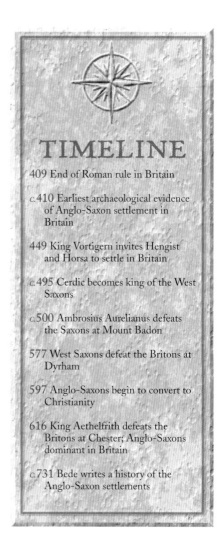

the flight of Britons really did happen, and the Anglo-Saxon warriors who caused the 'ethnic cleansing' brought their wives and families with them. The early medieval sources may contain some legendary tales but it now seems certain that they accurately portray the nature of the Anglo-Saxon conquest.

It has long been noticed that the incidence of Celtic place names gradually increases in England towards the west. This pattern is directly mirrored in the genes of the modern English. In the English Midlands the population is fairly evenly divided between those of Germanic ancestry and those of Celtic ancestry. In Cornwall, in the far west – the last part of England to be conquered by the Anglo-Saxons – the majority of the population is of Celtic ancestry. Most place names here are Celtic too, and spoken Celtic language died out only in the 19th century. This evidence tells us that, while in its early stages, the Anglo-Saxon conquest involved near complete population replacement, in its later stages it acquired a more political character.

Once the Anglo-Saxons had established kingdoms in the east, their westward advance involved smaller groups of settlers. The Britons were not driven out and over time they adopted the identity and language of their conquerors. The limited influence the conquered Britons had on the English language suggests they generally had low status under Anglo-Saxon rule. Most were probably enslaved, and slaves were more numerous in western England than in the east in Anglo-Saxon times. Many may have tended livestock: traditional shepherds' counting systems used in upland areas of western England are based on Celtic rather than English words. A few members of the Britons' ruling class may have been accepted into Anglo-Saxon aristocracy. The most successful was Cerdic (Caradoc), who became the first king of the Anglo-Saxon kingdom of Wessex and the earliest royal ancestor of Elizabeth II.

A seafaring tradition

The Anglo-Saxon migration was not only the first major migration to Britain since the end of the Ice Age, it was also the first major maritime migration to Britain. The first settlers who had arrived after the ice sheets melted had been able to walk because Britain did not become an island until around 6000 BC. The migration of whole communities to Britain would not have been possible without seaworthy ships. Because of their coastal homeland, the Angles and Saxons developed a seafaring tradition early in their history. One Saxon tribe, the Chauci, were launching pirate raids on the Roman empire early in the first century AD. By the fourth century their raids on the east coast of Britain had become so frequent that the Romans nicknamed it the 'Saxon Shore'. The Saxons also raided around the coast of France and, at the same time as they were settling in Britain, they also founded settlements around the Pas de Calais, in Normandy and in the Loire Valley. These were conquered by the Franks in the sixth century. Roman writers complained of the difficulty of protecting the coast against raiders who could strike without warning from the open sea. They also record that after a successful raid the

Saxons were in the habit of sacrificing prisoners to their gods to get a fair wind home.

Anglo-Saxon ships were built in a similar way to the Viking longships (see pages 110–115), with hulls fashioned from overlapping planks, and positions for oarsmen along the sides. But while Viking ships had high prows curving steeply upwards, the prows of Anglo-Saxon ships were long and raking. A replica of an early-seventh-century ship found in a royal burial mound at Sutton Hoo in Suffolk proved to be as fast and manoeuvrable under sail as a Viking longship.

In the early Middle Ages, travel by sea was much faster than travel by land. With a following wind, the 300-mile (500-km) crossing of the North Sea would have taken no longer than a 60-mile (100-km) journey overland, that is about two or three days. Hengist's appeal for reinforcements from his homeland could have been answered in little more than a week. Families would not have faced a long and gruelling journey and were probably able to take all their belongings, food stocks and livestock with them. Given the chaos on the continent, the accessibility of Britain and the power vacuum which had existed there since the Roman withdrawal, migration must have seemed an attractive option for the Anglo-Saxons.

It is not clear why the Anglo-Saxons were so successful. They possessed no military or technological advantage over the Britons. After the end of Roman rule, Britain was divided into rival kingdoms. Apart from a brief period around the time of the Battle of Mount Badon, these kingdoms never united to oppose the invaders, but the Anglo-Saxons were never politically united either. It may be significant that the south and east of Britain were where Roman influence had been strongest and the old tribal identities weakest. The Romans had strictly divided soldiers from civilians, who were not allowed to bear arms. When the Anglo-Saxon mercenaries rebelled against their employers, there were few Britons with military experience and no focus for popular resistance. Only when the Anglo-Saxons moved into the less Romanized west, where tribal identities were stronger, did British resistance stiffen.

Reconstruction of a ceremonial Anglo-Saxon helmet, part of the Sutton Hoo burial treasure excavated near Woodbridge, Suffolk in 1939.

The Arab Expansion
632–713

Arabs today form the ethnic majority of most Middle Eastern and North African states. Originally confined to the Arabian Peninsula, the spread of the Arab peoples is closely associated with the rise of the Islamic religion in the seventh century AD. In less than a century the Arabs, inspired by Islam, conquered an empire that stretched from India to Spain.

The faith of Islam ('submission to the will of God') was founded by Muhammad (*c.*570–632), a member of the Quraysh tribe of Mecca. Mecca had an important pagan shrine, and Muhammad's espousal of monotheism was opposed by the Quraysh. To escape persecution, Muhammad and his followers left Mecca in 622 and settled in Medina. This event, the *hijra* ('migration'), marks the beginning of the Muslim era. Muhammad used Medina as a base from which to attack Mecca, which surrendered to him in 630. Medina became the capital of a theocratic Islamic state, with Muhammad as both religious and political leader. In the last two years of his life, Muhammad united the Arab tribes under his rule, using a mixture of diplomacy and force. He was succeeded by his father-in-law Abu Bakr (r.632–4), who became the first caliph ('successor').

After defeating an anti-Islamic rebellion, Abu Bakr began to make raids on the Persian and Byzantine empires, probably hoping that success in war would help consolidate Arab unity. The raids met only weak opposition and under his successors Umar (r.634–44) and Uthman (r.644–56) Arab armies won a series of spectacular victories. The entire Persian empire had fallen under Arab control by 652, and the Byzantine empire lost the rich provinces of Egypt, Libya, Palestine and Syria by 642.

Early Umayyad gains

After Uthman's death, civil war broke out between supporters of the new caliph Ali (r.656–61), Muhammad's son-in-law and cousin, and Muawiya, a member of Uthman's Umayyad family. After Ali was murdered in 661, Muawiya (r.661-80) became caliph, founding the Umayyad dynasty. Ali's murder led to Islam's only major schism. On Muawiya's death, Ali's son Husain tried to seize the caliphate but was killed fighting the Umayyads at Karbala in Iraq in 680. Subsequently Islam split into two mutually antagonistic branches, the majority Sunnite (from *sunna*, meaning 'tradition of Muhammad') and the minority Shiite (from *shi'atu Ali*, 'party of Ali').

Territorial expansion continued under the early Umayyads, with the conquest of North Africa (698), Spain (711), the caravan cities of Samarkand and Bukhara in central Asia (710) and the Indus River Valley (713). Lacking institutions suited to the government of

what had become the largest empire the world had yet seen, the Umayyads co-opted the administrative systems of the empires they had conquered. Medina was too remote to be convenient, and the capital was moved to Damascus in 661 and then to Baghdad in 763.

Several factors explain the success of the Arabs in the seventh century. Among the pre-Islamic Arabs, war provided an important opportunity for young warriors to win wealth and status. Inter-tribal feuds lasted generations and raids on Byzantine or Persian territory were common. Arabs usually fought on horseback or on camels, giving them great mobility. Because of their ability to strike quickly without warning from the desert, the Arabs were a difficult enemy to deal with, but their raids were on a small scale and did little long-term damage. Internecine warfare was suppressed by Muhammad and his successors, but the social need for war remained and could now only be channelled outwards. Once united, the Arabs could field much larger armies than ever before.

The Arabs were also fortunate in their timing. The Byzantine and Persian empires had just fought a 20-year war and were unprepared for another. Both empires also had major internal problems. The Persian empire was wracked by civil war, and organized resistance collapsed quickly after the Arab victory at Nehavend in 642. The Byzantines' problem was religious disunity. The populations of Egypt, Palestine and Syria belonged to the Monophysite Church, which the Orthodox imperial government considered heretical. After years of persecution, the people of these areas welcomed the Arabs as liberators.

The Battle of Karbala of 680, represented in a late 19th-century painting. The large Umayyad army fought against 72 Arab soldiers led by Husain, Muhammad's grandson. Although heavily outnumbered, Husain's followers are said to have killed almost 20 percent of the Umayyad force before they themselves were slain.

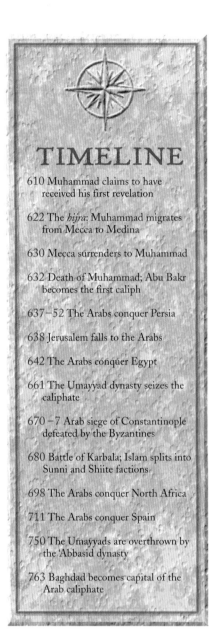

FRANKISH
KINGDOM

Loire
✕ Poitiers 732

Covadonga 718

LOMBARD
KINGDOM

VISIGOTHIC
KINGDOM

Narbonne

Rome

Lisbon

Toledo

Ecija 711 ✕   Córdoba

Cartha✕

Ceuta

Kairouan

Sahara

The Arabs believed their enemies' problems revealed the hand of God. Arab soldiers were motivated by plunder in this life and by the promise of immediate entry to paradise for those who died fighting for Islam. The defenders were exhausted and war weary.

Unsure of the loyalty of the conquered populations, the Umayyads settled Arab soldiers and officials in strategically sited *amsar*s (fortified military settlements), such as Qom, Iran; Basra, Iraq; Kairouan, Tunisia; and Cairo, Egypt, with easy escape routes to the desert. The government took possession of all land formerly owned by the Byzantine and Persian states. These extensive lands were granted on easy terms to Arab chiefs, who sub-let much of it for cultivation to settlers from their own tribes. The *amsar*s also attracted Arab (and local) merchants and artisans who hoped to make a living by supplying the needs of the garrisons. There was substantial migration even to the furthest extremities of the caliphate, in Spain and the Indus Valley. Several Arab tribes migrated into the Sahara, where they could continue to practise the traditional way of life of the nomadic Bedouin ('People of the Desert').

The unifying nature of Islam

Following Muhammad's teaching, the Arabs allowed 'People of the Book' (Jews, Christians and Zoroastrians) to practise their religions provided they paid the *jizya* (tribute) which was levied on unbelievers. For the Arabs, Islam was a symbol of national unity and superiority and they made little effort to convert the conquered populations because this would have reduced their tax income. Despite this official indifference, increasing numbers of non-Arabs converted to Islam. Because translation of the Koran was forbidden, converts learned Arabic. Islam is as much a way of life as a religion, so conversion also began the acculturation of the conquered population to Arab ways. The Arabs were in turn influenced by the culture of the peoples they had conquered, especially Greek science and philosophy, and Persian art and literature. Though they converted to Islam, the Persians resisted complete Arabization. While in Byzantine territories the ruling élite had been able to flee to unconquered areas, the rapid and total collapse of their state left the Persian élite nowhere to go. By accommodating themselves to the new regime, they retained considerable cultural and political influence.

New converts to Islam had always to become *mawali* (clients) of the Arab tribes. The purpose of this was to retain a hegemonic role in the caliphate for the Arabs. Converts

TIMELINE

610 Muhammad claims to have received his first revelation

622 The *hijra*: Muhammad migrates from Mecca to Medina

630 Mecca surrenders to Muhammad

632 Death of Muhammad; Abu Bakr becomes the first caliph

637–52 The Arabs conquer Persia

638 Jerusalem falls to the Arabs

642 The Arabs conquer Egypt

661 The Umayyad dynasty seizes the caliphate

670–7 Arab siege of Constantinople defeated by the Byzantines

680 Battle of Karbala; Islam splits into Sunni and Shiite factions

698 The Arabs conquer North Africa

711 The Arabs conquer Spain

750 The Umayyads are overthrown by the 'Abbasid dynasty

763 Baghdad becomes capital of the Arab caliphate

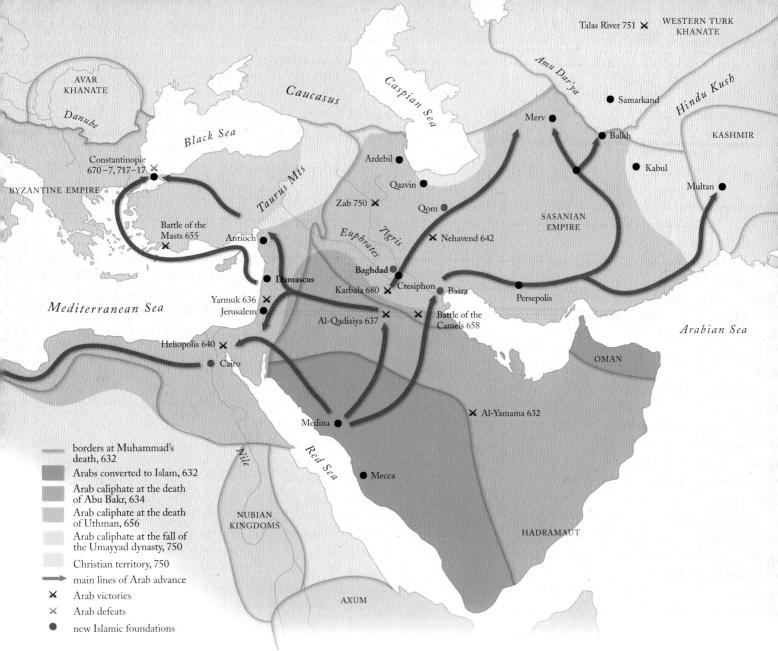

Map showing Islamic conquests in the seventh and eighth centuries.

were excluded from the highest offices of state, which were open only to people of pure Arab descent. New converts were resentful of the Arabs' privileged position and they became increasingly discontented with Umayyad rule. The caliphate, they argued, had been founded to further the message of Islam, which stresses the community of believers over ethnic differences, not to advance the Arabs' financial interests. There was also a growing class of half-Arabs, the product of marriages between Arab men and non-Arab women who also resented their inferior status.

The Sunnite–Shiite conflict and the re-emergence of feuding between Arab tribes caused by squabbles over the distribution of tribute also undermined the authority of the Umayyad dynasty. In 747 a rebellion broke out among new Muslims in Persia and in 750 the Umayyads were overthrown by the 'Abbasid dynasty. Under the 'Abbasids, Arab privilege was abolished, opening the way for the full Arabization of conquered populations. Muslim unity did not long survive the overthrow of the Umayyads, but few of the lands conquered by the Arabs in the century after the death of Muhammad have since been lost to Islam.

Vikings in the West
793–1000

In 793 Vikings – pagan Scandinavian pirates – sacked the monastery of Lindisfarne on an island off the northeast coast of England. Within a few years Viking pirates were active all around the coasts of western Europe. Success made them bolder and from the 840s they conquered lands and founded settlements in England, Scotland, Ireland and France. Fearless seafarers, the Vikings also pushed out into the North Atlantic, settling the Faeroe Islands, Iceland and Greenland, even founding the earliest known European settlement in North America.

The Vikings hailed from Norway, Sweden and Denmark. Tall, blonde and blue-eyed, it is the Norwegians who are often thought of as the archetypal Vikings but it was actually the Danes who were numerically dominant. Vikings from each country had their own preferred areas of operation: Norwegians were most active in Scotland, Ireland, northwest England and the North Atlantic; Danes in Germany, France and England; and Swedes around the Baltic Sea and in Russia (see pages 116–119).

Attacking from the sea without warning in fast sailing galleys called longships, the Vikings enjoyed all the advantages of surprise and their raids were very hard to prevent. Largely united under the rule of the Frankish emperor Charlemagne (r.768–814), western Europe was at its most peaceful and prosperous since the fall of the Roman empire. Ports, monasteries and towns were undefended. At first the Vikings launched hit-and-run raids using just a handful of ships. Around 835 the nature of Viking raiding changed. Much larger fleets are reported in contemporary chronicles and Vikings began making fortified camps in enemy territory, where they could spend the winter and make an early start raiding again the next spring. Most of these were abandoned after a few seasons but in Ireland a few developed into permanent settlements. The most important was Dublin, the first true town to develop in Ireland.

'Northmen' settle in the west

Dublin was founded as a raiding base in 841 but developed as a marketplace where Irish prisoners were sold to slave traders from as far away as North Africa. Limerick, Wexford and Waterford had similar origins. Irish resistance was tough, however, and the Vikings were never able to settle securely outside these fortified enclaves. By this time too, Norwegian Vikings were settling in Shetland and Orkney, and the Scottish Hebrides after conquering the native Picts. They had also begun to settle on the Faeroe Islands, which were uninhabited apart from a few Irish monks who used them as a retreat.

A fleet of Viking ships in rough seas, painted by the 19th-century American artist Edward Moran. The rigours of life at sea meant that the Vikings avoided making raids in winter, establishing bases in strategic locations overseas from which they could start early in the spring.

MARKLAND?

VINLAND?

L'Anse-aux-Meadows

NEWFOUNDLAND

TIMELINE

793 Vikings sack the monastery of Lindisfarne, off the northeast coast of England

799 First recorded Viking raids on France

*c.*825 Viking settlement in Orkney, Shetland and Faeroe Islands

841 Dublin is founded by Viking slave-traders

859–62 Viking raids in the Mediterranean

865 Danish 'Great Army' begins conquest of eastern England

*c.*870 Viking settlement of Iceland begins

878 Alfred the Great defeats the Vikings in Wessex

902–54 The Anglo-Saxons conquer the Danelaw

911 Viking settlement in Normandy

983 Erik the Red explores Greenland (settlement begins 987)

*c.*1000 Leif Eriksson becomes the first European to reach America

1066 Last major Viking attack on England defeated by King Harold

There was a further step change in Viking activity in the 850s when Viking fleets numbering 100 to 250 ships began raiding western Europe. England, at that time still divided into several kingdoms, was hit hardest. In 865 the largest Viking force yet, the Danish 'Great Army', landed in England intent not on plunder but on seizing land for settlement. In quick succession three Anglo-Saxon kingdoms – Northumbria, East Anglia and Mercia – were conquered and settled by the Danes. Only Wessex, led by Alfred the Great (r.871–99), survived. The areas settled by the Danes can still be identified today from place names ending in *-by*, as in Grimsby ('Grim's village') and *-thorpe*, as in Kettlethorpe ('Ketil's farm'). The area became known as the Danelaw, from distinctive legal customs that the Danes introduced. The Danes did not expel the native Anglo-Saxon peasantry from their villages, but they did take over royal and aristocratic estates and established themselves as the new social and political élite. Danish Vikings also settled on lands around the mouth of the Seine in France. Vikings were usually known as 'Northmen' on the continent and their settlement on the Seine became known as Normandy ('Northman's land').

Pushing across the Atlantic

Around the same time that the 'Great Army' arrived in England, Vikings also began to settle in Iceland. Although it may have been known to the Irish, the first Viking to reach Iceland, Gardar the Swede, did so by accident when he was blown off course on a voyage to the Shetland Islands in about 860. Other explorers followed up his discovery and by 870 settlement was in full swing. All the best land was soon taken and there was little immigration after 930, by which time the population is estimated to have been about 20,000. According to the Old Icelandic *Landnámabók* (The Book of the Settlements) most of the settlers came from western Norway, with substantial numbers from southern Norway and the Hebrides (the latter also brought Irish slaves with them) and a very few from Denmark and Sweden. The land was claimed by about 400 leading settlers, most of whom had been petty chieftains back home. Holding some land back to farm themselves, they shared the rest out among their followers and dependents. Though bleak, Iceland had good pasture land and there were no hostile natives to be fought for control of the land.

There was a further westward push to Viking settlement when Erik the Red (950 – *c.*1003) discovered the sheltered ice-free fjords of southwest Greenland in 983. Erik, a born salesman, chose the name Greenland because '*people would be much more tempted to go if it had an attractive name*'. About 3000 – 4000 people eventually settled there.

It was not long before Viking seafarers on their way to Greenland sighted land even further west. Around 1000, Erik's son Leif the Lucky (*c.*970 – *c.*1020) set out to

Areas of settlement
- Norwegians
- Danes

Viking raids and voyages
- Norwegians
- Danes
- uncertain origin

investigate and became
the first European known
to have reached North
America. Following his father's
practice, Leif called the land he
had discovered Vinland ('wine
land') but attempts to settle there
failed: the Vikings were too few, the
distances too great and the natives too
hostile for the settlement to succeed. The only known Viking settlement in the
Americas, at L'Anse-aux-Meadows in Newfoundland, was occupied for 20 years at most.
Newfoundland is too far north to fit Leif's description of Vinland, the exact location of
which remains uncertain.

Though over-population may have played a part in the Viking expansion, its main
causes were political. By the late eighth century Scandinavia was entering the first stages
of state formation. Chiefdoms and petty kingdoms were being amalgamated into larger
and more centralized kingdoms, and competition for power was becoming intense and
often violent. Viking raids were at first mainly a way for ambitious chiefs and kings to
win wealth and a military reputation to help them in their power struggles at home.
The big losers in this process were the district chieftains, who found their traditional
autonomy undermined by growing royal power. Emigration for this class began to seem
like a good opportunity to preserve their way of life. Members of the chieftain class were
prominent among the early settlers of Iceland, for example. Emigration was also
attractive for members of the royal families who were denied power at home. If they

*Viking raiders and settlers
swept across western Europe
from the ninth to the tenth
centuries, reaching as far as
the Mediterranean in the
southeast and the east coast
of North America in the
west. Until about 865, the
main motivation for
expansion was to gain
wealth and prestige at home
rather than territory abroad.*

could not rule at home, they could raise an army and try to conquer a kingdom abroad. Ivar, Halfdan, Ubba, Guthrum and other leaders of the 'Great Army' were such men.

Legacy of the Vikings

The Viking expansion was an entirely maritime movement. The Vikings are best known for their longships, on which they relied for piracy and war. Longships had sleek narrow hulls for speed under oars or sail and a shallow draft so that they could sail close inshore or up rivers without grounding. Once its crew of warriors and their war gear were onboard, there was little room in a longship for passengers and cargo. This was no problem for the armies of single men who intended to take everything they needed by force, but it made longships unsuitable for voyages of settlement to the uninhabited lands of the North Atlantic, where the men would have to take their families, livestock, tools and supplies with them. The type of ship used for these voyages was the *knarr*, a stout, broad-beamed trade ship which is known from trials with modern replicas to have been very seaworthy. Apart from carrying a few oars to help manoeuvre into and out of harbour, *knarrs* relied entirely on a single square sail for propulsion. Seaworthy or not, *knarrs* were just big open boats with no shelter for their passengers from wind, rain and spray and no place to light a fire or cook hot food. The danger of swamping or shipwreck in storms was considerable. Of 25 ships that set out from Iceland for Greenland with Erik the Red, only 14 arrived; some had turned back, but many disappeared without trace.

A 20th-century bust of Leif Eriksson ('Leif the Lucky') in America. Eriksson is thought to have been the first European to reach the coast of North America.

The only permanent extensions to the Scandinavian world to result from the Viking expansion were Iceland and the Faeroe Islands. The remote Greenland settlement died out in the 15th century, around the same time that Orkney and Shetland came under Scottish rule. Elsewhere, the Viking settlers were assimilated into the local population within a few generations through conversion to Christianity and intermarriage. Once settled, the Vikings lost their military advantages and their settlements were quite easily brought under the control of native rulers. In England, assimilation was made easier by the similarity between the Old English and Old Danish languages, which were mutually intelligible. The Danes had a lasting impact on the English language, which has hundreds of Scandinavian loan words, including 'sky', 'egg', 'skin', 'sister', 'skirt' and 'get'.

Recently, researchers have discovered genetic evidence of the Viking expansion. The most striking results have come from Orkney. A substantial Scandinavian settlement in Orkney has always been assumed from the dominance of Scandinavian place names in the islands. Norn, a Scandinavian dialect was also spoken by the islanders until the 18th century, when it was replaced by English. A majority of men in Norway and Sweden (but not Denmark) have a distinctive marker on their Y chromosomes called the M17 haplotype. In the Orkneys 55 percent of men also have this marker. Among Orcadian women, however, only one in ten have mtDNA which can be linked to Scandinavian lineages. This tells us that the Vikings who conquered Orkney were mainly single men. Some women came with them from Scandinavia but most took local women as wives or concubines. The prevalence of M17 Y chromosomes among today's male islanders indicates that the native Pictish men were not around to reproduce in any great numbers after the Viking conquest, meaning that they were either driven out, sold into slavery or simply killed. The Viking reputation for brutality was not undeserved, it seems.

Attempts to find a similar genetic imprint for the Danish Vikings in England have failed. This is probably because the Anglo-Saxons originated in much the same area as the Danes, so the two peoples were not genetically distinct. This means that it is not possible to estimate what proportion of the population they made up or if, as in Orkney, most of the settlers were men. At least some of the Danes are known from historical documents to have brought their wives and children with them, however. Results of genetic research in Ireland have produced results consistent with other historical evidence that the Vikings only settled in a few coastal enclaves in the east of the country. The M17 marker is rare in Irish men, but other genetic markers possibly indicative of Scandinavian origin are found in up to 6 percent of the population. Significantly, these markers are most common in the east, where all the historically attested Viking settlements were, and almost absent from the west.

By breaking up the existing power structures of western Europe, the Vikings were important agents of change in European history. Their destruction of the Anglo-Saxon kingdoms of Northumbria, Mercia and East Anglia paved the way for the unification of England under the leadership of Wessex. In northern Britain they helped turn Pictland into Scotland. Viking attacks weakened the native Picts, leaving them vulnerable to conquest by a bunch of recent Irish immigrants who called themselves Scots. The failure of Charlemagne's successors to stop Viking raids helped undermine their authority, contributing to the break-up of the Frankish empire and the emergence from its ruins of the kingdoms of France, Germany and Italy.

Replicas of a ship and a sod house stand at the site of the Viking settlement at L'Anse-aux-Meadows on the northern tip of Newfoundland.

The Swedes and the Origins of Russia
c.650–c.965

At the same time that Danish and Norwegian Vikings were carrying out raids and settling in western Europe, Swedish Vikings, known as Rus, were pushing into Russia in search of trading opportunities and tribute. By the end of the 9th century, the Rus had created a powerful state, based on Kiev, and given their name to one of the great nations of Europe.

Cemeteries containing Scandinavian merchant graves at the Slav trading centres at Elblag in Poland and Grobin in Latvia show that Swedish expansion east of the Baltic began *c.*650, over a century before the first Viking raids were launched against western Europe (see pages 110–115). Grave goods show that these traders were from Uppland in central Sweden and the island of Gotland. About a century later, Swedes were living at Staraja Ladoga on the Volkhov River in Russia, within easy reach of the Gulf of Finland, Lake Ladoga and the Russian interior. This trading and craft centre had a mixed population of Scandinavians, Slavs and Finns, each inhabiting their own quarter. The Swedes were probably drawn to the area by furs, wax and honey for the western European market.

Swedes venture into the interior

Around the end of the 8th century, Arab merchants began crossing the Caspian Sea and travelling up the Volga river to buy slaves and furs from the Khazars and the Volga Bulgars. The Arabs introduced into circulation high-quality silver coins called *dirhems*. When these coins started turning up at their trading posts around the Baltic, the Swedes began to press further inland, exploring Russia's many navigable rivers, to try to discover their source. By the 830s some enterprising Scandinavian merchants had made it all the way to Baghdad, others were travelling down the Dnepr River and crossing the Black Sea to Constantinople, the capital of the Byzantine empire. The wealth that flooded back to Sweden along these trade routes can be judged from the 80,000 Arab dirhems that have been found there in Viking Age coin hoards.

A fanciful 19th-century illustration of the possibly legendary figure Rurik, an early Rus ruler and the first king of Novgorod.

The Swedes came to be known as Rus, from which Russia gets its name. The word 'Rus' is most commonly thought to be derived from *Ruotsi*, the Finnish name for the Swedes. Ruotsi may in turn be derived from Scandinavian *rodr*, meaning 'a crew of oarsmen'. An attractive alternative view is that it derives from *Rusioi* ('blondes'), the Greek name for the Heruls, a well-travelled Scandinavian tribe who were active in the Roman empire between the 3rd and 6th centuries as mercenaries and pirates.

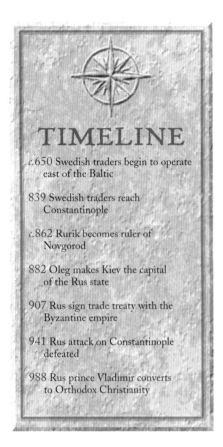

TIMELINE

*c.*650 Swedish traders begin to operate east of the Baltic

839 Swedish traders reach Constantinople

*c.*862 Rurik becomes ruler of Novgorod

882 Oleg makes Kiev the capital of the Rus state

907 Rus sign trade treaty with the Byzantine empire

941 Rus attack on Constantinople defeated

988 Rus prince Vladimir converts to Orthodox Christianity

A medieval Russian illumination showing Byzantine cavalry attacking Rus forces in the war fought by Oleg of Kiev against the Byzantine empire in 907.

Trading in this period was not without its dangers and merchants needed to be able to defend themselves. The merchants were particularly vulnerable to ambush by the local Slavs or roaming steppe nomads at portages, where they had to drag their ships overland from one river system into another or to avoid rapids. There was a very fine line between the merchant and the pirate in the Viking Age. During the course of the 9th century, the Rus began to take over Slav settlements, such as Novgorod and Kiev. These were used as bases from which to raid the surrounding countryside and force the local Slavs to pay tribute in the form of slaves, furs, wax and honey, which the Rus could then sell to Arab, Greek or western European merchants.

By 900 the Rus had established an extensive kingdom that gave them control over most of the river routes between the Baltic Sea, the Volga River and the Black Sea. Traditionally, this kingdom is considered to have been founded by Rurik, who became ruler of Novgorod in around 862. Some historians regard Rurik as an entirely legendary figure, however. Around 882, Oleg (Helgi), Rurik's successor expelled two rival warlords from Kiev and made it the capital of the Rus state. Oleg was killed fighting the Khazars in 913 but the Rus state continued to grow under his successor Igor (Ingvar). Igor attacked Constantinople in 941 and was killed on a tribute gathering raid four years later – a sign of the predatory nature of the early Rus state. Our knowledge of the early years of the Kievan Rus state comes from the *Primary Chronicle*, a manuscript compiled in Kiev in around 1113.

Assimilation with the Slavs

By the time of Igor's death, the Rus were beginning to be assimilated with the native Slavs. This is well shown in trade treaties agreed between the Rus and the Byzantine empire. All the signatories to the earliest treaties of 907 and 911 had Scandinavian names, but only half the names on a treaty of 945 were Scandinavian, the rest being Slavic. Even the ruling dynasty had adopted Slavic names by this time and

Igor was the last Rus ruler to have a Scandinavian name. Cemeteries show that the Rus were always a minority among the Slavic population even in the towns, and there is no evidence at all that they settled in the countryside. The Rus were, therefore, purely a warrior and merchant élite. Many of the Scandinavian graves found in Russia have belonged to women, suggesting that many of the Rus brought their families with them. The Arab traveller Ahmad ibn Fadlan, who visited Russia in 921, wrote that the Rus were also in the habit of taking local women as concubines and wives. Although he says they were usually well treated, ibn Fadlan describes how one slave girl was sacrificed at the funeral of her dead master and cremated with him in a Viking ship. This was a typical Scandinavian practice but by the mid-10th century Scandinavian religious beliefs were in decline. Sviatoslav's son Vladimir (r.978-1015) was a devotee of the Slavic gods Perun and Veles before he converted to Greek Orthodox Christianity in 988. By this time the majority of the Rus élite must have been Slavic speakers because Slavic became the language of the church.

Another sign of assimilation is that from the mid-10th century onwards Scandinavian merchants and mercenaries newly arrived in the east were called Varangians, to distinguish them from the Rus. The word 'Varangian' is probably derived from the Scandinavian word *vár*, meaning 'pledge', because bands of Viking warriors and merchants habitually formed sworn fellowships when embarking on a common enterprise. After 965 the number of Varangians arriving began to tail off. The Islamic world's silver mines were becoming exhausted and the trade routes began to fall out of use. Varangians continued to pass through on their way to sign on as mercenaries for the Byzantine empire until the 12th century, but long before this the Rus had become completely assimilated to Slavic culture and identity.

Map showing Scandinavian trading and colonization routes into the Russian interior.

Saami

NORWAY

Finns

Staraja Ladoga

Uppland

Novgorod

Volga

Birka

Volga Bulgars

Gotland

DENMARK

Grobin

Balts

Dvina

Gnezdovo

RUSSIA

Baltic Sea

Elbing

Hamburg

Wolin

Wends

Chernigov

Elbe

Oder

East Slavs

Kiev

Dnepr

FRANKISH KINGDOMS

Magyars

BULGAR KHANATE

Black Sea

Danube

Rome

Constantinople

BYZANTINE EMPIRE

areas of Scandinavian settlement

ARAB CALIPHATE

routes of Swedish expansion and trade

Mediterranean Sea

The foundation of the first Russian state was a key moment in the history of eastern Europe and it is undeniable that the arrival of the Rus was a great stimulant to the growth of towns in the region. Ultimately, however, the contribution of these Scandinavian immigrants to the development of Russian civilization was negligible, limited to a mere half dozen loan words in the Russian language. Far more important was Vladimir's decision to convert to Greek Orthodox Christianity and his subsequent marriage to Anna, the sister of the Byzantine emperor Basil II (r.976–1025). This brought Russia under the influence of the sophisticated Byzantine empire. Early Russia's alphabet, art, architecture, law, music and political ideology were all Byzantine in origin.

The Magyars
896–955

Hungarian is something of an oddity among European languages. Most European languages belong to the Indo-European language family, but Hungarian is a Uralic language; distantly related to Finnish, its closest relatives are Vogul and Ostyak, spoken in western Siberia. The Hungarians, or Magyars, as they have always called themselves, clearly have a different origin to most Europeans.

The Magyars were the most successful of a series of steppe nomad peoples who followed the Huns into Europe during the early Middle Ages. Most ventured no further than the Black Sea steppes but three – the Avars, the Bulgars and the Magyars – founded kingdoms in central Europe. They had very different fates.

The first to arrive were the Avars, a Mongol people. After being driven from their original homeland on the borders of China by the Turks in 553, they fled west towards Europe, crossing the River Volga in 562. Within six years they had conquered the Slav and German peoples living north of the River Danube. Like the Huns before them, they founded a kingdom on the steppes of the Carpathian Basin and began to raid the Byzantine empire and western Europe. Having suffered defeat at the hands of the Byzantines in 626, the power of the Avars declined and their kingdom was eventually destroyed by the Frankish emperor Charlemagne (r.768–814) in 796. The Avars were subsequently assimilated with the native Slav population (a few returned to the steppes and some still survive in the Caucasus), and they left no lasting legacy in Europe.

The Bulgars, a Turkic people, arrived in eastern Europe shortly after the Avars, dividing into two branches in the mid-seventh century. One branch migrated north and founded a khanate on the middle Volga, which survived until the 13th century, when it was conquered by the Mongols. The second, under its khan Asparukh, migrated west and seized the Byzantine province of Moesia, now northern Bulgaria. Unable to expel them, the emperor Constantine IV (r.668–85) recognized their possession in 679. Asparukh and his successors established their capital at Pliska and lived on tribute gathered from their mainly Slav subjects and plunder from raids on Byzantine territory. The Bulgars were converted to Orthodox Christianity by Greek missionaries in about 890, but they remained a thorn in the side of the Byzantines until they were finally conquered in 1018. The Bulgars survived this experience and regained their independence in the 12th century. They tried to preserve their separate identity through a system of apartheid whereby Bulgars and Slavs lived in separate settlements. Despite this the two populations had assimilated by the early ninth century, but while the Slavs adopted Bulgar identity, it was the Bulgars who adopted Slavic language and culture. As a consequence, the modern Bulgarians are essentially a Slav people.

'Ten-arrows' confederation

In contrast to the Avars and the Bulgars, the Magyars assimilated their subjects into both their identity and language. The Magyars originated in northern Russia or Siberia but migrated south to the Black Sea steppes in the seventh century and adopted nomadic pastoralism. Though they were divided into independent hordes, the Magyars formed a loose confederation called the On-Ogur ('Ten Arrows'); it is from the Slavic pronunciation of this name that the Magyars came to be called Hungarians by their neighbours. Under pressure from the Pechenegs, another nomad people, the Magyars migrated west towards the lower Danube, where the Byzantines encouraged them to attack the Bulgars.

Arnulf, the king of Germany (r.887–99), enticed the Magyars further west by persuading them to help him destroy the Slav principality of Great

These impressive bronze statues of chieftains were erected in Heroes' Square, Budapest, in 1896 to mark the millennium of the Magyar conquest of the Carpathian Basin.

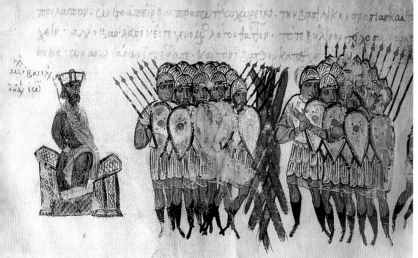

The final defeat of the Bulgars by the Byzantine emperor Michael IV the Paphlagonian (seated on his throne) is depicted in this 11th-century manuscript.

Moravia. Under the leadership of Árpád (c.850 – 907), the Magyars crossed the Carpathian Mountains in 896, and by 906 they had taken the Carpathian Basin from the Moravians. The area soon became known as Hungary (or Magyarország to the Magyars). No sooner was this accomplished than Árpád turned on Arnulf and raided Bavaria, followed by northern Italy. Though Árpád died in 907, the success of his raids encouraged more, and bolder, raids in the future.

The Magyars were attracted to the Carpathian Basin for the same reasons that had drawn the Huns and the Avars to settle the area before them: it was the most westerly area of steppe that had sufficient grazing for the vast herds of horses on which the nomads depended. The basin's westerly position also made it an ideal base for raiding the western European kingdoms. The Magyars were typical nomad warriors, light cavalry who relied on speed and mobility rather than armour for protection, and whose preferred weapon was the bow. On campaign, the Magyars forced their slower-moving opponents off balance by making frequent and unexpected changes of direction, making it difficult to predict where they would strike next.

Magyar raids

In 910 the Germans under Louis IV (r.899–911) were defeated by the Magyars at the Battle of Augsburg after they fell for the oldest trick in the nomad book of war. Confronted by the heavily armoured German cavalry, the Magyars feigned panic and fled – only to turn on their pursuers and annihilate them once they had become thoroughly disorganized and exhausted. For the next 30 years Italy, Germany and France were all savagely and repeatedly raided. The Magyar raids were far more wide-ranging than those of the Huns or Avars, reaching Otranto on the 'heel' of Italy in 921, the foothills of the Pyrenees in 924 and the suburbs of Constantinople in 942.

Magyar raiding began to decline gradually from the 930s because of widespread fortress-building in western Europe. The German kings Henry the Fowler (r.919–36) and Otto I (r.936–73) put considerable resources into fortifying Germany's eastern border against the raiders, and in 933 Henry inflicted the first defeat on the Magyars at the Battle of Riade. This did not significantly affect Magyar power, however. The raids reached a climax in 954, when a horde of 50,000 Magyars rampaged through Germany, France, Burgundy and Italy before returning to Hungary. When the Magyars tried to repeat the raid next year,

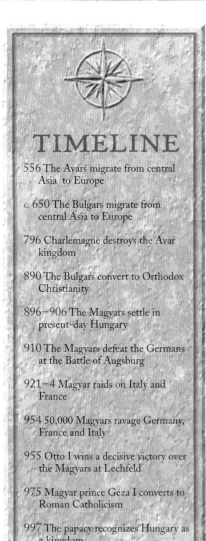

TIMELINE

556 The Avars migrate from central Asia to Europe

c. 650 The Bulgars migrate from central Asia to Europe

796 Charlemagne destroys the Avar kingdom

890 The Bulgars convert to Orthodox Christianity

896–906 The Magyars settle in present-day Hungary

910 The Magyars defeat the Germans at the Battle of Augsburg

921–4 Magyar raids on Italy and France

954 50,000 Magyars ravage Germany, France and Italy

955 Otto I wins a decisive victory over the Magyars at Lechfeld

975 Magyar prince Géza I converts to Roman Catholicism

997 The papacy recognizes Hungary as a kingdom

1018 Byzantine empire conquers the Bulgars

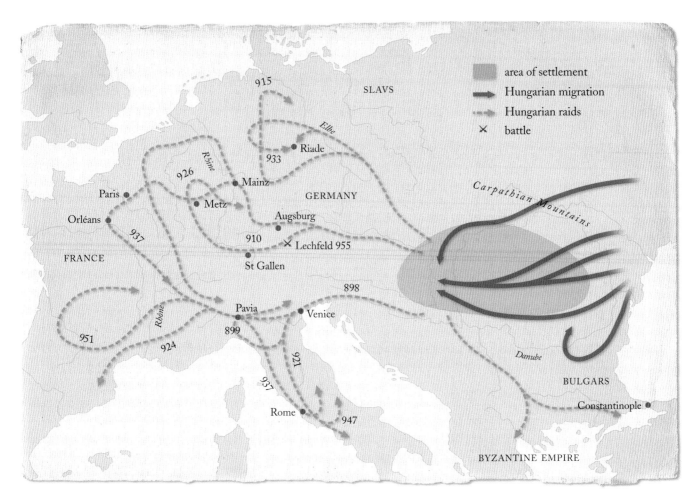

Map showing areas of Hungarian settlement and raids on their neighbours during the tenth century.

however, they were forced to battle by Otto I at Lechfeld near Augsburg and crushingly defeated. Otto's victory proved decisive, ending Magyar raids once and for all. In 975 Prince Géza I (*c.*940–97) converted to Roman Catholicism, beginning the normalization of the Magyars' relations with their neighbours. Under Géza's son Stephen I (St Stephen; r.997–1038), who was granted a crown by the pope, Hungary took its place among the Christian kingdoms of medieval Europe.

An élite ruling class

The Magyars' achievement was all the more remarkable because genetic studies indicate that they must have been outnumbered at least 20:1 by their mainly Slavic subjects. A genetic marker typical of northern mongoloids and most common in the Buryat people of central Siberia, known as the ab3st haplotype, is found in about 3 percent of modern Hungarians but not in the general European population. This confirms both the Asian origin of the Magyars and that they were a small warrior élite. In this respect they were probably no different from the Bulgars and Avars but the Magyars successfully resisted assimilation, while the others did not. The reason for this is probably linked to the Magyars' early conversion to Christianity, after they had been settled for only three generations. The Avars only converted after they had been conquered by Charlemagne and the Bulgars only after they had become Slavicized. The support of the church and of other European ruling houses consolidated the prestige of the Magyar ruling class at just the point when they might otherwise have begun to merge with the Slavs.

Pioneers of the Pacific
2000 BC—AD 1000

The Pacific islands were among the very last places to be settled by humans. By the time European navigators began to explore the vast spaces of the Pacific Ocean, they found that almost every habitable island they sighted, no matter how remote, had already been discovered and populated by the Polynesians.

The jumping-off point for the settlement of the Pacific was the large island of New Guinea, first settled by early Papuan peoples around 40,000 years ago. East of New Guinea a continuous chain of mountainous islands extends for nearly a thousand miles out into the Pacific. None is separated from another island by more than about 40 miles (64 km) of open sea so there is a high degree of intervisibility between islands. This allowed the Papuans to island-hop as far out into the Pacific Ocean as the Solomon Islands without ever sailing out of sight of land. This they had accomplished by around 28,000 years ago. It was to be more than 20,000 years before the human settlement of the Pacific islands progressed any further. Beyond San Cristobal (Makira) Island, the most easterly of the Solomons, there is a gap of over 200 miles (320 km) before the Santa Cruz Islands are reached. The Papuans' simple rafts or boats were not seaworthy enough to allow them to make voyages of exploration to search for land which might (or might not) lie beyond the horizon.

The Lapita people

About 2000 BC a new group of peoples arrived in New Guinea from the Philippines. These people were Austronesians, whose descendants include the modern Malays, Javanese and Filipinos, among others. They found it hard to find anywhere to settle because the Papuans had long ago settled the best places, but they had better luck in the Solomon Islands. Here a mixed culture developed to which both the Austronesians and the original Papuan settlers contributed. This is known as the Lapita culture.

Around 1500 BC the Lapita people made a great technological breakthrough, which finally opened the Pacific to human settlement. They invented sails and two new kinds of boat which were seaworthy enough to make long voyages on the open ocean: the outrigger canoe and the twin-hulled voyaging canoe. Voyaging canoes could make open-sea crossings of hundreds of miles and within a few centuries the Lapita people had discovered and settled the Santa Cruz Islands, Banks Islands, New Caledonia, Fiji, Tonga and Samoa. About 500 BC the Lapita people split into three groups: the Melanesians, who lived on the islands of the western Pacific (Fiji west to New Guinea); the Micronesians, who spread through the islands north of the Melanesians; and the

Small outrigger canoes are still used throughout the Pacific region for fishing and short voyages. This craft is from Tahiti in French Polynesia.

An early 19th-century lithograph showing a European visitor being carried on a large Tahitian ocean-going canoe.

Polynesians, who lived on Tonga and Samoa. The Polynesians continued to move out into the Pacific and by 200 BC they had reached Tahiti, 1500 miles (2400 km) from Tonga. The Pacific islands were very restricted environments. Voyages of settlement were a way for the Polynesians to deal with problems caused by overpopulation and civil war. When two chiefs fought for control, the loser could set sail with his followers to look for a new place to live. By about AD 400 Polynesians had reached Hawaii and Easter Island, the most remote inhabited place on earth. There is a certain amount of evidence that a few Polynesians even reached South America hundreds of years before Europeans did.

The last great voyage of Polynesian settlement was from Tahiti to New Zealand. According to Maori legend New Zealand was discovered in *c.*1000 by Kupe who lived in the mythical land of Hawaiki (generally thought to be Tahiti). Kupe was out fishing octopus. When one stole his bait he gave chase. New Zealand got its Maori name Aotearoa ('Land of the Long White Cloud') from the fact that Kupe saw the clouds that formed over the mountains long before the land came into sight. A 'Great Fleet' of eight huge canoes set sail from Hawaiki to settle Aotearoa. Each was captained by a chief and crewed by his followers and their families. The Maori tribes are all able to trace their ancestry back to the people who came in one of these canoes. At first, the Maori got to eat a lot more meat than other Polynesians because New Zealand was populated by giant moas, flightless birds about twice the size of an ostrich. Moas were easy prey – not being used to humans, they did not run away – and they were hunted to extinction by 1800.

Canoes for crossing oceans

Outrigger canoes, the smaller of the two types of craft used by the Polynesians, were small, light, fast and very manoeuvrable. They were used mainly for shorter sea trips and fishing. Most had only one outrigger but some had two, one on each side. For voyages of settlement they used big double-hulled canoes, up to 30 metres (100 ft) long. These were very stable and seaworthy and could carry over 100 people. Both types were built of planks which were sewn together with ropes. The gaps between the planks were made watertight by caulking with the thick, sticky sap of the breadfruit tree. Boats carried a single sail, most often of a triangular or 'claw' shape, made of matted pandanus leaf fibres. These gave Polynesian boats the ability to sail across the wind and, by tacking, even make headway against it.

Polynesian boats could carry enough supplies to stay at sea for up to six weeks. Water supplies were carried in bamboo stems or hollowed out coconuts. Lots of coconuts were carried as these provided both food and drink. The main foods were dried pandanus fruit (an orange, segmented fruit vaguely resembling a pineapple) and fermented breadfruit (a green, starchy fruit). Wrapped in palm leaves, these could last months. Hard tack was provided by dried molluscs, which kept almost indefinitely, but were almost as tough to chew as rubber. Large boats had hearths made of clay and stone for cooking fish caught by the crew. There was no need to carry fire wood, since old coconut husks were used for fuel. Pigs, chickens and dogs were the only domesticated animals that could survive long voyages. Rats were inevitable stowaways and they played havoc with ground-nesting birds on the islands where the Polynesians landed.

The direction of migration was largely determined by that of the prevailing winds, though not in the way that the landlubber might expect. Voyages of exploration were usually made against, not with, the prevailing wind, which across most of Polynesia blows from the east or southeast. Setting sail into the unknown with the prevailing wind brought with it the danger that a navigator might not be able to find a favourable wind to bring him home again. In 1492, Columbus set sail across the Atlantic Ocean using the easterly trade winds knowing that if he failed to make a landfall he could simply sail

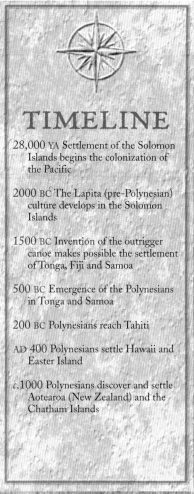

TIMELINE

28,000 YA Settlement of the Solomon Islands begins the colonization of the Pacific

2000 BC The Lapita (pre-Polynesian) culture develops in the Solomon Islands

1500 BC Invention of the outrigger canoe makes possible the settlement of Tonga, Fiji and Samoa

500 BC Emergence of the Polynesians in Tonga and Samoa

200 BC Polynesians reach Tahiti

AD 400 Polynesians settle Hawaii and Easter Island

c.1000 Polynesians discover and settle Aotearoa (New Zealand) and the Chatham Islands

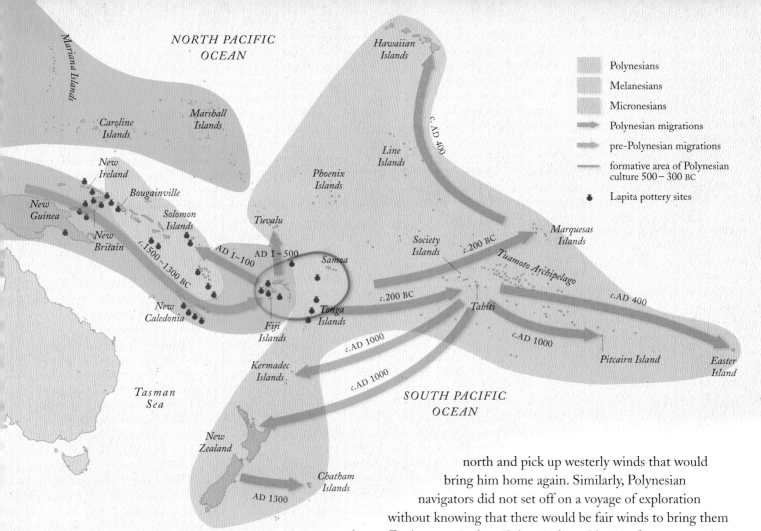

NORTH PACIFIC
OCEAN

Mariana Islands

Caroline Islands

Marshall Islands

New Ireland

Bougainville

New Guinea

New Britain

Solomon Islands

Tuvalu

Hawaiian Islands

Line Islands

Phoenix Islands

Society Islands

Samoa

Marquesas Islands

Tuamoto Archipelago

New Caledonia

Fiji Islands

Tonga Islands

Tahiti

Kermadec Islands

Pitcairn Island

Easter Island

Tasman Sea

New Zealand

Chatham Islands

SOUTH PACIFIC
OCEAN

c. AD 400

c. 1500–1300 BC

AD 1–100

AD 1–500

c. 200 BC

c. 200 BC

c. AD 400

c. AD 1000

c. AD 1000

c. AD 1000

c. AD 1000

AD 1300

	Polynesians
	Melanesians
	Micronesians
→	Polynesian migrations
→	pre-Polynesian migrations
—	formative area of Polynesian culture 500–300 BC
•	Lapita pottery sites

The peopling of the Pacific region by the descendants of the Lapita people: Polynesians, Melanesians and Micronesians.

north and pick up westerly winds that would bring him home again. Similarly, Polynesian navigators did not set off on a voyage of exploration without knowing that there would be fair winds to bring them home. Explorers waited until the wind was blowing from a westerly direction and then set off, confident in the knowledge that when the winds changed back to their normal direction, they would be taken back towards home.

Masters of navigation

The Polynesians were the most accomplished of all pre-modern navigators. Though they never knew about the magnetic compass, they were able to navigate accurately over hundreds or even thousands of miles of open ocean. Polynesian navigators depended on an excellent knowledge of the movement of the sun and the stars to navigate. They learned the positions on the horizon where bright stars or constellations (like the Pleiades or Orion's belt) rose and set in every season of the year. This allowed them to work out easily whether they were sailing north or south relative to their starting point. They also knew the rising and setting points of these stars as seen from all the surrounding islands. With this knowledge it was easy for a navigator to work out whether he reached the same latitude as the place he was trying to sail to. He could adjust his course north or south every night until he reached his destination. This knowledge was accumulated by practical experience over centuries and passed down by word of mouth from one generation to another.

Navigators were also helped by their detailed knowledge of the marine environment. They knew a lot about the swell, which is the general direction in which the waves flow. They knew that this varied much less than wind direction, so it was possible for them to get their bearings just by looking at the angle between the boat and the swell. For example, if, when it grew dark in the evening, the boat was heading straight into the swell and then, when it got light the next morning, the swell was coming straight at the side of the hull, it would most likely mean that the boat had changed course by 90 degrees during the night. This was especially useful if the night had been cloudy and the sailors had not been able to take star bearings.

Navigators could often detect the presence of land, even in poor visibility, by reflected waves. When a large wave hits the shore, a small wave is reflected back out to sea. These could be nearly invisible but an experienced navigator could detect them from their vibrations in the water. To do this he lowered himself into the water just as far as his scrotum, the most sensitive part of the male anatomy. Some islanders made charts using sticks and shells representing the exact pattern of reflected waves around different known islands. These allowed a navigator to be able to identify an island long before he could see it just from the pattern of reflected waves.

Experienced navigators could recognize many other clues indicating the proximity of land. High islands could be detected by the build-up of clouds over mountains. Even coral atolls can be detected long before they can be seen. Light reflecting onto the bottom of clouds from the shallow water in the atoll's lagoon is a different colour from that reflecting from the deep water of the open sea. The colour is different for every atoll, depending on the size and depth of the lagoon, so an island could be identified when it was still over the horizon just by observing the colour of the reflected light. Changes in sea colour could indicate the presence of land. Open ocean is deep blue but when the sea is shallower than 30 fathoms (180 feet or 55 metres), it starts to turn greener.

A 19th or early 20th century navigational chart from the Marshall Islands (Micronesia). The diagonal and curved sticks represent wave swell patterns. This type of chart was called a 'mattang' and was used for training people to become navigators.

Sailors recognized that particular parts of the ocean were favoured by shoals of fish, turtles or whales (usually because currents brought nutrients to the surface). Sailing through one of these areas gave sailors a rough idea where they were even when they were hundreds of miles from land. The flight of birds which feed at sea but nest on land can point the way to land. Some birds, like boobies (a type of gannet), fly as much as 30 miles (48 km) out from land searching for food, but return to land to roost at night during the breeding season.

Although islands were small specks in a vast ocean, these signs, for someone who knew how to recognize them, magnified their size by over ten times. Easter Island is only 12 miles (19 km) long but the target zone is 124 miles (198 km) wide. Even so, this is still a small target in a vast expanse of ocean. Migration was a dangerous business because often no one knew when they set out that there were any more islands out there that could be settled. Many people must have set out and died of thirst and hunger on the open ocean without finding land.

The Normans
1017–1099

A French-speaking people of Viking descent, the Normans
were the most influential migrants of 11th-century Europe.
Normandy became the most powerful feudal principality
in France and had a major impact not only on that nation's
history, but also on that of England, Italy and the Holy Land.

The Normans were descended from Danish Vikings who
settled around the mouth of the River Seine at the end of
the ninth century. In 911 their leader Rollo (*c.*860–932), or
Hrolf, reached an agreement with the French king Charles
the Simple (r.893–923). Rollo would become a
royal vassal, convert to Christianity and keep
other Vikings out of the Seine, in return for which
Charles would recognize him as count of Rouen
(Norman rulers did not use the title 'duke' until
1006). The Viking settlement became known as
Normandy, 'Northman's Land'. Over time, the
Normans lost their Scandinavian identity and
adopted French culture and language.

*A 12th-century mosaic icon
in Martorana Church,
Palermo, depicts Roger II
being crowned king of Sicily
by Christ himself, reflecting
the belief that his royal
authority came direct
from God.*

Fortune-seeking nobility

The early 11th century was a time of intense competition within the
Norman aristocracy. This resulted in an often violent redistribution of land
in favour of an emerging élite. Members of the lesser nobility feared for their
future status. They also found their resources were becoming too meagre to
provide an adequate inheritance for all their sons. Normandy, therefore, had
relatively large numbers of young men with little or no land and few
prospects of getting any. As part of their noble upbringing they had all been
trained as knights, so many left to serve as mercenaries for foreign rulers. An extreme
example of this was the family of Tancred of Hauteville, a minor landowner whose 12
sons all emigrated to seek their fortunes.

The main destination was southern Italy which was being fought over by the Lombards,
Byzantines and Arabs. The first Normans to serve here were a band of 40 men under
Rodulf (d.1052) who fought for the Lombard duchy of Benevento against the
Byzantines in 1017. In 1047 Robert Guiscard (d.1085), one of the Hauteville brothers,
arrived in Italy. He established himself in Calabria, where he was joined by his younger

RVNT ARVIERANT C

brothers Roger (d.1101) and Richard (d.1078). Together they had conquered the Lombard duchies by 1072, as well as driving the Byzantines and Arabs out of Italy and Sicily.

The Norman lands in Italy were united by Roger's son Roger II (r.1130–54), who was crowned king of Sicily in 1130. The culture of Roger's court was an eclectic mix of Latin-Italian, Norman, Arab and Byzantine, and has left a legacy of outstanding architecture and religious art. In the longer term, the Normans had little influence on the Italian population. Both peoples were Catholic Christians so there were no barriers to intermarriage and the Normans were gradually assimilated by the Italian majority. Norman rule continued in Italy until 1190– 4, when the kingdom of Sicily was conquered by the German emperor Henry VI (r.1190–97).

Detail from the Bayeux Tapestry (c.1077), showing a Norman horseman killing a huscarl *(household warrior) from King Harold of England's army at the Battle of Hastings in 1066.*

Conquest of England

The Normans' most successful colonizing venture was in England. Small numbers of Normans had entered the service of the pro-Norman king Edward the Confessor (r.1042–66), but their arrogance made them unpopular with the English. Edward was childless and he offered to make Duke William of Normandy (c.1027–87) his heir.

Map showing the extent of Norman lands, 11th century.

When Edward died in 1066, the English rejected William's claim and chose Harold Godwinson (r.1066) as king instead. William, a good soldier who had already earned his nickname 'the Conqueror', raised an army, invaded England and defeated and killed Harold at Hastings.

Further English resistance was crushed with extreme brutality and William was in firm control of England by 1071. William gave his border barons complete freedom to enlarge their territories at the expense of the Welsh, but by the 1090s their advance had stagnated. The Welsh retained their independence for another 300 years. In the 12th century, King David I of Scotland (r.1124–53) invited Normans to settle in the wilder parts of his kingdom and help bring them under firm royal control.

The Norman conquest of England is a good example of the way small numbers of immigrants can have a disproportionately large impact on the host community. It is clear from documentary evidence that only around 10,000 immigrants came to England after the conquest. The population of the country at this time was around 1.5 million. Most of the immigrants were from Normandy, but some were from France, Brittany and Flanders, and the majority were male. The most immediate consequences of the conquest were a revolution in land-holding and the imposition of a new French-speaking ruling class. Most of William the Conqueror's troops were landless younger sons. The Normans initially claimed the land by right of conquest. All the English landowners who had fought against William at Hastings were dispossessed and the land was distributed among the victors. The majority of the remaining English landowners were dispossessed as a result of their unsuccessful rebellions in the years immediately after the conquest. To further legitimize their claims to the land, Normans were ordered to marry the widows of men who had died fighting against William. The changes at the top had little effect in the lower reaches of society, and English peasants stayed put. There were no Norman peasant immigrants.

Pre-conquest England had been an integral part of northern Europe and had forged close cultural and political links with Scandinavia and the Celtic kingdoms. William and his successors continued to rule Normandy as dukes after the conquest, so making England part of a cross-Channel polity. For the next 400 years all kings of England would also rule lands in France. In this way, the Normans decisively drew England into the French cultural and political sphere of influence. English culture was both changed and immeasurably enriched by the introduction of French artistic, architectural and literary fashions. The English stubbornly refused to learn French, but thousands of French loan words found their way into the English language, eventually enabling English to compete with Latin as a language for learned discourse.

By the early 12th century, Normans who had been born in England were beginning to think of themselves as English, even though they remained French in language and culture. However, in 1154, on the death of Stephen (r.1135–54), the last Norman king of England, the count of Anjou acceded to the throne as Henry II (r.1154–89). Though he had a Norman mother, Henry was thoroughly French in identity and outlook. When he took up the English throne, he brought with him his Angevin cronies who reinforced the French character of the English ruling class, so much so that it would be the 14th century before English reasserted itself as the language of the élite.

Attempts to identify genetic traces of the Norman conquerors in the English population have so far failed. This is probably because, despite being French-speaking, the Normans were ultimately of Danish origin. Many Anglo-Saxons, and later Viking settlers in England, hailed from Denmark so the Normans were not genetically distinct from the English. Languages, cultures and genes do not always march in step. The fact that so many Normans, including William the Conqueror's own son, Henry I (r.1100–35), married English women, further diluted any genetic distinctiveness they might once have had.

Normans in the Holy Land

The final phase of Norman expansion was in the Middle East. This came about as a result of the First Crusade (1096–9). Two of its five leaders were the eldest sons of Robert Guiscard and William the Conqueror: Bohemund of Taranto (c.1057–1111) and Robert of Normandy (c.1051–1134). Both took with them to the Holy Land substantial numbers of Norman knights. After Jerusalem was taken in 1099 most of the crusaders went home, leaving pitifully few to garrison the land recaptured from the Muslims. Bohemund was one of those who stayed. He became prince of the Syrian city of Antioch but he was joined by only a few hundred settlers. In 1119 Antioch could raise only 700 knights. There was a large native Christian minority in Syria but they belonged to churches that the Catholic Normans regarded as being schismatic, so they remained aloof from them. With their Muslim subjects, there was even less interaction. The Normans remained an isolated military aristocracy, unable even to recruit local Christians into its ranks. Strong castles made up for the shortage of manpower to some extent, but in 1268 Antioch finally fell to the Muslims.

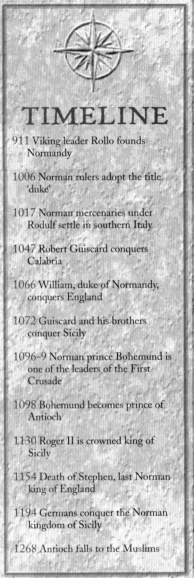

TIMELINE

911 Viking leader Rollo founds Normandy

1006 Norman rulers adopt the title 'duke'

1017 Norman mercenaries under Rodulf settle in southern Italy

1047 Robert Guiscard conquers Calabria

1066 William, duke of Normandy, conquers England

1072 Guiscard and his brothers conquer Sicily

1096–9 Norman prince Bohemund is one of the leaders of the First Crusade

1098 Bohemund becomes prince of Antioch

1130 Roger II is crowned king of Sicily

1154 Death of Stephen, last Norman king of England

1194 Germans conquer the Norman kingdom of Sicily

1268 Antioch falls to the Muslims

The Turks
552–1095

As commonly used in the West today, the terms 'Turk' and 'Turkish' describe the citizens of the Republic of Turkey. However, Turks also form the majority of the populations of the former Soviet republics of Azerbaijan, Kazakhstan, Turkmenistan, Tajikistan, Kyrgyzstan and Uzbekistan. There are significant Turkish minorities in Russia, Mongolia, China, Afghanistan and Iran. The wide spread of the Turks is a result of migrations during the Middle Ages.

The Turks share a common origin with the Mongols somewhere in northeast central Asia. Turks formed part of the great Xiongnu nomad confederation that launched plundering raids on China in the last centuries BC. When this confederation broke up in the first century AD, its constituent peoples scattered across the steppes. One group, the Huns, finished up in Europe, another, the Ephthalites, in India. The Turks were swept up in another nomad confederation, the Mongol-dominated Juan-Juan, in about AD 400 and they were instrumental in its overthrow in 552. In the aftermath, the Turks created the Türküt khanate that stretched from Manchuria in the east to the Aral Sea in the west.

The Türküt khanate split into eastern and western halves in the seventh century before breaking up. One of the more important groups to emerge from the breakup of the khanate was the Oguz (or Ghuzz), a confederation of around 24 Turkish tribes. In the eighth century they were living in Mongolia but after a period of inter-tribal warfare they migrated west to the steppes between the Caspian and Aral Seas. Here they came into contact with the Samanid emirate of Persia. As a result of Samanid influence the shamanist Oguz began to convert to Sunni Islam around 970.

As can be seen in this relief sculpture, the Seljuk Turks were warrior peoples. Their defeat of the Byzantines at the Battle of Manzikert in 1071 paved the way for the Turkish occupation of Anatolia.

Mamluk dynasties

The Muslim world had long been familiar with the Turks; since the time of the caliph al-Mu'tasim (r.833–42) it had been importing Turkish boy slaves to be given an Islamic education and brought up as Mamluks, slave-warriors who served as the élite bodyguards for Islamic rulers. Slavery of this sort carried no social stigma in the Islamic world and, as Mamluks, Turks often reached positions of great power and influence. On occasions, they were able to overthrow their masters and found their own dynasties. One of the most remarkable of these was Mahmud of Ghazni (r.997–1030), who founded a militant Islamic state in Afghanistan. These were the achievements of individuals.

In Egypt, Mamluks overthrew the Ayyubid dynasty and established themselves en masse as a ruling class which held power until 1516, when Egypt was conquered by the Ottomans. Usually, the strongest general among them was chosen to rule as sultan. The Mamluks did not abandon a system that had served them so well and they continued to import boys from the steppes until they were overthrown. This helped prevent the Mamluk class from being assimilated into the Egyptian population. Turkish remained their first language, and many Mamluks knew little or no Arabic.

Service as mercenaries familiarized the Turks with the riches of the Middle East. In 1038–40 Tugril Beg (r.1038–63), leader of the Seljuk clan, led the Oguz on a successful invasion of Iran and founded the Seljuk Turk sultanate. In 1055 Tugril added the caliphate of Baghdad to his dominions. In theory, the caliph was the leader of the Muslim world; in practice he was a puppet of a Shia group called the Buyids. Tugril gained much Arab support by posing as the champion of Sunni orthodoxy against the heretical Shia but after his victory he did not return any real power to the caliphs. The success of the Seljuk Turks attracted more Turks from central Asia. These nomads proved disruptive to attempts at creating a stable government so they were sent to the frontiers, thus perpetuating the tide of Turkish conquests.

The Qaitbay citadel at Alexandria, Egypt, was built c.1480 by the Mamluk sultan Al-Ashraf Qaitbay as part of his coastal defences. The Mamluks were a dynasty of Turkish slave-warriors who ruled Egypt from 1250 to 1516.

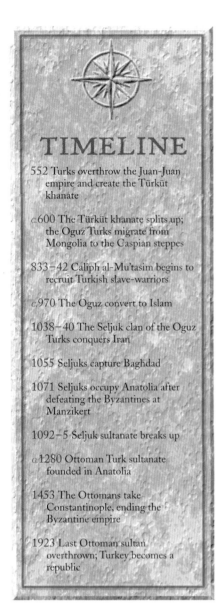

TIMELINE

552 Turks overthrow the Juan-Juan empire and create the Türküt khanate

c.600 The Türküt khanate splits up; the Oguz Turks migrate from Mongolia to the Caspian steppes

833–42 Caliph al-Mu'tasim begins to recruit Turkish slave-warriors

c.970 The Oguz convert to Islam

1038–40 The Seljuk clan of the Oguz Turks conquers Iran

1055 Seljuks capture Baghdad

1071 Seljuks occupy Anatolia after defeating the Byzantines at Manzikert

1092–5 Seljuk sultanate breaks up

c.1280 Ottoman Turk sultanate founded in Anatolia

1453 The Ottomans take Constantinople, ending the Byzantine empire

1923 Last Ottoman sultan overthrown; Turkey becomes a republic

Tugril's successor, Alp Arslan (r.1063–72), conquered Syria and, in 1071, routed the Byzantines at the Battle of Manzikert. After Alp Arslan was killed fighting off an invasion by the Qarakhanid Turks, his successor Malik Shah (r.1072–92) occupied Byzantine Anatolia and drove the Egyptians out of Palestine. As new converts to Islam, the Seljuks were less tolerant of Christians than the Arabs had been and they began to harass pilgrims on their way to Jerusalem. It was this, and the Byzantine emperor's plea for help in recapturing Anatolia, that led to the calling of the First Crusade in 1095.

Malik Shah's death sparked a civil war and the Seljuk sultanate broke up. In 1095 the Seljuks in Anatolia set up two independent states: in the west the sultanate of Rum and in the east the Danishmend emirate. The civil war helped the crusaders reconquer the Holy Land. It also helped the Byzantines recapture much of Anatolia from the Seljuks of Rum, but they failed to expel the Turks completely. Elsewhere in the Middle East, Turkish influence began to wane, the Arabs and Persians reasserted themselves, but Turkish domination of Anatolia became permanent.

Rise of the Ottoman Turks

The sultanate of Rum fragmented in the 13th century but the Turks of Anatolia were reunited in the 14th century by the Ottoman dynasty. By the time Sultan Mehmet II (r.1444–6; 1451–81) captured the Byzantine capital Constantinople (modern Istanbul) in 1453, the Ottomans had already overrun Greece and the Balkans. They eventually extended their rule also to Syria, Palestine and most of North Africa and Arabia. Many Turks settled in the Balkans and Greece but few did so in the conquered Arab lands to the south.

A portrait of Sultan Mehmet II, painted c.1453. As well as being a military leader, Mehmet was a patron of literature and fine art.

Because of the success of the Ottomans, Anatolia became the centre of the Turkish world, while the old central Asian homeland was first marginalized and then conquered by the Russian and Chinese empires. From the 18th century onward the Ottoman empire gradually declined, until by the end of the First World War (1914–18) it was reduced to Anatolia and a foothold in Europe, where Turks formed the ethnic majority. After the last sultan was overthrown in 1923, this rump became the Republic of Turkey. Almost all ethnic Turks living in former Ottoman provinces migrated to Turkey during this period.

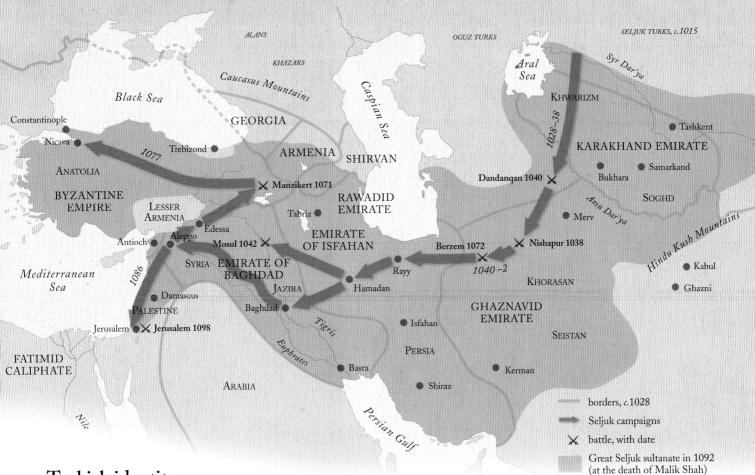

Map showing the extent of the Seljuk sultanate in 1092 and the Seljuk campaigns of the early 11th century.

Turkish identity

Turks vary considerably in appearance. Turkish peoples in central Asia, such as the Uighurs of Xinjiang in western China, have a mongoloid appearance, while at the opposite end of the Turkish world, most Turks in Istanbul look like southeastern Europeans. Writers of the time describe the Turkish conquest and occupation of Anatolia as a process of infiltration by small warrior bands. Because of this it has long been thought that the contribution of Turkish immigrants to the population of modern Turkey as a whole was relatively small. There were certainly few obstacles to the conquered Byzantine Christians adopting Turkish identity once they had converted to Islam. Converts gained equal rights with Turks and it then only required them (or, more likely, their children) to become fluent Turkish speakers for the transition to be complete.

However, research into the DNA of the Anatolian population has shown that a substantial proportion – around 30 percent – of the inhabitants are of central Asian ancestry. Significantly, the percentage is the same for female mtDNA lineages and male Y chromosomes. This means that there were equal numbers of male and female immigrants, not at all what would be expected if Anatolia had been conquered and settled by a warrior élite alone. The results are best explained by an undocumented, small-scale, but long, sustained trickle of Turkish immigrants from central Asia lasting for many generations after the initial conquest. Immigration to Anatolia forced major changes of lifestyle on the Turks. To fit in with established settlements they had, for the most part, to give up nomadism and become settled farmers. A vestige of the old ways survives in mountain areas, where some practise transhumant pastoralism, moving their herds between mountain and valley pastures with the seasons. These pastoralists have permanent villages in the valleys, however, and also grow crops.

The Medieval German Drive to the East

IOTH–I5TH CENTURIES

Until the Second World War the Germans were among the most widespread peoples of Europe. As well as in their core areas of Germany, Austria and Switzerland, pockets of German speakers were to be found in Poland, Hungary, Czechoslovakia, Romania, the Baltic states and Russia. This was the result of a sustained movement of colonization which began in the 11th century and continued until after the end of the Middle Ages.

A contemporary manuscript illumination showing the coronation of Henry the Lion, one of the most powerful German princes of the 12th century.

The events of the migration period are so dramatic that it is easy to overlook the fact that at its end the area settled by Germanic-speaking peoples was much smaller than it had been before the arrival of the Huns had thrown Europe into chaos. In 370 German-speaking peoples had inhabited a vast territory that extended from the Rhineland to the River Don in the east. Less than 200 years later, migrating Slavs had moved into the lands vacated by the Germans as they fled from the Huns, and the eastern border of the German-speaking area stood on the River Elbe. To compensate, the only permanent extensions of the German-speaking area had been in the Low Countries and south of the Danube into Bavaria and the Alps.

The German reoccupation of some of these lost territories, known to German historians as the *Drang nach Osten*, the 'Drive to the East', began in the late tenth century. Yet the popular designation is misleading, since this was no medieval equivalent of the Nazis' blitzkrieg against the USSR in 1941. There was never an imperial blueprint for German domination in the east, just a succession of individual initiatives over several centuries. Germany was the heart of the medieval Holy Roman Empire. The empire, which had pretensions to be the successor of the Roman empire, was a decentralized feudal state, comprising several sub-kingdoms, princely duchies and counties, all owing allegiance to the Holy Roman Emperor. For much of the Middle Ages, the emperors were preoccupied with enforcing their authority over the rich but rebellious cities of Italy, and the princes and counts were left with considerable freedom to expand their own territories eastward.

Conquest, conversion and colonization

In the mid-tenth century Herman Billung, margrave of Saxony, and Gero, margrave of Thuringia, conquered the Wends, as the Slavs who lived between the Elbe and the Oder were called. The area was divided into marches (from the German *mark*, meaning border), highly militarized territories with garrisons to control the conquered population and which could be used as bases for raids into as yet unconquered territory. The Wends were forced to pay tribute, and burgwards were established to encourage German peasants to settle. A burgward was a fortification (burg) with ten to 20 dependent settlements in the surrounding district (ward). The fortification provided a refuge for the settlers in the event of native rebellions but was also a centre for secular and ecclesiastical government, with a church, a court and tax collector. Hand in hand with conquest went evangelization of the still pagan Wends under the guidance of German missionaries. In 983, the Wends rebelled against their treatment; most of the burgwards were destroyed, missionary activity ceased and German expansion was set back for over a century.

German expansion began again in the middle of the 12th century under the leadership of Henry the Lion, duke of Saxony and Bavaria, who set about reconquering the Wends. Henry was helped by the church, which agreed to recognize campaigning against the

Founded in 1274 on the bank of the River Nogat by the Order of the Teutonic Knights, Malbork (formerly Marienburg) Castle in Poland became the seat of the order and Europe's largest Gothic fortress.

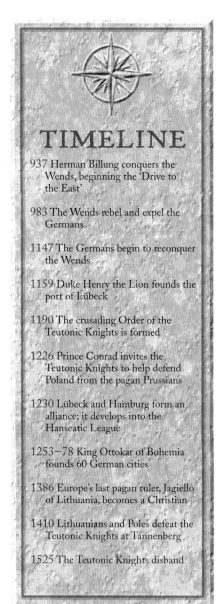

pagan Wends as an extension of the crusades then being waged to recover control of the Holy Land from the Muslims. Henry's pretensions led the emperor to overthrow him in 1183, but by this time the Germans had established their control over the Baltic Sea coast as far east as the River Vistula. Around the same time, German expansion was proceeding in the southeast, across the Alps and into the northern Balkans.

Conquest was followed by colonization. To encourage German peasant settlement, surveyors identified suitable locations to found new villages. The settlers were guaranteed free status – an attractive privilege at a time when most European peasant cultivators were unfree serfs – and the right to treat their farms as heritable property. Settlers lived rent-free until the settlement was properly established; thereafter they paid rent in cash or grain. Monasteries of German monks and nuns were also used as agents of Germanization in the countryside. Secular lords granted estates to monasteries primarily for the benefit of their souls, but they would contribute to conversion of the Slavs and, as centres of literacy, they also played a role in the administration of conquered territories.

Urbanization and expansion

German merchants and artisans were attracted by the foundation of cities, which from the outset were given autonomous status under German law. Slavs as well as Germans lived in these cities but the former were specifically excluded from the best-paid crafts and commercial activities to prevent them competing with the colonists. These new cities, Berlin and Vienna among them, became centres for trade, religion and culture, acting as powerful agents of Germanization. The system was so successful in promoting urbanization that it was adopted by Slavic rulers who recognized the economic benefits that German settlers could bring to their kingdoms. King Ottokar of Bohemia (r.1253–78), for instance, founded 60 German cities in his kingdom.

New German towns on the Baltic, such as Lübeck, founded by Henry the Lion in 1159, greatly stimulated trade in the region. By 1250, the German trading towns had banded together in the Hanseatic League (from *Hanse*, German for 'guild'), which negotiated trading privileges for its members, organized convoys for protection against pirates, produced navigational charts and even waged war. By 1300 colonies of German merchants were settled in the most important northern and eastern European cities. In many, such as Novgorod, Bergen, Bruges and London, the league had self-contained enclaves, called Kontore.

A major agent of German expansion was the Order of the Teutonic Knights (German: *Deutscher Orden*), a crusading order of warrior-monks that had been founded in Acre in 1190 to protect German pilgrims to the Holy Land. In 1226 the Polish prince Conrad invited the knights to help him defend his borders against the pagan Prussians. In 50 years of warfare, the knights conquered the Prussians and forcibly converted them to Christianity.

The knights had agreed to serve as vassals of the Polish rulers but they soon reneged and set up their own power base at the castle of Marienburg (now Malbork). The knights encouraged German peasant farmers to settle in Prussia, and founded new towns such as Königsberg (Kaliningrad) and Danzig (Gdansk) for German artisans and merchants.

While German settlers enjoyed privileged status, the native Prussians laboured as serfs on the knights' estates. Conversion and German settlement began the process of Germanizing the Prussians, who were originally a Baltic-speaking people. By the 20th century the Prussians had come to be seen as the archetypal efficient, militaristic Germans.

The Teutonic Knights were an unusual colonizing organization. As an arm of the church, the knights had taken vows of celibacy, so theirs was not a self-sustaining community. The only way they could maintain their numbers was by recruitment. To attract idealistic young knights, the order continued to crusade against Europe's last remaining pagans, the Lithuanians, who came to know Christ simply as 'the German god'. To try to bring an end to the order's attacks, the Lithuanian prince Jagiello converted to Christianity in 1386 and, by marrying a Polish princess, also became king of Poland. Rather than welcoming Jagiello's conversion, the knights claimed that it was their right to evangelize the Lithuanians and they continued their attacks. The knights' defeat by the Lithuanians and Poles at the Battle of Tannenberg (also known as the Battle of Grünwald) in 1410 was a severe blow to the order's prestige. The flow of recruits began to dry up and the order was wound up during the Reformation, when its Grand Master, Albert of Brandenburg, converted to Protestantism in 1525.

Map key:

- area of German settlement, *c.*962
- expansion of settlement by 1250
- expansion of settlement by 1300
- expansion of settlement by 1400
- border of the Holy Roman Empire, *c.*962
- border of the Holy Roman Empire, *c.*1400
- land of the Teutonic Knights, 1390
- • new German towns
- × battle

Map showing the pattern of German settlement in eastern Europe during the Middle Ages.

The Gypsies
10TH–20TH CENTURIES

The Gypsies, or Roma, are unique: they are the only nomadic people in recorded history who have not been either hunters or herders. They are believed to have originated in the north of the Indian Subcontinent but are now found in all European countries, the Middle East, North Africa, North and South America and Australia.

The exact origins of the Gypsies are unknown. Their name reflects the widespread but mistaken medieval European belief that Gypsies came from Egypt. The name most commonly used by Gypsies to describe themselves, 'Rom', is a reflection of the fact that for centuries Romania, and the Balkans more generally, has been the main Gypsy centre in Europe. The Gypsy language, Romani, shows a strong Romanian influence but its basic vocabulary and grammar point to a north Indian origin. Iranian and Armenian influences on the language are a sign that the Gypsies also spent a long time in the Middle East before they reached Europe.

It is not known when or why the Gypsies left India but they were living in Iran by the tenth century AD. The Iranian poet Firdausi (c.930–1020) wrote of the Gypsies in his epic history of the Iranians, the *Shah Nama* (Book of Kings), that they were originally a tribe of musicians who had been sent to the ruler of Iran by an Indian king. Once they had eaten the ruler out of house and home, the Gypsies took to the roads. By the 11th century Gypsies were living in the Byzantine empire and soon afterwards were spreading through the Balkans. When the Ottoman Turks began to overrun the Balkans in the 14th century, groups of Gypsies dispersed across western Europe, reaching Bohemia in 1399, Bavaria in 1418, Paris in 1421, Rome in 1423 and Spain in 1425. In the early 16th century Gypsies spread to Britain, Scandinavia, Poland and Russia, but the Balkans remained the main Gypsy centre. At first Gypsies were protected by the authorities. Early in the 15th century Sigismund, king of Hungary and Bohemia (r.1387–1437), gave letters of protection to Gypsies in his lands. It was these letters which caused Gypsies to be called 'Bohemians' in many European countries and why today people with unconventional lifestyles are described as Bohemians.

An independent lifestyle

Medieval Europeans, who rarely travelled far from their native villages, found the Gypsy lifestyle totally alien. Dressing distinctively, travelling and living in brightly painted horse-drawn wagons, Gypsies made their living by horse-trading, metalworking, music and dance, healing and fortune-telling. Until

TIMELINE

*c.*1000 Gypsies have left India and are living in Iran

*c.*1200 Gypsies living in the Balkans

1399 King Sigismund of Bohemia gives protection to Gypsies

1421 First Gypsies recorded in France

1500 Anti-Gypsy laws passed in Germany

1501 First Gypsies recorded in England

1710 Austrian emperor Joseph I orders all male Gypsies to be hanged

1880s Eastern European Gypsies emigrate to the US

1943–5 400,000 Gypsies killed in Nazi death camps

1989 Mass migration of eastern European Gypsies to western Europe

people got wise to them, they were also very successful at conning alms from the pious by pretending to be pilgrims. Although they might work as seasonal labourers, they were generally disdainful of working for wages, seeing this as a loss of independence. Gypsies were greeted with a mixture of curiosity and hostility. Their skills, especially their knowledge of horses, made them useful but, in the case of fortune-telling and healing, gave rise to suspicion of witchcraft and black magic. Their curses were feared and they were even thought to steal children to bring up as Gypsies. The Gypsies' unwillingness to become wage slaves was seen as indolence and a sign of criminality.

A Gypsy Family by the Austrian painter Matthäus Loder, c.1759.

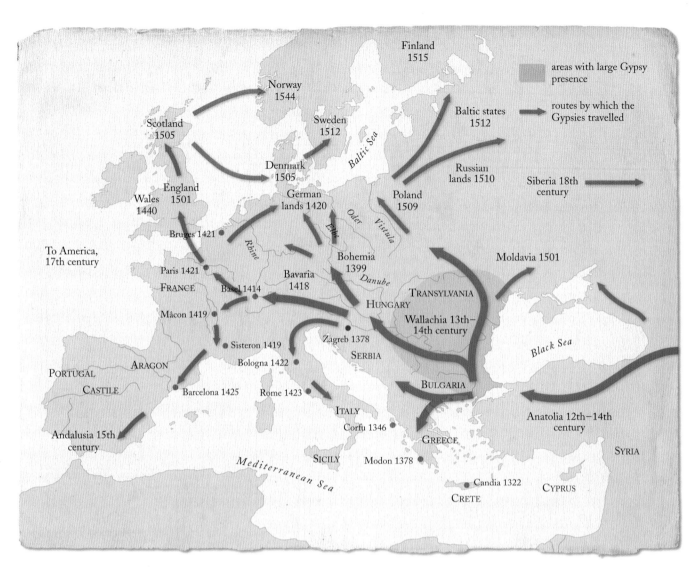

Map showing the dispersal of Gypsies across Europe, 12th–16th centuries.

As early as 1449, Gypsies were expelled from Frankfurt in Germany; laws expelling Gypsies from the rest of Germany were passed in 1500. The fact that over the next 200 years German states frequently re-enacted such laws, often with savage penalties, such as hanging, branding and mutilation, shows they were ineffective or not rigorously enforced. Similarly harsh laws were enacted against Gypsies in Spain several times after 1499 and remained in force until the death of the fascist dictator Franco in 1975. In the 19th century the Spanish government deported Gypsies to Argentina; the Portuguese deported them to Brazil. In England in 1530 Gypsies were given a choice of settling and adopting a trade, or leaving the country. But Gypsies were still there in 1546, when some were forcibly shipped across the Channel to France, and presumably also in 1554 and 1562, when the laws were reissued. France also introduced punitive laws against Gypsies in 1504, condemning them to become galley slaves if they did not settle permanently. These ineffective laws were repeatedly re-enacted until 1803. In Romania, Gypsies were enslaved and were emancipated only in 1856. Many Gypsies from eastern Europe emigrated to the US in the 1880s to escape hostility but were often refused entry.

This history of intermittent persecution pales beside the persecution of the Gypsies by the Nazis. They regarded Gypsies as sub-human and in 1943 ordered their systematic extermination in all territories under their control. Up to 400,000 Gypsies may have been killed in Nazi death camps by the end of the Second World War. After the war,

Gypsies faced further persecution by the communist regimes of the Soviet bloc. A ban on nomadism, forced settlement, dispersion and deportation were used to try to destroy the Gypsies as a distinct ethnic group. When the Cold War ended in 1989, there was an exodus of East European Gypsies to Germany and other western European countries.

A more insidious threat to the Gypsy way of life emerged in the 19th century. As European countries industrialized and steam engines and internal combustion engines began to replace horsepower, the Gypsies' traditional economic role diminished in importance. At the same time, the intensification of land use for farming, housing, industry and recreation greatly reduced the number of places where Gypsy camps were tolerated. Gypsies gradually became concentrated around urban centres. Seasonal movements were abandoned and Gypsies became semi-settled. In the second half of the 20th century, Gypsy families began living in caravans drawn by motor vehicles. Horse-trading remains an important activity for a small minority of Gypsies but most are now engaged in scrap-metal collection and construction.

A closed society

Despite all difficulties, Gypsies still retain a distinct ethnic identity after something like 1000 years as a wandering stateless people. This is in part because their mobility has been a barrier to assimilation into their host communities. The values of Gypsy society, which still show traces of their Indian origins, have also stood in the way of their assimilation. Gypsy society is organized in clans based on occupation, each with its own chief. Marimé, the Gypsy code of ritual purity, incorporates taboos on food, parts of the body, relations between the sexes and even topics of conversation. Traditional Gypsy society is therefore a closed one which shuns contacts with non-Gypsies (gadjés), who are regarded as impure, as well as potentially hostile. Marriages to non-Gypsies are extremely rare.

If they have remained socially separate, the Gypsies have always been partially assimilated into the culture of their host communities; for example, they adopt the language and religion of the country they are in. Their folklore and music are also usually strongly influenced by that of the local settled population. The Romani language survives because it is useful as a means of secret communication, incomprehensible to non-Gypsies. Because so many are now sedentary, and because of their partial cultural assimilation, estimates of the Gypsy population vary wildly, from 8 to 12 million worldwide and from 3 to 8 million in Europe.

Women of a Gypsy tribe from southern India, photographed in around 1928.

Peopling the Far North
2500 BC–AD 1500

No one has adapted to life in the Arctic with so much skill and ingenuity as the Inuit (or Eskimo), whose most northerly settlements, in Greenland, are little more than 400 miles (644 km) from the North Pole. Their achievement is all the more remarkable as they are descended from Siberian farming peoples who migrated to North America 4500 years ago.

The high Arctic of North America is the toughest environment to be permanently inhabited by humans. The land is treeless, barren tundra where all but the top few inches stays frozen all year round. The sea freezes in winter and does not entirely thaw out in the summer leaving ice floes and icebergs to make sailing dangerous. The winters are long, dark and bitterly cold, with temperatures down to −74°C (−100°F). The short summers have 24-hour daylight and are dry and sunny for a few weeks but the tundra turns into an unpleasant mosquito-infested swamp. Travel, whether by land or sea, is actually much easier in winter when everything is frozen hard.

Hardy nomadic hunter-gatherers

Life under such conditions is extremely arduous, so much of the Arctic remained unpopulated until *c.*2500 – 2000 BC when a new culture, the Arctic Small Tool Tradition, appeared in Alaska and spread quickly through the islands of the Canadian Arctic to Greenland. The Arctic Small Tool Tradition was not an indigenous development: similarities in the designs of stone tools show that it was introduced by migrants from the Yakutia region of Siberia who most authorities accept were the immediate ancestors of the Inuits. The migrants brought with them a technological innovation, long used in the Old World by this time, that would revolutionize hunting: the bow and arrow. Why the Inuit settled in the Arctic is not known – their ancestors had been farmers – but it may simply be that all the more attractive ecological niches in the Americas had been occupied by earlier migrants by this time. Not that the Arctic was lacking in attractions for people who could adapt to the harsh climate, which the Inuit soon did. The tundra supported herds of caribou and musk oxen, and, in summer, vast flocks of migratory birds. The seas swarmed with seals, walrus and whales and there were rivers full of salmon and char. There were berries to be collected in the autumn but no other plant foods. Animals provided everything necessary for life, not just food. Furs for warm clothing; hide for tents, ropes and boats; antler and bone for tools; fat and oil for fires and lamps. Big animals like whales even provided somewhere to live – huts could be built with their huge bones. Timber that had been washed down to the Arctic Ocean by the great rivers of Siberia and Canada was available as driftwood.

Inuit artefacts and tools. From top to bottom: a driftwood box, an adze (called a 'kepun') and a curved ivory knife ('cavik').

The Arctic Small Tool people were nomadic, staying in one place for a long time only for the harshest months of midwinter. They hunted mainly land mammals, especially musk oxen. Later Inuit cultures became progressively more focused on hunting marine mammals as they learned that could provide not only meat and hides but oil for lamps and stoves. The people of the Dorset tradition (c.550 BC–AD 1100) of the eastern Arctic relied heavily on hunting seals by ambushing them at their breathing holes in the sea ice. The Norton tradition (c.1000 BC–AD 800), which developed on both shores of the Bering Strait, shows a further shift towards hunting marine mammals. One of its innovations was the ingenious toggling-head harpoon. Earlier types of harpoon relied on the barbs on its tip to hold the prey; with the new type, the head was tied loosely to the shaft so that on impact it would catch beneath the skin and blubber and be impossible to remove. The head was attached by a line to an inflated seal skin float, which impeded the wounded animal's escape. These harpoons were deadly against larger mammals like walrus and whales. Food was easy to store in an environment where freezing temperatures were the norm, so a single whale could keep a family in fuel and food for months.

The range of Inuit settlement expanded and contracted as they migrated according to the twin pressures of population growth and climate change. The Arctic environment can sustain only very low population densities, less than one person per 100 square miles (260 sq km) even in favourable areas. Even small population increases could put severe pressure on natural resources and force some groups of hunters to search out new hunting grounds.

Though the terrain of the Canadian high Arctic appears harsh and barren, it harbours many natural resources that the Inuit skilfully exploited.

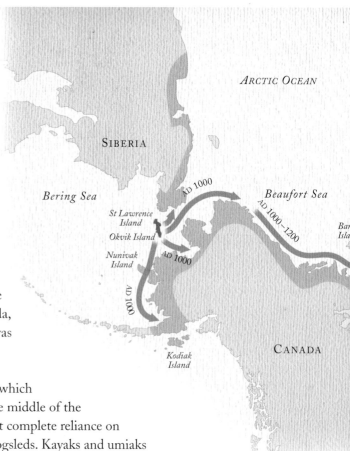

In colder periods, such as the 'Little Ice Age' which lasted from around 1400 to 1800, extreme northerly areas like Ellesmere Island and northern Greenland became practically uninhabitable and had to be abandoned. The range of favoured prey animals also shifted south and the Inuit followed, sometimes settling as far south as Newfoundland, and Kodiak Island in the Pacific. When the climate became milder, the Inuit followed their prey back north again. Occupation along both the Alaskan and Siberian shores of the Bering Strait, the Arctic Ocean coastline of Alaska and Canada, northern Hudson Bay, northern Labrador and Baffin Island was continuous.

The most sophisticated Inuit culture was the Thule tradition, which originated *c.*AD 1000 on St Lawrence and Okvik Islands in the middle of the Bering Strait. The Thule tradition was characterized by almost complete reliance on marine mammals and by the use of kayaks and umiaks, and dogsleds. Kayaks and umiaks were boats made of waterproofed hide stretched over a wooden frame. Kayaks, built for one or two people, were preferred for fishing and seal hunting, while the larger umiaks were used for hunting whales and long distance group travel. Light in weight, kayaks and umiaks could easily be carried over ice floes or land if necessary. Dogsleds were adopted by the Thule through contacts with Siberian peoples. Earlier Inuit cultures had used sleds but they were pulled by people. The Thule's transport innovations gave them exceptional mobility at sea and overland in winter, allowing them to range widely on hunting trips. On hunting expeditions the Thule lived in tents or aputiaks (the snow houses commonly but inaccurately called igloos) but their mobility made it practical for the Thule to inhabit permanent villages of circular stone or turf houses.

Map showing Thule Inuit migration across the Arctic from AD 1000 onwards.

This 19th-century engraving depicts Inuits hunting seals and whales from umiaks and kayaks.

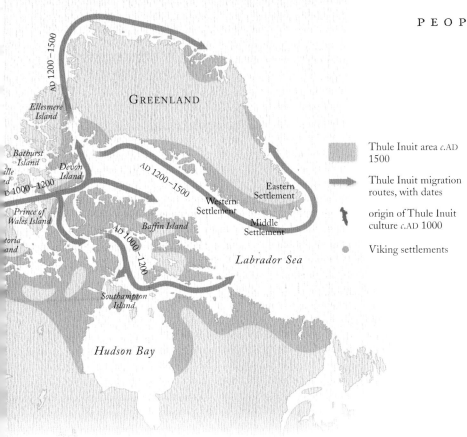

Thule Inuit area *c.*AD 1500

Thule Inuit migration routes, with dates

origin of Thule Inuit culture *c.*AD 1000

Viking settlements

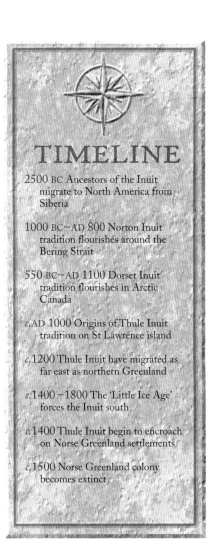

TIMELINE

2500 BC Ancestors of the Inuit migrate to North America from Siberia

1000 BC–AD 800 Norton Inuit tradition flourishes around the Bering Strait

550 BC–AD 1100 Dorset Inuit tradition flourishes in Arctic Canada

***c.*AD 1000** Origins of Thule Inuit tradition on St Lawrence island

***c.*1200** Thule Inuit have migrated as far east as northern Greenland

***c.*1400–1800** The 'Little Ice Age' forces the Inuit south

***c.*1400** Thule Inuit begin to encroach on Norse Greenland settlements

***c.*1500** Norse Greenland colony becomes extinct

Encounters with white settlers

From St Lawrence Island, the Thule tradition spread quickly to the Chukchi peninsula in Siberia and north to Point Barrow in Alaska. From here the Thule migrated east, displacing or assimilating the indigenous Dorset Inuit. By *c.*1200 the Thule Inuit had reached Labrador, Ellesmere Island and northern Greenland. Here they encountered Norse Greenlanders who made summer trips to the high Arctic hunting polar bears for their furs and walrus for their ivory and hide. The Vikings traded iron tools with the Inuits in return for furs. The Vikings called the Inuits *skraelings* ('screamers'), while the Inuits referred to the Vikings as *kavdlunaits* ('white men').

In the 15th century the climate deteriorated as the 'Little Ice Age' (*c.*1400–1800) took a grip. The Thule Inuit began to migrate south, encroaching on the Viking settlements. Conflicts became increasingly common. An Inuit folk tale tells how they made a surprise attack on a Viking farm by camouflaging their boats as icebergs. By 1500 the Viking settlements had been abandoned. It is not clear what role conflict with the Thule played in this. For such an isolated community any losses in battle would have been a serious blow. However, the main reason for the Vikings' demise was probably economic. The Greenland Vikings found it hard to carry on with their European farming way of life but they were too proud to learn from the pagan Inuits. As the summers got shorter and the winters longer, the Vikings could not grow enough food to survive and they starved to death. With the settlement of southern Greenland, the Thule tradition reached its greatest extent. It survived until the 18th century, when contact with European traders and missionaries began to undermine Inuit traditions.

The Toltecs and Aztecs
c.800–1325

The greatest empires of ancient Central America, those of the Toltecs and the Aztecs, were founded by migrant farming peoples. There are a number of striking parallels between the two migrations, with both peoples taking advantage of the collapse of foregoing great empires to gain control over highly fertile agricultural lands in the Valley of Mexico.

The Toltecs did not have a fully literate civilization and most of what is known of their history comes from legendary traditions preserved by the Aztecs, who liked to think of themselves as their heirs. The Toltecs were descended from two farming peoples, the Chichimeca and the Nonoalca, who migrated into central Mexico c.AD 800. The dominant group, the Chichimeca, originated in the highlands of northwest Mexico and migrated to the Valley of Mexico under the leadership of their semi-mythical king Mixcoatl. The Nonoalca, from the southern Gulf coast, were regarded as skilled artisans. The main cause of their migration was probably the collapse of the great Teotihuacán empire in the eighth century. Teotihuacán had dominated the Valley of Mexico for nearly 700 years and its fall left the area divided between dozens of small city states The ensuing power vacuum gave migrant groups the opportunity to seize lands in this fertile area.

Rise and fall of the Toltecs

Under Mixcoatl's son Topiltzin (born 935 or 947), the Toltec established their capital at Tula, just north of the Valley of Mexico. According to later Aztec tradition, Topiltzin was a devotee of the agricultural god Quetzalcóatl ('Feathered Serpent'), and he later became identified with him. Topiltzin was opposed to human sacrifice but this offended the sun-god Tezcatlipoca, who overthrew him. Topiltzin fled with his supporters east over the sea on a raft of serpents, vowing that one day he would return to his kingdom. Intriguingly, Mayan texts record that a man called Kukulcán, which means 'feathered serpent' in the Mayan language, conquered the Yucatán peninsula in 987. It is impossible to say whether Kukulcán was the Toltec Topiltzin-Quetzalcóatl but archaeological evidence confirms that the dominant Maya city of Chichén Itzá was occupied by Toltecs around that time. Much of the city's art and architecture is modelled on that of Tula. Typical Toltec influences include chacmools, recumbent stone figures thought to have been used as altars; tzompantlis, low platforms covered with relief carvings of human skulls used to display war trophies; and feathered serpent imagery. Toltec rule lasted at Chichén Itzá until 1221, when it was conquered by the native Mayan king Hunac Ceel.

After Topiltzin-Quetzalcóatl's overthrow, the Toltecs became the dominant power of central Mexico, while Tula gained a reputation for fabulous opulence. Toltec merchants travelled widely and had a trading post at Casas Grandes, less than 100 miles (160 km)

south of the present-day border between Mexico and the USA, where they traded tropical bird feathers for turquoise. These contacts introduced many Mexican customs to the ancestral Pueblo peoples of the American Southwest. This prosperity came to an end in the 12th century following a prolonged drought. Conflict broke out between the Chichimeca and the Nonoalca and then in 1168 Tula was sacked. The last Toltec king Huemac tried to establish a new capital in the Valley of Mexico but soon gave up and committed suicide. The fall of their empire made refugees of the Toltecs. Some groups conquered Cholula and other cities in central Mexico, others travelled as far as the Guatemalan Highlands and Belize before settling. Following their dispersal, the Toltecs lost their identity as a people and disappeared but with their passing they attained almost mythical status and their state became the model for all later Central American states, including the Aztec empire.

Carved pillars depicting warriors in the ceremonial centre at the Toltec capital of Tula.

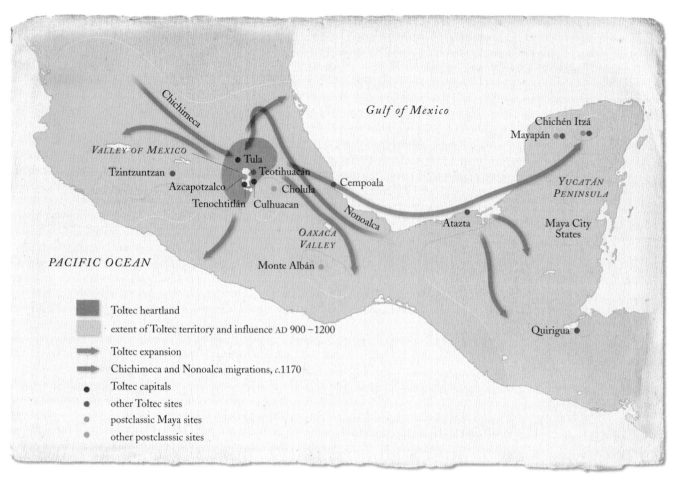

Map showing the
migrations of the
Chichimeca, Nonoalca and
Toltecs in Mesoamerica.

The warlike Aztecs

Like the Toltecs, the Aztecs were migrants, a farming people from western Mexico.
The Aztecs were only one of over a dozen different peoples who exploited the fall of the
Toltec state to settle in the fertile Valley of Mexico. According to their own traditions,
the Aztecs began their migration in 1111, led by their tribal war god Huitzilopochtli
('Hummingbird on the left') whose talking idol was carried before them on the
shoulders of four priests. Before the arrival of Europeans, the peoples of Mexico had
neither wheeled vehicles nor beasts of burden. Little in the way of equipment or stores
could be carried so the Aztecs migrated in a series of short annual steps. Pioneers were
sent ahead of the main body to find a suitable camp site and to plant and tend crops
there. Once the harvest had been taken in the Aztecs trekked to the new site where they
would remain for a year while the pioneers prepared the next year's camp site.

It was probably sometime in the 13th century that the Aztecs finally entered the Valley
of Mexico. All the best sites in the valley were already occupied so for a long time the
Aztecs were forced to live a semi-nomadic existence as squatters. Women were scarce
among the Aztecs and they made themselves unpopular by raiding the settled peoples
for wives. A punitive expedition was mounted against the Aztecs, after which they were
forced to settle as serfs on a barren site in the territory of the city of Culhuacan.

After they acquitted themselves well in battle, Coxcox, the ruler of Culhuacan, gave the
Aztecs' chief one of his daughters as a wife. The delighted Aztecs promptly sacrificed
the unfortunate girl to their gods, apparently hoping that she would be transmuted into
a war goddess. The Aztecs had invited Coxcox to the ceremony; having expected to

witness a wedding, he was outraged. The Aztecs were quickly driven out of Culhuacan and resumed their wandering existence. They finally settled permanently on a marshy island near the western shore of Lake Texcoco in around 1325. Their chief Tenoch ordered the construction of a city, which was named Tenochtitlán after him; the site now lies under Mexico City. This was apparently in fulfilment of a tribal prophecy that the Aztecs would found a city where they saw an eagle sitting on a cactus with a snake in its mouth. The small island allowed little scope for expansion of agriculture so the Aztecs took to building *chinampas*, artificial islands made of fertile mud dredged from the lake bed. These became the basis of a highly productive system of agriculture.

In 1367 the Aztecs began serving as mercenaries in the armies of Tezozomoc, the king of Azcapotzalco. Sharing in war booty, the Aztecs grew rich, their egalitarian tribal society became more hierarchical, and in 1375 Acampitchtli became their first king. By the time Tezozomoc died in 1426 the Aztecs were becoming a power in their own right. Tezozomoc's son Maxtlatzin tried to rid himself of the Aztecs but was crushingly defeated by their third king Itzcóatl. Tenochtitlán supplanted Azcapotzalco as the dominant city of the Valley of Mexico. During the remainder of his reign Itzcóatl reduced the cities of the valley to vassal status. Expansion continued under Itzcóatl's successors. By the time the empire was at its peak under Moctezuma II (r.1502–20) the Aztecs ruled over 11 million people. The Aztecs did not found colonies in their empire but they had a hereditary class of merchants, the pochteca, who travelled throughout Central America trading in obsidian (a black, volcanic glass used for making blades), feathers, cocoa and cloth. All Mesoamericans practised human sacrifice but none to the extent of the Aztecs. The Aztecs believed that Huitzilopochtli needed the hearts of captured enemy warriors to keep the sun moving in the heavens. The near constant warfare and heavy demands for tribute made the Aztecs feared and hated.

When Hernán Cortés (1485–1547) and his small army of Spanish conquistadors landed in Mexico in 1519, he had little difficulty in recruiting native allies. Moctezuma vacillated, fearing that Cortés might be the exiled god Quetzalcóatl, whom the legends described as fair-skinned and bearded, returning to reclaim his kingdom. By the time Moctezuma realized that Cortés was all too human, his empire was already collapsing around him (see pages 154–159).

An Aztec golden mask from Tenochtitlán, thought to represent the god Quetzalcóatl.

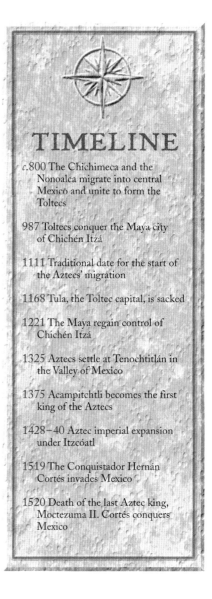

TIMELINE

*c.*800 The Chichimeca and the Nonoalca migrate into central Mexico and unite to form the Toltecs

987 Toltecs conquer the Maya city of Chichén Itzá

1111 Traditional date for the start of the Aztecs' migration

1168 Tula, the Toltec capital, is sacked

1221 The Maya regain control of Chichén Itzá

1325 Aztecs settle at Tenochtitlán in the Valley of Mexico

1375 Acampitchtli becomes the first king of the Aztecs

1428–40 Aztec imperial expansion under Itzcóatl

1519 The Conquistador Hernán Cortés invades Mexico

1520 Death of the last Aztec king, Moctezuma II. Cortés conquers Mexico

For God and Gold: the Spanish in the Americas 1492–c.1800

The European colonization of the Americas resulted in the transformation of two continents. Indigenous peoples everywhere suffered demographic collapse and in vast areas were replaced entirely by immigrant populations of European and African descent. In the process, dozens of ancient civilizations and cultures were destroyed and supplanted by new ones based largely on European traditions. This great movement of colonization was begun by the Spanish after Columbus' discovery of the Americas in 1492.

Of course, Columbus was not looking for the Americas – he was trying to pioneer a new route to the spice islands of the East Indies, and remained convinced that he done so right up to his death in 1506. Other explorers quickly realized that he had discovered a 'New World'. Spain's first permanent colony in the New World was founded by Columbus at Santo Domingo on Hispaniola in 1496. By 1518 Cuba, Puerto Rico and Jamaica had been colonized and, in the following year, the first mainland colony was established at Panama. Up to this point, the Spanish had been somewhat disappointed by the apparent paucity of gold in the New World. Stock rearing and sugar-cane plantations were the main economic activities.

The conquest of the Aztec empire of Mexico by Hernán Cortés (1485–1547) in 1519–24, and of the Inca empire of Peru by Francisco Pizarro (1471–1541) in 1531–5, changed the situation dramatically. Vast amounts of gold and silver began to be shipped back to Spain, where they altered the balance of power in Europe and placed the continent at the centre of a new globalized trading system. All this wealth also made emigration to the New World an attractive prospect. The conquests continued apace throughout the 16th century, so that by 1609 the Spanish-American empire controlled a contiguous territory that extended from Santa Fe in the north to Patagonia in the south.

The Aztec ruler Moctezuma II greeting the Spanish conquistador Hernán Cortés at the city of Tenochtitlán in 1519. Within a decade, the Aztec empire lay in ruins.

It was no part of the conquistadors' plans to displace the native peoples; they wanted to govern them, exploit them and convert them to Christianity. However, the conquest had a devastating impact on the indigenous population. The ancient traditions of civilization that had endured for centuries in Central and South America were wiped out almost overnight. Temples and holy sites were destroyed and replaced with churches. Forced

conversion to Christianity followed. The Indian population of Mexico, which was over 11 million at the time of the conquest, had slumped to 2.5 million by 1600 and just 1.5 million by 1650. Similar demographic collapses occurred throughout the Spanish-American empire. The cause was not maltreatment by the Spanish (though it was rife) but the accidental introduction of European diseases, such as smallpox, influenza and measles, against which the Indians had no natural immunity. Epidemics swept through the Americas far faster than the conquistadors. Smallpox first broke out in Hispaniola in 1518 and quickly killed around two-thirds of the indigenous Caribs. One of Cortés' soldiers took smallpox to Mexico with him, where it wreaked havoc among the Aztecs. The disease spread to Panama in 1520 and from there to the Inca empire in 1525. One victim of the epidemic was the emperor Huayna Capac (r.1493–1527), whose death sparked a damaging civil war that had only just ended when Pizarro invaded.

Establishing an empire

The conquistadors were few in number. Cortés had only about 400 men with him when he invaded Mexico, Pizarro only about half that for the conquest of Peru. Their success was only in small measure due to their technological superiority. Metal swords and armour, plus a few firearms, could not have prevailed against millions of Indians had many of them not been willing to ally with the Spanish and had the Indians not been demoralized by the epidemics depleting their ranks.

The normal procedure after territory had been conquered was to distribute it among the conquistadors, and any allied Indian leaders, as *encomiendas*. These were semi-feudal landholdings in which the native population retained ownership of their farms and villages but were forced to pay tribute to the *encomendero*, who could also call on their forced labour. This was not a new system; it had been developed by the Spanish during the Middle Ages to consolidate control over territory reconquered from the Muslims. The *encomienda* system was most effective in the former Aztec and Inca empires, where Indians were used to paying tribute and labouring for their imperial masters. Cortés' own *encomienda* of the Oaxaca Valley gave him 23,000 tributary families, but around 2000 was the norm. Indians were rarely forcibly expelled from their lands but Indian land could be bought very cheaply by Spanish settlers because of the declining population. The value of *encomiendas* was much reduced by the decline of the Indian population, which also created a labour shortage for the Spanish colonies. The Spanish tried to make up for this by importing slaves from Africa. African slavery was mostly confined to the Caribbean, where Africans became the majority of the population, and to tropical coastal areas on the mainland where plantation agriculture was practised.

The conquistadors were consciously inspired by the chivalric exploits of Spanish knights during the wars of reconquest, and they shared their spirit of militant Catholicism, but very few of them actually came from the nobility. Some leading conquistadors, like

This 18th-century caricature shows Francisco Pizarro gloating over the riches he has amassed. Bullion fleets carried huge amounts of silver and gold back to Spain from her American colonies.

Cortés and Vasco Nuñez de Balboa (1475–1519), were of the hidalgo (lower nobility) class but most were commoners, often professional soldiers, who were willing to take very high risks in the hopes of striking it rich. The majority of Spanish emigrants were middle-ranking townspeople and artisans looking for new economic opportunities. Spanish landowners actively sabotaged attempts to encourage peasant farmers to emigrate. The wealthier emigrants took their families and servants of both sexes with them. Unlike English servants who emigrated to America, they were not indentured and were free to leave their masters and set up on their own, which many did.

An important group of emigrants were missionaries, mostly from the mendicant orders and the Jesuits. The urge to convert pagan peoples was almost as important a motive in Spanish expansion as greed for material wealth. Most missionaries were sincerely concerned for the physical as well as the spiritual well-being of the Indians and they enjoyed some success in persuading the Spanish crown to curb the worst excesses of the conquistadors.

Around one-third of all Spanish emigrants came from Andalucia, with another third from Castile and Extremadura. Seville sent more migrants than any other city. Many were chain migrants, people joining family members who had already emigrated. Initially 94 percent of emigrants were male, falling to about two-thirds by 1550 and to a half in the 18th century. The number of emigrants was large in relation to the Spanish population but small relative to the size of the territory conquered by Spain. From a home population of about eight million, an average of 2500 people emigrated from Spain every year between 1500 and 1600. Emigration peaked between 1600 and 1650, when 4000 people left each year on average. Between 1650 and 1800 about another 250,000 Spanish people emigrated, making a total of around 700,000 over 300 years. Europeans suffered high mortality in the Caribbean, but Mexico and Peru were healthier and wastage from disease did not seriously hinder the growth of the colonial population. After its American colonies became independent in the early 19th century, emigration from Spain virtually ceased. Foreigners were officially excluded from the Spanish empire but this was not strictly enforced; small numbers of Portuguese, Italians, Irish and Germans settled in the Spanish Americas. And, as trade between the Spanish Americas and East Asia increased, so too did Filipino, Chinese and Japanese immigrants.

Map showing the extent of the Spanish empire in the Americas, which endured for 300 years.

Because of their backgrounds, most voluntary immigrants to the Spanish Americas settled in towns. There they were joined by Indians, who left the land in large numbers to escape paying tribute, and freed African slaves. Even *encomenderos* preferred to live in towns rather than on isolated haciendas among a resentful Indian population. Indians, therefore, remained the majority in the countryside. A Spanish colonial town was governed by a cabildo, a council of elected and appointed representatives. The cabildo was the main point of contact between settlers and the Spanish government. Most Spanish colonial towns were built on virgin sites, planned using a similar grid pattern of streets with a central plaza surrounded by the main public buildings. Where the site of a native town was used, as at Mexico City, the old town was levelled first. Architectural styles, and often architects, were imported from Spain. Early colonial architecture includes elements of the late Gothic, Italian Renaissance and southern Spanish Mudéjar styles. Later, the Baroque style predominated. Indian influences persisted in domestic buildings and in folk art there was a fusion of European and native traditions.

The caste system

The three main ethnic groups of the Spanish Americas, the whites, Indians and Africans, became only partially integrated. Because there were more Spanish male emigrants than females, mixed marriages were common but it was impossible for anyone to escape from their racial background. The Spanish were obsessed with limpieza (purity of blood). This had developed during the Reconquista, when noble families took great pride in being of Christian descent and having no taint of Muslim blood. The Spanish Americas developed a complex caste system based on skin colour and the origins of a person's parents. At the top were the Spanish. To be Spanish someone had to be born in Spain of Spanish parents, so guaranteeing that they were 'pure white'. Though they were always a tiny minority (1 percent in 1760), the Spanish monopolized the most important posts in the empire. Below the Spanish were the Creoles. These were white Europeans who were descended from Spanish settlers. The Creoles resented the Spanish for looking down on them – after all, were they not descended from the conquistadors? – and for excluding them from political power. Creoles became the leaders of the revolutions that overthrew Spanish rule in the early 19th century.

Below the whites were two mixed-race castes, the mestizos and the mulattos.

Jesuit missionaries undertake the conversion of Amerindians. Jesuit missions ('reducciones') later became the chief protectors of Indian populations in Paraguay and northern Argentina against attacks by slavers from Brazil.

The mestizos had mixed European and Indian ancestry, the more European the better. Many mestizos were wealthy and aristocratic descendants of conquistadors who had married women from Indian royal families and they naturally resented their inferior status. Mulattos were of mixed European and African ancestry. They had lower status than mestizos because the Africans had been brought to America as slaves but they had higher status than Indians because they were at least part white.

The lowest castes were those who could claim no white ancestry, the Indians, Africans and Zambos. Indians were the largest caste in the Spanish Americas, making up 60 percent of the total population of 3.75 million in 1760. Most Indians continued to live much as they had done before the arrival of the Spanish. Many even managed to preserve their traditional beliefs under a veneer of imposed Christianity. Below the Indians were the Zambos, of mixed Indian and African ancestry. The lowest status of all was reserved for Africans, because of their black skin and because, even if they were lucky enough not to be slaves themselves, they were still descended from slaves. However, slaves in the Spanish Americas had more legal rights than in the USA. The language of the whites and mixed castes was Spanish, but it made only slow headway among rural Indians. In some Latin American countries, like Guatemala and Bolivia, most people still speak native languages such as Quechua and Aymara.

Changing the landscape

The environmental impact of the Spanish colonization of the Americas was also enormous. The Spanish settlers adopted many native foods but still demanded their familiar diet, especially wheat flour, olive oil and wine. As these were expensive to import, efforts to produce them locally soon began. Wheat cultivation was established by the 1540s, while the first New World wine was made in 1551 in Peru. Olive groves are very slow-growing, so olive oil production did not begin until the late 16th century. Another economically significant crop was sugar cane, which was grown in vast slave-worked plantations in tropical areas. European domestic animals were also introduced. Cattle and sheep flourished on grasslands that had never been systematically grazed before. Horses and mules revolutionized transport (llamas were used as pack animals in the Andes but beasts of burden were unknown elsewhere in the pre-Columbian Americas). Horses, which had escaped from Spanish expeditions into North America in the 1770s and bred in the wild, transformed the lives of the Indians on the Great Plains, enabling them to become nomadic bison hunters. On the pampas, the South American equivalent of the North American prairies, a whole new ecosystem developed based on feral horses, cattle and sheep, all hunted by dogs, which had escaped from failed settlements. Native crops like potatoes, sweet potatoes, maize (corn), chilli peppers, tomatoes, cocoa and pineapples found their way into Old World agriculture. Few migrations have had such a far-reaching effect on the world's diet.

TIMELINE

1492 Columbus' first voyage to the Americas

1496 First Spanish colony in the Americas founded at Santo Domingo, Hispaniola

1511 Spanish settlement of Cuba begins

1517 The Spanish first import African slaves to their American colonies

1518 Smallpox epidemic breaks out on Cuba

1519–24 Cortés conquers the Aztec Empire

1520 Smallpox spreads to the mainland, killing millions of native Americans

1531–5 Pizarro conquers the Inca Empire

1536 Buenos Aires, Argentina, founded

1539–43 Coronado explores New Mexico

1545 World's richest silver mine discovered at Potosí, Bolivia

1551 First New World wine produced, in Peru

1565 First European colony in North America founded at St Augustine, Florida

1609 Santa Fe, New Mexico, founded

The Portuguese Colonies
1418–1580

Portugal was the pioneer of European overseas expansion, founding its first colonies in the 15th century. Many thousands of Portuguese emigrated to colonies in South America, Africa and Asia. These colonies helped transform the pattern of global trade but it was only in Brazil, now South America's most populous country, that a large Portuguese-speaking colonial population was established.

Portuguese maritime expansion was initiated in 1418 by Prince Henry the Navigator (1394–1460). Henry's motives were twofold. He wanted to find new trade routes which could end Muslim control of trade with Asia, the source of valuable commodities such as spices and silk. A deeply religious man, Henry also hoped to strengthen Christendom by converting pagan peoples to Christianity and recruiting them as allies in the struggle with the Muslim powers that threatened Europe. The first Portuguese maritime discoveries were Madeira (1419) and the Azores (1427). These Atlantic islands were colonized shortly after their discovery: their sub-tropical climate made them ideal for producing sugar, which was at that time still an expensive luxury in Europe. In 1456 the Cape Verde Islands were discovered and colonized. The Atlantic slave trade was begun soon after, when the Portuguese began buying African slaves from Sierra Leone to work on new sugar plantations in the Cape Verde Islands. Before the invention of modern medicines, West Africa was a lethally unhealthy place for Europeans and it was not until 1482 that the Portuguese founded a permanent settlement on the mainland, at Elmina ('The Mine') on the coast of Ghana.

To commemorate the 500-year anniversary of the death of Henry the Navigator, the caravel-shaped Monument to the Discoveries *was inaugurated in Lisbon, Portugal, in 1960.*

In 1487–8 Bartolomeu Dias (c.1450–1500) rounded the southern tip of Africa and entered the Indian Ocean, proving that it was possible to sail directly from Europe to India. After Columbus (1451–1506) reached the New World in 1492, Portugal and Spain agreed the Treaty of Tordesillas (1494) to avoid conflict over the astonishing new maritime discoveries. This divided the world along a line drawn 1185 miles (2000 km) west of the Cape Verde Islands: the Spanish were to keep to the west of the line, the Portuguese to the east. The treaty allowed Portugal to claim Brazil after its discovery in 1500. Portuguese influence in the east increased rapidly

after Vasco da Gama (*c.*1460−1524) made the first direct voyage from Portugal to India in 1497−8. By 1557 the Portuguese had founded a chain of colonies which gave them control of the lucrative spice trade with the East Indies: Mozambique, Muscat (Oman), Diu and Goa (India), Malacca (Malaysia) and Macao (China). In 1542 they also became the first Europeans to open trade links with Japan. The success of the Portuguese was due in part to the superiority of their ships and cannon, in part to the lack of political unity in Asia. Though few in number, the Portuguese were able to deal with their enemies one at a time.

Spice trade monopoly

Spices could command such high prices in Europe that it was said a merchant could lose five out of six cargoes and still make a handsome profit. The Portuguese crown exercised a monopoly over the spice trade, and the majority of those who emigrated to the Asian colonies in the hope of making a fortune had to do so as servants of the crown, either soldiers or officials. Only after eight years could they leave crown service and become settlers or merchants in their own right. Most emigrants were townspeople or members of the lesser nobility. Averaging around 4000 a year in the 16th century, the number of emigrants was considerable for a country with a home population of only 1.4 million.

Accounts of voyages to the New World had huge appeal for a European public hungry for news about the colonies. This engraving depicts an episode recounted in Grand Voyages to America *(1593) by Hans Staden, a German soldier who sailed twice to Brazil on Portuguese ships.*

Relative to its population, this was nearly ten times greater than emigration from Spain in the same period. Portugal was, however, a much poorer country than Spain.

Despite the high level of emigration, the Portuguese struggled to establish a viable colonial population in Africa and Asia. A major reason for this was that the crown actively discouraged women from emigrating. In Macao in 1636 there was, for example, only one Portuguese woman. Officials rarely took their wives with them and, if they took any of their children, it was usually only the boys. The main exceptions were 'Orphans of the King' – orphaned girls of marriageable age who were sent to Goa at crown expense. Their numbers were far too small to make much difference to the Portuguese population of the east. Portuguese men could usually make advantageous marriages with daughters of wealthy Eurasian families but the children of such marriages, known as *mestiços*, faced official discrimination. Sexual relationships with female slaves were also extremely common but, again, the mixed race children of slave mothers were socially disadvantaged irrespective of the status of the father.

Conditions in the colonies

Another factor was the unhealthy conditions of many of the Portuguese colonies. Diseases such as dysentery, cholera and malaria took a heavy toll. Few Portuguese who emigrated to Asia lived long enough to leave crown service. The Royal Hospital at Goa recorded 25,000 Portuguese deaths from tropical diseases between 1600 and 1630 alone, not including deaths while on military service or people dying of disease without being admitted to hospital. There were only about 3000 Europeans at Goa at any one time, so this was equivalent to an annual mortality rate of nearly 30 percent. Portugal could ill afford such enormous loss of life. Further losses occurred from disease and malnutrition on the six- to seven-month voyage to the east. The government tried to make good the manpower shortages by conscripting convicts, but they often deserted to the natives after they arrived. African slaves were also imported and trained as soldiers.

Portugal's eastern colonies remained male dominated and military in nature but its colony in Brazil was very different. A labour-intensive economy developed, based on logging, stock raising, gold mining, and sugar and tobacco plantations, and requiring the importation of millions of African slaves and raids into the American interior to capture and enslave indigenous peoples. Africans eventually made up one-third of Brazil's population. Portuguese planters and cattle barons became a politically influential rural aristocracy. The practice of deporting gypsies and convicts to the colonies gave rise to a transient class of poor whites. Craftsmen were always in short supply and the jails of Portugal were scoured to find blacksmiths and stonemasons to send to Brazil and Africa.

The growth of Portuguese trade routes and overseas settlements in the 15th and 16th centuries.

Mostly male, these involuntary emigrants took Indian and African women as wives or concubines, leading to a growing population of Portuguese-speaking *mestiços* and mulattos. Brazil developed a caste system not unlike that of the Spanish American empire, where highest status was reserved for those born in Portugal and then for Creoles of pure European descent. Mulattos and Africans had the lowest status and were barred from entering the church or government service.

Jesuit missionaries were an influential group of emigrants to the Portuguese colonies. In Brazil they enjoyed great success in Catholicizing the indigenous Indians and African slaves (though many African religious customs survive). Small Christian communities were established in India and China but their activities in Japan led to the expulsion of the Portuguese in 1641. By this time, the Portuguese had transformed Japan in another way. Their introduction of firearms in 1542 revolutionized Japanese warfare and made possible the uniting of the country by the Tokugawa shoguns in 1568–90. The Portuguese colonies in Asia and Africa also, as had been hoped, broke the Muslim stranglehold on trade between East Asia and sub-Saharan Africa and Europe. This gradually impoverished the Muslim world and shifted the balance of power in favour of Christian Europe. These are major achievements for a relatively short-lived colonial movement. From 1580–1640 Portugal was under Spanish rule. Spain neglected Portugal's colonial interests and other European powers undermined its monopoly on trade with the East Indies. Brazil became independent in 1821 but the remainder of Portugal's colonial empire survived into the 20th century, its last possession, Macao, being handed back to China only in 1999.

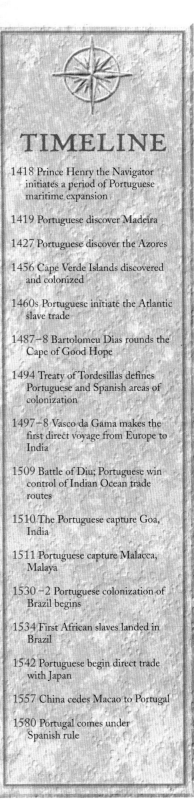

TIMELINE

1418 Prince Henry the Navigator initiates a period of Portuguese maritime expansion

1419 Portuguese discover Madeira

1427 Portuguese discover the Azores

1456 Cape Verde Islands discovered and colonized

1460s Portuguese initiate the Atlantic slave trade

1487–8 Bartolomeu Dias rounds the Cape of Good Hope

1494 Treaty of Tordesillas defines Portuguese and Spanish areas of colonization

1497–8 Vasco da Gama makes the first direct voyage from Europe to India

1509 Battle of Diu; Portuguese win control of Indian Ocean trade routes

1510 The Portuguese capture Goa, India

1511 Portuguese capture Malacca, Malaya

1530–2 Portuguese colonization of Brazil begins

1534 First African slaves landed in Brazil

1542 Portuguese begin direct trade with Japan

1557 China cedes Macao to Portugal

1580 Portugal comes under Spanish rule

The Plantations
1532–1653

Over a period of nearly 500 years English governments tried to turn Ireland into an extension of England through policies of colonization, plantation and Anglicization. These policies ultimately failed but the English learned valuable lessons which they later applied in the creation of their colonial empire in the New World.

The history of English colonization in Ireland began when the Anglo-Norman baron, Richard FitzGilbert de Clare (113–76), popularly known as 'Strongbow', won control of Leinster in 1171. His overlord, King Henry II of England (r.1154–89), was not prepared to let one of his vassals acquire an independent kingdom of his own, so he invaded Ireland and forced both Strongbow and the native Irish rulers to recognize him as Lord of Ireland.

When Henry left Ireland in early 1172 he had established English rule in Dublin and the southeast, and it was left to opportunistic Anglo-Norman barons to complete the conquest. At first they seemed invincible: their armoured knights and archers easily overcame Irish soldiers equipped with spears and shields and little armour. The English consolidated their rule with castles and settlements. The ancient Irish landscape of dispersed settlements and pasture was supplanted by the English manorial system, with its nucleated villages and plough lands. These villages were populated by English and Irish peasants attracted by favourable terms. Walled towns, like Galway and Athenry, were founded and peopled by English merchants and artisans.

An uphill struggle

After 1200 the English conquest stalled as the Irish learned to avoid open battle and adopted guerrilla tactics. Discouraged by continuing resistance, English immigration slowed. There was also a geographical obstacle to Anglicization; outside the fertile southeast, most of Ireland was not suited to the imposition of the manorial system and the English could not easily dominate areas that did not have a settled peasantry. England's frequent wars against France and Scotland also diverted resources from Ireland. The arrival of the Black Death in Ireland in 1348–50 was another major blow. The plague flourished in the crowded, unhygienic medieval towns, so the highly urbanized English suffered far more than the rural Irish. English losses could not be made up by immigration. The Black Death had created a labour shortage in England and wages were rising fast. Faced with insecurity in Ireland and new opportunities in England, many colonists packed up and left.

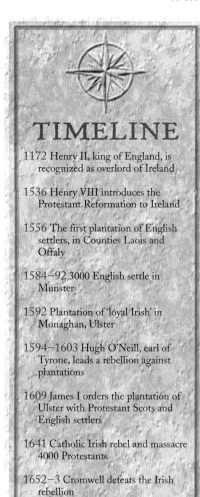

TIMELINE

1172 Henry II, king of England, is recognized as overlord of Ireland

1536 Henry VIII introduces the Protestant Reformation to Ireland

1556 The first plantation of English settlers, in Counties Laois and Offaly

1584–92 3000 English settle in Munster

1592 Plantation of 'loyal Irish' in Monaghan, Ulster

1594–1603 Hugh O'Neill, earl of Tyrone, leads a rebellion against plantations

1609 James I orders the plantation of Ulster with Protestant Scots and English settlers

1641 Catholic Irish rebel and massacre 4000 Protestants

1652–3 Cromwell defeats the Irish rebellion

The remaining colonists clung tenaciously to their English identity but intermarriage with Irish families and the multitude of everyday contacts meant that they were gradually becoming Gaelicized. In 1366 the English government introduced the Statutes of Kilkenny in an attempt to prevent the English in Ireland being assimilated by the Irish. All those living in the English colony were required to use only the English language, English personal names and English law. Intermarriage was outlawed. Playing Irish sports and employing Irish minstrels were banned, as was selling arms and horses to the Irish. Other measures provided for maintaining a permanent state of military readiness and for avoiding unnecessary wars.

By the end of the 15th century the area controlled by the English crown had shrunk to the Pale, the highly Anglicized area surrounding Dublin. The Protestant Reformation following the Tudor king Henry VIII's (r.1509–47) break with Rome in 1532–6 lent new urgency to the subjugation of Ireland, since England now found itself politically isolated with no major continental ally. Rebellious Ireland had rejected Protestantism as an English imposition and

A view of Carrickfergus Castle in County Antrim, Northern Ireland. Built by the Norman knight John de Courcy in 1177, Carrickfergus was an important stronghold in the first period of English colonization of Ireland.

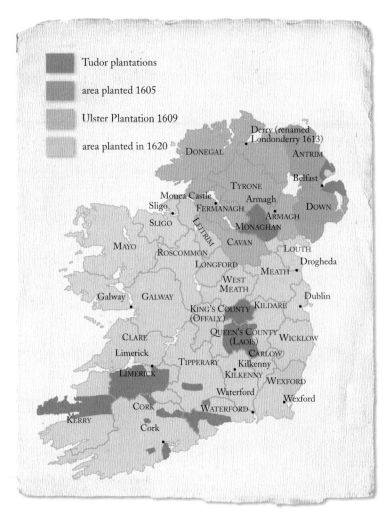

Tudor plantations

area planted 1605

Ulster Plantation 1609

area planted in 1620

Map showing the expansion of plantations in Ireland in the 16th and 17th centuries.

was now an obvious back door through which the Catholic powers might try to launch an invasion of England. It was in this context that the English government conceived the idea of plantations.

The first plantations

Plantations were not at first intended to be a means of ethnic cleansing. The lands of rebellious Irish lords were confiscated and handed over to English and, sometimes, loyal Irish lords. The new English lords would provide islands of authority and Protestantism, and, it was hoped, exercise an Anglicizing influence over the Irish peasantry, who were allowed to stay on their land as tenants. Inevitably, there was resistance by former landowners, who waged guerrilla warfare against the planters. The English government was forced to send ever more troops to Ireland. The largest of the Tudor plantations was ordered by Elizabeth I (r.1558–1603) in Munster in 1584 on more than 250,000 acres (101,175 ha) of land confiscated after the defeat of a Catholic rebellion. The lands were awarded to 35 undertakers (chief planters), many of whom were happy simply to live off the rents of the existing Irish tenants. Other planters expelled the Irish from their lands altogether and introduced English agricultural practices and English tenants. In 1592 a new plantation, of 'loyal Irish', was made on lands in Monaghan in Ulster. Alarmed by this development, the greatest Irish landowner, Hugh O'Neill, the earl of Tyrone (c.154–1616), led a rebellion in Ulster (the Nine Years' War) that was defeated with difficulty by the English only in 1603, just days before Elizabeth I died.

Systematic dispossession

The new king James I (James VI of Scotland; r.1603–25) continued the policy of plantation on lands in Ulster seized after the war and for the first time the displacement of the native population became official policy. The Articles of Plantation, passed by James in 1609, provided for most of the Irish population of Donegal, Derry, Tyrone, Armagh, Fermanagh and Cavan to be removed to designated reservations to release Ulster's best land for plantation with Protestant Lowland Scots and English tenant farmers. The scheme foundered, as previous schemes to colonize Ireland had done, on its reputation for rebellion. The undertakers who were appointed by the government to oversee the plantation found that it was both necessary and profitable to retain the original Irish tenants because they were willing to pay high rents to stay on the land. Although a Protestant majority – mainly of Lowland Scots – was established in Antrim and Down, in the rest of Ulster they were a minority among a resentful Catholic population. The bawns (defensive courtyards with towers) and fortified houses that the settlers built across the countryside testify to their insecurity. Efforts were also made to strengthen the Munster plantation, which had suffered badly during the Nine Years' War.

In 1641 Irish discontent flared into another rebellion and around 4000 of the estimated 36,000 Protestant settlers were massacred. The outbreak of civil war in England between King Charles I (r.1625–49) and his parliament in 1642 meant that it was not until 1649–53 that the Catholic rebellion was crushed by Oliver Cromwell (1599–1658), the leading general of the short-lived English republic.

Cromwell planned to solve the Irish problem with new plantations on estates confiscated from rebel landowners, comprising about 50 percent of Ireland's fertile land. Counties Dublin, Cork, Kildare and Wicklow were reserved for use by the government; ten others – Antrim, Down, Armagh, Meath, West Meath, Laois, Offaly, Waterford, Tipperary and Limerick – were allocated to around 1500 adventurers (investors who had funded the Irish campaign) and nearly 35,000 veterans of the parliamentary army, who were given debentures (land bonds) in lieu of back pay. The plan was that the new landowners would expel their Catholic Irish tenants, who would be transplanted to reservations in Mayo, Galway, Roscommon and Clare, and replace them with English Protestants. The Cromwellian settlement destroyed the Catholic landowning class but the influx of English settlers never materialized. England's new colonies in North America and the West Indies were much more attractive prospects for would-be emigrants than rebellious Ireland (see pages 168–173). Moreover, less than a third of the army veterans took possession of their lands. Most sold out to the adventurers or established Protestant landowners and returned to England. Because the new landowners wanted a quick return on their investments, very few Catholic Irish tenants were actually expelled and most of those were soon allowed back. Everywhere outside Ulster there remained a majority of native Catholic Irish. Except in the growing popularity of the English language, which was gradually replacing Gaelic, Anglicization had clearly failed, and there were no more plantations.

The ancient castle on the Rock of Dunamase in County Laois (Queen's County) was sacked by Oliver Cromwell in 1650 during his pacification of Ireland.

Profit and Puritanism: the Beginnings of English Colonialism 1587–1707

England was a late starter in Europe's overseas expansion, but it became the leading colonizing nation in the 17th century, laying the foundations of the British empire. Of the English colonies founded in this period it was those in North America that were most important for the future, as it was from these that the United States of America developed.

In the 16th century, the English watched with undisguised envy as wealth flooded back to Spain and Portugal from their colonial empires. Successful voyages of exploration (and piracy) by navigators like Francis Drake (*c.*154–96), and their victory over the Spanish Armada in 1588, encouraged the English to aspire to found their own colonies. After a failed attempt at Roanoke (North Carolina) in 1587, the English founded their first successful colony in Virginia in 1607. A second North American colony was settled in Newfoundland in 1610 (claimed for England in 1497 by John Cabot; 145–*c.*98) and a third in Massachusetts, New England, in 1620. England founded its first major colony in the Caribbean on Barbados in 1625, and a permanent presence was established in India, at Surat, in 1618. By 1700 England had 14 colonies in North America, nine island colonies in the Caribbean and a string of trading posts along the coasts of Africa, India and the East Indies. In total over 60,000 English emigrated in the first half of the 17th century, and nearly 200,000 in the second half.

For the English, founding colonies was partly a matter of national prestige, and for many there were strong religious motives. Some saw colonies as a way to spread Anglicanism, others as opportunities to put into practice their own religious and social ideals. The New England Puritans are the most famous of these, but later in the 17th century Quakers founded settlements in Pennsylvania, and Catholics in Maryland. The main motive, however, was always economic. Colonies would strengthen the national economy by becoming suppliers of raw materials – metals, timber and foodstuffs – and in return they would stimulate English industry by purchasing manufactured goods.

The expectation of profit meant that English colonialism was funded mainly by private, rather than government, capital. Many colonies were founded by chartered companies,

A painting by American artist Jean Leon Gerome Ferris (1863–1930) of the Pilgrim Fathers at Massachusetts Bay, entitled The First Sermon Ashore, 1621.

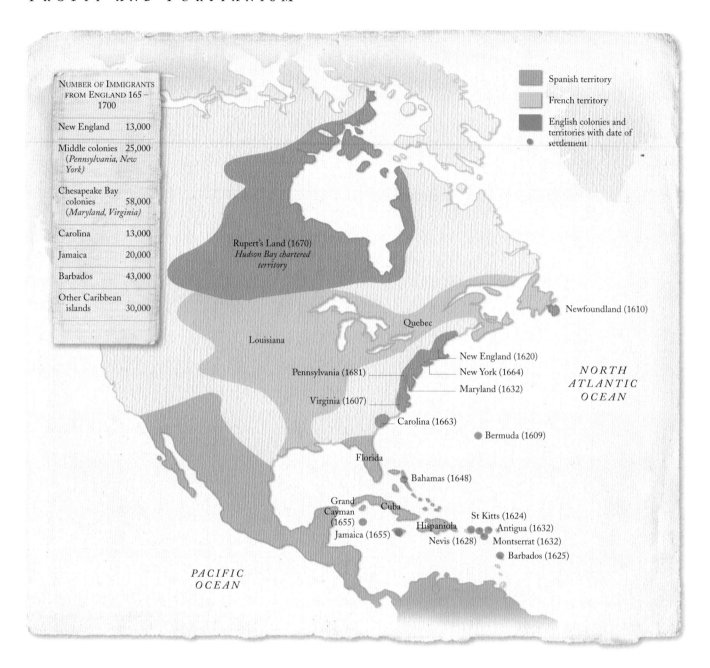

Number of Immigrants from England 165 – 1700	
New England	13,000
Middle colonies (Pennsylvania, New York)	25,000
Chesapeake Bay colonies (Maryland, Virginia)	58,000
Carolina	13,000
Jamaica	20,000
Barbados	43,000
Other Caribbean islands	30,000

Spanish territory

French territory

English colonies and territories with date of settlement

Rupert's Land (1670)
Hudson Bay chartered territory

Newfoundland (1610)

Quebec

Louisiana

New England (1620)

Pennsylvania (1681)

New York (1664)

Maryland (1632)

Virginia (1607)

NORTH ATLANTIC OCEAN

Carolina (1663)

Bermuda (1609)

Florida

Bahamas (1648)

Grand Cayman (1655)

Cuba

St Kitts (1624)

Jamaica (1655)

Hispaniola

Antigua (1632)

Nevis (1628)

Montserrat (1632)

Barbados (1625)

PACIFIC OCEAN

Map showing the extent of English, French and Spanish colonization of the New World in around 169 – 1700.

which had paid the crown for a monopoly on the right to trade with a specified area. The costs of colonization were so great that many of these companies ran into financial difficulty and, from the 1630s, the crown granted charters to wealthy private landlords instead. Colonies were expected to produce social benefits, too, by creating more employment in manufacturing and opportunities for the poor to start new lives overseas.

Tied labour

Almost half of all emigrants from England in the 17th century went to the Caribbean, which was seen as a more glamorous destination than North America. Most were indentured servants, young single men and women who mortgaged their labour for a term of four to seven years in return for payment of their passage. Labour was so scarce that servants were put up for auction on arrival, though, unlike slaves, they were free when their term was up. It was the ambition of most servants to set up their own farms or plantations when their terms expired but most died of tropical diseases before this happened. Those who survived received only small cash grants at the end of their terms, so most finished up as wage labourers. Others went to Virginia, where land on the frontier was plentiful for those willing to take risks. A bold few became buccaneers.

The economic staple of the English Caribbean colonies was sugar cane. Sugar production was both capital and labour intensive. Plantation owners found that the quickest way to build up their labour force was to import African slaves, who had greater resistance to tropical diseases than Europeans and so survived for longer despite relentless hard labour and maltreatment. Land was in short supply in the islands and the huge profits to be made from sugar pushed prices up by 1000 percent in the 1640s. It soon became obvious to even the most optimistic emigrant that the islands offered few prospects for anyone who was not already rich, and it became harder to recruit indentured labour.

The unhealthy reputation of the islands also discouraged emigration. Fear of slave rebellions made plantation owners anxious to increase the islands' white population. Increasingly, indentured servants were convicted criminals who had been given a choice between emigration and the gallows. It was not uncommon for people to be kidnapped and transported against their will to the Caribbean. None of these measures did much more than replace wastage from disease. By 1700 the English Caribbean colonies had developed a polarized society, with a majority of Africans, most, but not all, of whom were slaves, a tiny élite of rich white plantation owners and a transient population of English government officials, merchants, overseers, soldiers and seamen, most of whom were hoping to survive long enough to go home with whatever money they had made.

Tobacco, slavery and racial tension

With its plantation-based economy, the Virginia colony had much in common with the Caribbean colonies but its healthier climate allowed a viable English population to be established. As in the Caribbean, a high proportion of settlers were indentured servants. The first colony was founded in 1607 by the Virginia Company at Jamestown, close to Chesapeake Bay. At first the colony struggled to survive. Too much emphasis was put on prospecting for precious metals and too little on food production. The colony also had a poor fresh-water supply and mortality was high. Under the leadership of John Smith (158–1631) the colony became more self-sufficient and the successful experiments of John Rolfe (c.1585–?1622) with tobacco production in 1612 finally gave the colony a valuable cash crop.

Gaining confidence as its economy improved, Virginia established a precedent for all future English colonies in North America when it established its own elected assembly

In this undated woodcut an African slave couple plants sugar cane, threatened by a supervisor wielding a whip. The growing demand in Europe for sugar and tobacco fuelled the economies of the newly founded colonies, which depended on imported slave labour to keep up the supply of these valuable products.

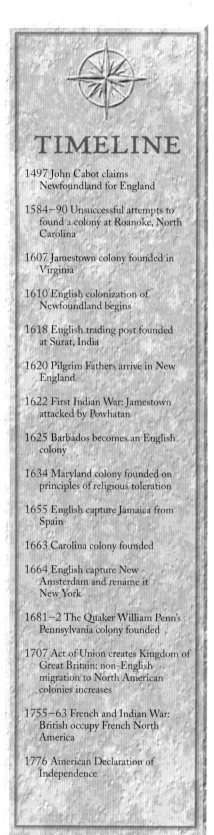

in 1619 to represent freeholders. In this year 1200 new settlers arrived and the colony began to expand as new land was taken for tobacco production. Plantations spread and tobacco production rose rapidly. Growing profits meant that investors were more willing to advance capital to recruit and transport labour to Virginia. Because of the frontier, most indentured servants did eventually become freeholders. Despite increasing immigration, tobacco plantations soon employed all available family and indentured labour, leading to the importation of increasing numbers of African slaves.

Expansion led to a dramatic worsening of relations with the Indians, whose numbers had been much depleted since 1607 by epidemics of European diseases. In 1622 an attack led by the native chief Powhatan killed 350 settlers, but many more American Indians were killed in English reprisals. The attack led the settlers to develop an attitude of racial and cultural superiority that they felt justified the expulsion of indigenous peoples from their lands. The costs of the 'Indian War' bankrupted the Virginia Company, which after 15 years had still not returned a profit: it was dissolved in 1624 and Virginia became a royal colony, so assuring its long-term future.

The Pilgrim Fathers

The settlement of New England began on 21 November, 1620 with the arrival at Cape Cod of the 'Pilgrim Fathers', 102 Puritan settlers, on board the *Mayflower*. Shortly afterwards they founded the Plymouth colony on Massachusetts Bay. Puritans regarded England's state church, the Church of England, as being too close to the Roman Catholic Church in its practices. With the backing of the Plymouth Company, a group of them decided to found a colony in Virginia, where they could practise their religion in freedom. When they arrived at Cape Cod it was too late in the year to continue the voyage safely, so they decided to stay where they were. None of the Pilgrims had a farming background, and help from the American Indians was essential for their survival. Within a few years the settlers had established a prosperous mixed economy based on farming, fishing and fur trading with the local people. In only 12 years they had repaid their financial backers. While on the voyage the Pilgrims had agreed the Mayflower Compact, committing the male settlers to form a *'civill body politick; for our better ordering and preservation'*, and establishing from the start a strong tradition of self-government and local democracy in New England.

After the foundation of the Massachusetts Bay colony by 1000 Puritans at Boston in 1630, the 'Great Migration' saw over 20,000 settlers arrive in New England during the 1630s. Boston developed into a flourishing port. The settlers of the bay colony wanted to create a Bible Commonwealth; until 1664, citizenship, and with it the right to vote for the governor and the representative assembly, was restricted to full church members only. Dissenters were expelled, to found their own colonies, including Rhode Island, New Hampshire and Connecticut, where greater religious tolerance was practised.

Healthy population growth

The rate of natural population growth was much higher in New England than either Virginia or the Caribbean. New England had a healthy climate and was relatively disease-free so the settlers had a better life expectancy than they would have had at home. Settlers in New England were much more likely to have emigrated as families than as single indentured servants, so women formed a higher proportion of the population, which was obviously good for the birth rate. The availability of land also made it easier for a young couple to set up an independent homestead.

As the population grew and settlers began to spread inland, relations with the American Indians became worse, culminating in the Pequot War in 1637. The New England colonies co-ordinated their military effort and defeated the natives. In 1643 the colonies formed the New England Confederation for mutual defence. It showed its worth during King Philip's War of 1675–6. Although 500 settlers were killed and many towns burned, the Indians were again defeated with heavy losses. This was the last serious native challenge to English colonization – the settlers were by now too numerous and too entrenched to be dislodged. These wars were fought and won entirely by local militias as the government would commit troops only to defend the colonies against other European powers.

By 1700 the English population of North America exceeded 400,000, with some 40,000 in the Caribbean and a home population of 5 million. France, with a home population of 20 million, had only 70,000 colonial subjects. England's success as an exporter of people laid strong foundations for the long struggle with France for dominance of North America in the 18th century. England (after 1707, Great Britain) would win this conflict but would later lose its most populous American colonies. The English government generally left the colonists to govern themselves, but the exact nature of their rights and responsibilities vis-à-vis the crown was never defined. It was this oversight that led eventually to the American Revolution and the creation of the United States.

A late 16th-century map by the Flemish traveller Theodore de Bry, showing the English settlement at Chesapeake Bay, Virginia, thought to be a copy of an original by John Smith. Along the right border is the figure of an American Indian holding a bow. The illustration in the upper left corner depicts the residence of Powhatan.

New France
1534–1763

France was England's principal rival in the race to found colonies in North America in the 17th and 18th centuries. French adventurers were at the forefront of exploration of the New World and soon established control over extensive territories. Yet despite having a larger population than England, France was far less successful in encouraging emigration to its colonies.

French exploration of the Americas began in the late 15th century, when Basque and Breton fisherman began crossing the Atlantic to take cod from the Grand Banks. In the 16th century, French, English and Dutch pirates plundered Spanish ships and colonies in the Caribbean, and in 1534–6 Jacques Cartier (1491–1557) became the first European to journey down the St Lawrence River. Cartier used two names for the lands he explored: 'Canada' (an Indian term) and 'New France'. His attempts to found colonies in New France failed but a trade in furs was established with the Indians, who were keen to acquire metal tools and other European goods.

A vital foothold in the Americas

France's first successful New World colonies were founded in Acadia (Nova Scotia and New Brunswick) in 1604 and at Quebec in New France in 1608. Further colonies were founded in the Caribbean at Haiti and Martinique, Dominica and Guadeloupe, and in South America at Cayenne (French Guiana). In 1682 Sieur de la Salle (1643–87) claimed the Mississippi basin for France, naming it Louisiana, in honour of King Louis XIV (r.1643–1715). Permanent French settlement began in 1714 and was boosted by Acadians (Cajuns) expelled by the British in 1755. France lost its North American colonies to Britain in the French and Indian War (1754–63) – an extension of the Seven Years' War in Europe – but there remain over eight million French speakers in Canada and, though French is no longer widely spoken there, the Cajuns and Creoles of Louisiana retain many French cultural traits.

Like the English, the French saw colonies as a source of tropical products, minerals and other valuable natural commodities, as an outlet for surplus population and as captive markets for home-produced goods. Also in common with the English, chartered companies played an key role in sponsoring colonization. In 1627 the Company of New France was founded by Cardinal Richelieu (1585–1642) with the intention of recreating a version of French rural society of aristocratic seigneurs and a servile peasantry, who would rent smallholdings from the seigneurs and perform labour duties for

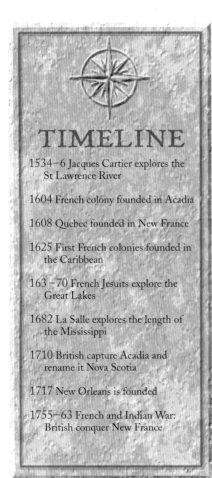

TIMELINE

1534–6 Jacques Cartier explores the St Lawrence River

1604 French colony founded in Acadia

1608 Quebec founded in New France

1625 First French colonies founded in the Caribbean

163 –70 French Jesuits explore the Great Lakes

1682 La Salle explores the length of the Mississippi

1710 British capture Acadia and rename it Nova Scotia

1717 New Orleans is founded

1755–63 French and Indian War: British conquer New France

them. The French state also hoped to emulate Spain and Portugal by spreading Catholicism to the native peoples. However, the Indians were hostile to the Jesuit missionaries who were sent to preach to them and many were killed.

Total emigration to France's overseas colonies in the 17th and 18th centuries was probably only around 6–70,000, out of a home population averaging about 20 million. The most popular destination for French emigrants was the Caribbean and, like the English, once there they perished in considerable numbers from tropical diseases. To solve their labour problems, French plantation owners imported African slaves. Louisiana was also unhealthy and immigration barely maintained the population. French settlers at first struggled to survive the harsh winters in Canada, and relied heavily on bartering with the Indians for their food supplies. But as they learned to adapt to the environment, the settlers began to prosper. The ready availability of land led to a low age of marriage and a high birth rate. In the early 18th century, the average French-Canadian women brought up eight children, compensating to some extent for the shortage of female emigrants. Despite this, by the time of the British conquest New France had a French population of only 55,000, little more than one-fortieth the population of British North America. Louisiana had a French population of 4000, the Caribbean colonies around 25,000 and Cayenne only 1000.

The majority of French emigrants were *engagés* (indentured servants) who were recruited by seigneurs, companies, merchants and sea captains, who were paid commission by the government for every settler they sent. This encouraged unscrupulous practices.

Jacques Cartier Discovering the St Lawrence River in 1535, *by Theodore Gudin (1847). Harsh winter conditions and native hostility forced Cartier to abandon the settlement he established on the St Lawrence after barely a year.*

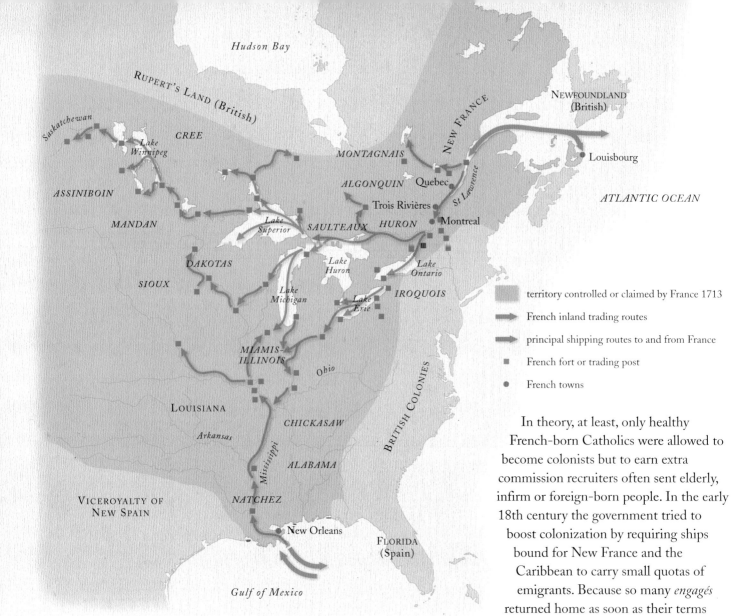

Map showing the territory of New France at its height in the early 18th century, including key trade routes and forts.

In theory, at least, only healthy French-born Catholics were allowed to become colonists but to earn extra commission recruiters often sent elderly, infirm or foreign-born people. In the early 18th century the government tried to boost colonization by requiring ships bound for New France and the Caribbean to carry small quotas of emigrants. Because so many *engagés* returned home as soon as their terms (usually of six years) expired, the authorities began recruiting whole families, a move that encouraged more emigrants to stay in the colonies. Petty criminals were also deported to New France and Louisiana but in such small numbers (only about 2000 in total) that it had little impact.

Most emigrants to the French colonies came from coastal areas of Brittany and Normandy and the hinterlands of the ports of Bordeaux and La Rochelle. Over half of all emigrants came from urban areas, although only 15 percent of the French population lived in towns at that time, and were from poor artisan families. However, the peasant farmers who might have fulfilled the government's vision of New France could not be persuaded to emigrate in any numbers. Many female emigrants were orphans, sent overseas at state expense as *filles du roi* ('daughters of the king') to provide wives for the predominantly male settlers. Higher-ranking colonists would not consider marriage to women of such low social status but their demands for more suitable women could not be met. In frontier zones intermarriage between French men and Indian women (mainly from the Cree and Ojibwa nations) was common. These marriages gave rise to the Métis people, from the French word for 'mixed', who were marginalized by settler society and migrated west, adopting a nomadic lifestyle as traders, trappers and hunters.

Founded by the French navigator Samuel de Champlain in 1608, Quebec (shown here in a contemporary print) became an important commercial centre on the French fur trading route from the Great Lakes. After the city was captured by the British in 1759, France ceded its claims to Canada.

Defeated by demography

France's lack of success in populating its colonies was a decisive factor in its defeat by Great Britain in their long struggle for supremacy in North America. The result was that North America became a mainly English-speaking continent. Once it had been isolated by British naval dominance, New France lacked the manpower to sustain a long war, while the British could reinforce their regular troops with colonial militias. The relative lack of emigration from France was due in part to its agricultural system. Because of agricultural reforms, 17th-century England had large numbers of landless poor for whom emigration was an attractive option. This was not the case in France. Most French peasant farmers were serfs under the jurisdiction of their seigneur. Unlike England's free peasantry, however, French peasants had security of tenure and had the absolute right to pass their farms on to their heirs. As a result French peasants had little incentive to emigrate to a wild and dangerous frontier region, where they would still be under the thumb of a seigneur. Recruitment among poor artisans was more successful because they were promised recognition as master craftsmen when they had served their indentures. However, all too often they returned home to practise their trades.

Another obstacle to recruiting settlers was competition from the French army, which needed large numbers of young healthy men for its many continental campaigns. France in the 17th century was at the height of its wealth and power and this made emigration unattractive to aristocrats and other high-ranking people. One group of French people who did have a strong incentive to emigrate were the Huguenots (French Protestants), who faced growing persecution by the Catholic French monarchy. Huguenots had much the same virtues as the English Puritans, but Protestants were expressly forbidden to settle in the French colonies. Consequently, the 200,000 and more Huguenots who left France in the 17th century went to Switzerland, the Netherlands and, especially, to England and its American colonies – a huge loss for France and its colonial enterprise.

Russia's Wild East
1581–1914

In a mirror image of the westward migration of Europeans to the Americas, the 16th century saw the beginning of eastward migration of Russians across Siberia. In what was one of the greatest population shifts in European history, Russians conquered and marginalized the native Siberian peoples to become the dominant ethnic group across the whole breadth of northern Asia as far as the Pacific Ocean.

Siberia comprises nearly 12 percent of the earth's land area, extending west to east over 3500 miles (5600 km) from the Ural Mountains, which mark the eastern border of European Russia, to the Bering Straits. The greater part of this vast region is frozen tundra or swampy pine forest but it also contains large areas of steppe grassland, fertile farmland, temperate rainforest and high glaciated mountains, and it contains enormous mineral wealth. Except in the mild Pacific southeast, Siberia has a harsh climate, with extremely cold winters, with temperatures frequently below −20°C (−4°F), and warm, humid summers with swarms of biting insects. The challenging environment has always made exploiting Siberia's natural resources very difficult.

Subjugating Siberia

The opening up of Siberia to Russian settlement was initiated by Tsar Ivan IV 'the Terrible' (r.1533–84), who sent his Cossack general Yermak Timofeyevich (c.1537–85) on an expedition to conquer the Tatar khanate of Sibir on the Irtysh river in 1581–2. Russian pathfinders had pioneered a route to the Pacific Ocean by 1637 but the process of subjugating the native Siberian peoples and settling the region with ethnic Russians would take another 300 years. The initial motivation for Russian expansion into Siberia (and later into Alaska) was the search for 'soft gold', that is furs. Expansion into Siberia was directed by the Siberian Department in Moscow but there was also room for private initiatives. Sometimes an expedition ordered by Moscow would be the first to explore a region; on other occasions trappers or fur traders might explore a region on their own and then report their discoveries to the local military governor. As travel overland was extremely arduous, expeditions used river systems as much as possible. First contact with a native Siberian people would be followed by a military expedition to force them to pay tribute in the form of furs. A small fort would be built and a garrison stationed there to collect

An early 19th-century illustration showing the town of Yakutsk on the River Lena in the Russian Far East. Russian pioneers first established a fort (Ostrog) here in 1632.

the furs and protect fur traders. Forts were also built at strategic points along the main travel routes, at the confluences of rivers, for example, or at portages, where boats were carried overland from one river system to another. Small communities of soldiers' families, traders and craftsmen began to develop around forts at key strategic locations, growing eventually into fully fledged towns. Some of Siberia's most important modern cities, such as Tobolsk, Tomsk, Krasnoyarsk and Irkutsk, developed in this way. Because of their isolation, and the vast distances involved, supplying garrisons was a problem. It was because of this that the government began to encourage peasant settlement in Siberia, so that garrisons could be supplied with produce from nearby fields. The Orthodox Church also participated in the process of colonization, founding monasteries, which, like the forts, became the focus for the growth of new communities.

Even in the 18th century, conditions on the frontier were so insecure that towns were fortified and blockhouses were built among the fields to provide refuges for peasant farmers in case of surprise native attacks. Native resistance was punished by reprisal raids, hostage taking and the killing of domesticated reindeer. Young native women were often

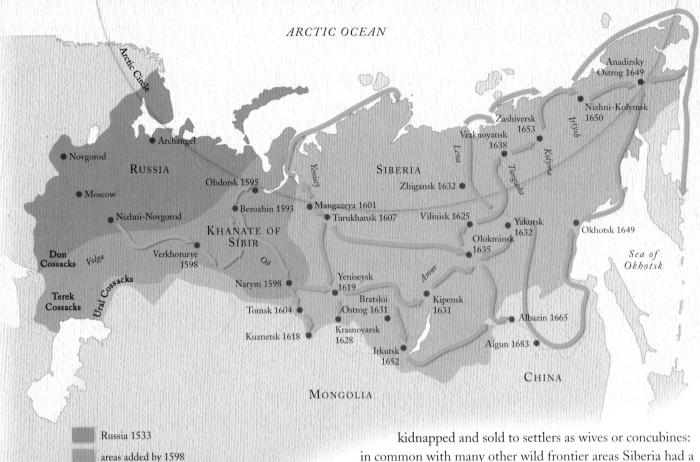

Map showing the expansion of Russia into Siberia in the 16th and 17th centuries.

kidnapped and sold to settlers as wives or concubines: in common with many other wild frontier areas Siberia had a shortage of female settlers. As was the case in the Americas, European diseases had a more severe impact on Siberia's indigenous population than violence. Smallpox was the big killer. The first outbreak, in 1630, killed around 50 percent of the Ostyak, Tungus, Yakut and Samoyed peoples. Later outbreaks were even worse. These epidemics demoralized the native peoples and greatly aided the Russian conquest. The Yukhagir people of Kamchatka have a legend that the Russians were unable to conquer them until they brought smallpox in a box. When they opened the box the land was filled with smoke and the people began to die.

A place of banishment and hard labour

Siberia is best known as a chilly place of exile and punishment for political dissidents. The tradition of using Siberia as a place of exile developed early and by the end of the 17th century about 11 percent of the population were exiles. Most exiles up to this time were members of the ruling classes who had committed political misdemeanours or, in the case of former lovers and favourites, simply become an embarrassment. A new element was introduced by Tsar Peter the Great (r.1682–1725). This was *katorga* or forced labour as a punishment for common criminals. *Katorga* for a specified number of years followed by perpetual exile in Siberia remained the harshest punishment of the tsarist regime until the revolution. Many exiles were joined voluntarily by their families. As popular opposition to the tsarist regime grew in the 19th century, increasing numbers of middle class intellectuals and working class activists, such as trade unionists and striking workers, were also exiled to Siberia. By the middle of the 19th century between 17,000 and 19,000 people were being deported east of the Urals every year for political offences, not counting common criminals. Though not as terrible as the Gulags of the Soviet era, conditions in the the tsarist penal system were harsh. The novelist Fyodor

Dostoyevsky (1821–81) described Siberia as the 'House of the Dead'. Forced labour was generally used on infrastructure projects, such as roads, and mining and transport.

To secure supplies for the military garrisons, large numbers of peasant farmers were forcibly resettled in Siberia in the 17th and 18th centuries. However, most Russians who migrated there were neither political exiles, criminals nor deportees. Contrary to its popular image, Siberia was a place of freedom and opportunity for many in the tsarist period. Thousands of peasants who were weary of the burdens of serfdom in European Russia fled across the Urals. These migrants usually began by working as labourers for established settlers until they had saved up enough money to set up a farm of their own. Offers of free land were also used by the government to entice freed serfs to migrate to Siberia. Another important group of migrants had religious motives. These were the 'Old Believers', Russian Orthodox Christians who faced persecution for their refusal to accept liturgical reforms in the 17th century. They sought out remote areas to settle and, by avoiding contact with outsiders, preserved an essentially 17th-century way of life into the 20th century. Other categories of migrant included industrialists, administrators, miners, craftsmen, general merchants, prostitutes, fugitives from justice and draft dodgers.

Migration began as a trickle but by 1724 there were already 400,000 Russians in Siberia, outnumbering the natives two to one. By 1858 this figure had grown to 2.3 million. After the abolition of serfdom in 1861 migration to Siberia began to increase and became a flood after the construction of the Trans-Siberian Railway between 1893 and 1903. Between 1880 and 1914 over 5 million Russians settled in Siberia. With higher living standards than in European Russia, they had a high birth rate. By 1914 ethnic Russians formed 85 percent of the total 10.5 million population of Siberia. In the preceding 15 years alone over 6400 new communities had been founded and nearly 45 million acres (18 million hectares) of land brought under the plough. Most immigrants settled in the mixed forest-steppe zone to the south, where the best farmland was, along the track of the Trans-Siberian Railway. Most of Siberia remained (and still remains) virtually uninhabited, the domain of the surviving indigenous reindeer herders and trappers. The advantages to the Russian state of the settlement of Siberia were many. Wealth from the sale of Siberian furs and minerals underwrote royal absolutism, while the vast size of the region helped establish the perception of Russia as a world power.

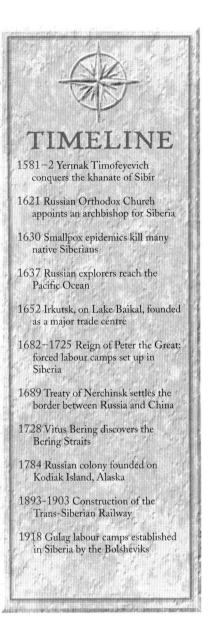

TIMELINE

1581–2 Yermak Timofeyevich conquers the khanate of Sibir

1621 Russian Orthodox Church appoints an archbishop for Siberia

1630 Smallpox epidemics kill many native Siberians

1637 Russian explorers reach the Pacific Ocean

1652 Irkutsk, on Lake Baikal, founded as a major trade centre

1682–1725 Reign of Peter the Great: forced labour camps set up in Siberia

1689 Treaty of Nerchinsk settles the border between Russia and China

1728 Vitus Bering discovers the Bering Straits

1784 Russian colony founded on Kodiak Island, Alaska

1893–1903 Construction of the Trans-Siberian Railway

1918 Gulag labour camps established in Siberia by the Bolsheviks

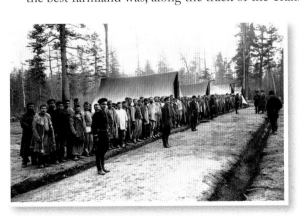

In 1895, a gang of convict labourers assemble at a camp set up in the Ussuri region near Vladivostok to advance the construction of the Trans-Siberian Railway.

The Atlantic Slave Trade
c.1460 – 1882

The largest forced migration in history, an estimated 14 million Africans, were transported by slavers to work on plantations in the Americas between the 16th and 19th centuries. As a result of this trade, people of African descent form the majority population of all the modern Caribbean nations, as well as nearly half the population of Brazil and 12 percent of the population of the USA. In addition they are significant minorities in many Central and South American countries. In all there are estimated to be over 120 million people of African descent in the Americas.

The Atlantic slave trade began in a small way in the 1460s when the Portuguese began transporting West African slaves to work on sugar plantations in the Cape Verde Islands. The first African slaves were transported across the Atlantic by the Spanish in 1517 to work on sugar plantations in the Caribbean and Mexico. The Spanish had initially enslaved native Indians, but found them unsuitable because of their vulnerability to European diseases. Being in their own homeland, Indian slaves could also easily escape or resist. Africans were physically well adapted to tropical climates and had a much lower death rate than Europeans, despite their often brutal treatment, while the experience of transportation to a distant land in awful conditions left them feeling disorientated, dispirited and cowed. After they too had tried enslaving Indians, other European colonizers began importing Africans to the Americas. In 1534 the Portuguese started to transport African slaves to Brazil to work on sugar and, later, coffee plantations. Brazil became far the biggest importer of slaves: over 3.6 million Africans would be transported there in total (see pages 154–159; 160–163).

In the 17th century other European powers, including England, France, the Netherlands and Denmark, began shipping slaves to their Caribbean and North American colonies (see pages 168–173). By the end of the century, Africans already greatly outnumbered Europeans in the Caribbean. In the English colony of Jamaica, for example, in 1700 there were 45,000 African slaves to only 7000 Europeans. In the 18th century the gap widened further, as the European population declined and the number of Africans grew through importation and, as slaves were allowed to marry, from natural reproduction.

The slave trade to North America

In 1619, the first African slaves had been imported into the English Virginia colony and by the end of the century there were African slaves in all of England's North American colonies, but in small numbers only. Numbers of slaves were greatest in the Virginia

White slavers bartering with an African agent over a shipment of slaves from the West African coast, from an 18th-century engraving.

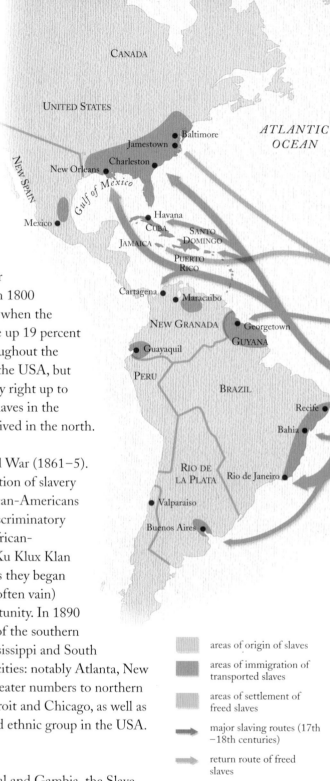

colony, where tobacco plantations dominated the economy, but even here there were less than 2000 slaves in 1680. Slave numbers increased rapidly after 1700 because of a boom in the tobacco trade and by 1740 one third of Virginia's population of 180,000 were African slaves. Although the northern states abolished slavery after the Revolution, the institution became even more important in the south, thanks to the boom in cotton planting that followed the invention of the cotton gin in 1793. This led to a great increase in demand for field hands to grow and pick cotton. Imports peaked between 1800 and 1808, when 108,000 slaves arrived in the USA. In 1808, when the government banned the importation of slaves, Africans made up 19 percent of the US population. This proportion declined steadily throughout the 19th century, due to the flood of European immigrants into the USA, but thousands of African slaves continued to be imported illegally right up to the Civil War. By this time there were four million African slaves in the USA and 400,000 free Africans, most, but not all, of whom lived in the north.

The future of slavery was one of the major causes of the Civil War (1861–5). The defeat of the southern Confederacy resulted in the abolition of slavery throughout the USA, but it was another century before African-Americans had equal civil rights with white Americans. In the south, discriminatory 'Jim Crow' laws were used to introduce racial segregation, African-Americans were denied their voting rights and subjected to Ku Klux Klan lynch law. The distribution of African-Americans changed as they began to migrate from the south to other parts of the USA in the (often vain) hope of enjoying greater social mobility and economic opportunity. In 1890 almost 90 percent of African-Americans lived in rural areas of the southern states and made up over 50 percent of the population in Mississippi and South Carolina. In the 20th century there was a steady drift to the cities: notably Atlanta, New Orleans, Memphis and Houston in the south, and in even greater numbers to northern cities such as New York, Washington DC, Philadelphia, Detroit and Chicago, as well as Los Angeles. African-Americans are now the most urbanized ethnic group in the USA.

Slaving by proxy

The main sources of slaves for the Atlantic trade were Senegal and Gambia, the Slave Coast (now part of Nigeria), the Gold Coast (now Ghana), and the Ivory Coast (now Côte d'Ivoire) in West Africa. Angola and Mozambique in southern Africa were also an important source, used almost exclusively by the Portuguese for export to Brazil. Slavery and slave trading were already widespread in West Africa at the time of the first contact with Europeans. However, in African societies, slaves had rights and were not treated as mere chattels as was the practice of European slave traders and owners. Only rarely did Europeans themselves enslave Africans. Endemic tropical diseases made West Africa a

areas of origin of slaves

areas of immigration of transported slaves

areas of settlement of freed slaves

major slaving routes (17th –18th centuries)

return route of freed slaves

international frontiers

GREAT
BRITAIN

FRANCE

PORTUGAL   SPAIN
Mediterranean Sea

AFRICA

Arguin

Gorée
SIERRA LEONE
LIBERIA   Lagos
Monrovia   Bonny
Elmina   Calabar

Gulf of Guinea

Cabinda

Luanda

ANGOLA

Map showing the major transatlantic slave routes and the return routes of emancipated slaves in the 18th century.

fatally unhealthy place for Europeans before modern medicines became available in the late 19th century.

European traders visiting West Africa therefore tried to make their visits onshore as brief as possible, preferring to conduct their business through African agents. Agents were usually paid a year in advance so that they could purchase a cargo of slaves ready to load onto the slave ship as soon as it arrived, thus reducing to a minimum the time the vessel had to stay in West African waters. African rulers were happy with these arrangements, which made it easy for them to control, and profit from, trade with Europeans.

Until the 18th century, Spain and Portugal were the leading slave trading nations and other Europeans were prevented from trading with their colonies. Following its victory in the War of the Spanish Succession (1701–13), Britain quickly became the leading slaving nation. The British established the so-called 'triangular trade'. British manufactured goods, including cloth, rum and firearms, were first exported to West Africa, where merchants would exchange them for a cargo of slaves. On the second leg of the triangle, known as the 'middle passage', the slaves were shipped to the Caribbean or North America and exchanged for foodstuffs, such as sugar, coffee and rice, and raw materials, such as cotton and dyes to supply British factories. In this way the slave trade made an important contribution to Britain's Industrial Revolution.

Effects of the slave trade

The steady growth of European demand for slaves had a huge impact on West Africa. Many of the kingdoms on the coast, such as Asante and Benin, were enriched by trade with the Europeans, but others became victims of raids by the stronger kingdoms to take prisoners who could be sold as slaves. In the 17th and 18th centuries over 14 million West Africans were sold to European slave traders. This massive loss of population held back economic growth. The effects were made worse because the slave traders took only the healthiest and strongest young people.

TIMELINE

1460s Portuguese begin transporting African slaves to the Cape Verde Islands

1517 Spanish import African slaves to the Caribbean and Mexico

1522 African slaves in Hispaniola rebel against the Spanish

1534 Portuguese begin transporting African slaves to Brazil

1619 The first African slaves imported to the English Virginia colony

1713 Britain wins control of the Atlantic slave trade

1787 Sierra Leone established as a colony for freed slaves

1791–1803 Slave rebellion overthrows French rule in Haiti

1793 Invention of the cotton gin increases demand for slaves in the USA

1807 Britain bans the slave trade

1808 US government bans the importation of slaves

1831–2 Slave rebellion in Jamaica

1834 Slavery is abolished throughout the British empire

1865 Slavery abolished in the USA

1888 Brazil becomes the last American country to abolish slavery

The impact of the Atlantic slave trade was, of course, greatest on the slaves themselves. Conditions on slave ships were appalling. Slaves were crammed into the dark holds of sailing ships for six weeks or more, chained together with barely enough room to lie down. With poor food, no chance to wash or exercise, and no proper toilet facilities, about one in five slaves died of disease during the Atlantic crossing. If they survived the crossing, all slaves could expect was a life of unrelenting toil and maltreatment. Average life expectancy for an adult male field slave on a sugar plantation was as little as seven or eight years. Slaves in other occupations generally fared better, but any disobedience was liable to be punished with a severe beating at least. Young female slaves were highly likely to be sexually abused by male slave owners.

The psychological impact of slavery was just as devastating as its physical effects, if not more so. Slaves were separated from their families and communities, stripped of personal freedom, status and all possessions, and transported thousands of miles to live in an alien culture with no hope of return. Not surprisingly, suicide was a common reaction. Slaves were bought and sold with no regard for their family relationships or ethnic and linguistic backgrounds. Slaves from different African peoples frequently worked together on the same plantations. Under such circumstances, the need to communicate with one another as much as with their European overseers, led them and their descendants to adopt the language of their masters. Slave culture also became Europeanized to varying degrees. This was greatest in the USA where, unlike in the Caribbean, Africans were always a minority of the population. In many areas, traditional African folklore and religious beliefs survived. Combined with the Christianity that masters imposed on their slaves, and with native Indian beliefs, this spawned new syncretic religions, such as the Trinidadian shango cult, Cuban santeria and – probably the most widely misunderstood religion in the world – Haitian voodoo. African musical traditions also survived and were influenced by European musical traditions. In the USA this led to the development of spirituals and Jazz and Blues music.

Slaves picking cotton on a plantation in the southern state of Georgia, USA. The invention of the cotton gin mechanized the separation of cotton fibres from seeds, but slaves continued in ever greater numbers to do the back-breaking work of picking the crop.

Abolition and rebellion

Revulsion at the treatment of slaves led to the growth of anti-slavery movements in Britain and the USA in the late 18th century. Denmark was the first European country to abolish the slave trade, in 1802, followed by Britain in 1807. Other European nations gradually followed suit, with Portugal being the last country to outlaw the slave trade, in 1882. Slavery itself took longer to disappear: it was abolished in the British empire in 1834, in the USA in 1865 and in Brazil, the last American country to do so, in 1888.

Nor did slaves themselves accept their lot passively. Because their masters believed them to be intellectually inferior, slaves were often able to commit acts of deliberate sabotage to property and pass them off as the result of stupidity or clumsiness. There were also

many large-scale slave rebellions – the first being in Haiti in 1522 – but they were all defeated, and punished with savage reprisals, until rebel slaves led by the freed slave Toussaint L'Ouverture (1743–1803) overthrew French rule in Haiti in 1797. A major slave rebellion in Jamaica in 1831–2 hastened the British government's decision to abolish slavery, but rebellions in 1800, 1822 and 1831 in the USA simply led to the introduction of harshly repressive legislation to control slave behaviour. In the larger Caribbean islands and Brazil many slaves, known as Maroons, escaped to the interior and set up independent communities. In the USA, free African-Americans helped slaves escape to freedom in the northern states and Canada using the 'Underground Railroad' network of safe houses.

Most migrations involve an element of counter-migration, that is emigrants who, for whatever reason, decide to go home. This was even the case with the forced slave migration. In 1787 British anti-slavery activists established the colony of Sierra Leone in West Africa for emancipated African slaves. In 1821 a second colony for emancipated slaves was founded in Liberia by American anti-slavery campaigners. About 20,000 freed slaves were resettled in Liberia and 74,000 in Sierra Leone. Many of the settlers in Sierra Leone eventually succeeded in returning to their original homelands. The ideal of a return to Africa has remained influential among slave descendants: it has been an important element in the development of the Rastafarian religion of Jamaica and in the Black nationalism movement in the USA.

Negroes in the Bilge (1835) by the German painter and engraver Johann Moritz Rugendas. Scant regard was paid by slavers to their human cargoes, and conditions on slave ships were often far more squalid and cramped than those illustrated here.

Chinese Peasants on the Move

C.AD 1 – 2007

The Chinese have a long history of migration, both within China and beyond its borders. The overseas migrations are often referred to as the 'Chinese diaspora', because emigrants have, to a great extent, retained much of their original cultural identity and become only partially assimilated within their host communities.

Ethnic Chinese, known as Han, are a Mongoloid people of northeast Asian origin. At the time of the earliest historically attested Chinese dynasty, the Shang (c.1766 – 1122 BC), the Han homeland centred on the fertile Yellow River Valley, in the north of modern China. Southern China was inhabited by tribal farming peoples related to the modern Thais and Vietnamese. Later Chinese dynasties began military expansion into this area and China achieved an approximation of its modern southern borders under the Han dynasty (206 BC – AD 220), from whom the Han Chinese take their name.

Compared to the densely settled Yellow River Valley, southern China was relatively sparsely populated. Beginning in the early centuries AD, Chinese peasants began to migrate south, settling in river valleys where they could practise intensive rice farming in paddyfields. In the process, the indigenous peoples were either assimilated or were confined to mountain areas, which were unattractive to Chinese settlers. Even today, there remain over 50 ethnic minority peoples in southern China. This migration was on such a massive scale that by the Tang dynasty period (618 – 907) more than 50 percent of the total Chinese population of around 140 million lived in the south. This proportion increased to 90 percent in the 13th century. Migration to the south was encouraged by northern China's exposure to invasion by steppe nomads. In the 14th century there was a counter-migration back to the north, to repopulate areas devastated by the Mongol invasions of the previous century. The conquest of China in 1644 by the Manchu (who ruled as the Qing dynasty 1644–1911) offered more opportunities to peasant migrants. Many Manchu migrated south, while a mass migration of Han farmers into Manchuria turned the Manchu there into an ethnic minority in their own homeland. As a result, the Manchu soon became highly Sinicized and their language is now virtually extinct.

Under Manchu rule, China expanded deep into Central Asia following the conquest of the Mongols, the Turkish Uighurs and the Tibetans in the 18th century. These newly conquered territories consisted mainly of open steppe, desert, high-altitude plateau and

glaciated mountain ranges and were not attractive to Han settlement because traditional Chinese agriculture could not be practised in these harsh environments. After the establishment of the People's Republic of China in 1949 the communist government began to introduce financial incentives to encourage Han settlement in Central Asia for strategic and political reasons. Both the Tibetans and the Uighurs have resisted Sinification and the Chinese government's intention is to turn them into ethnic minorities in their own countries by swamping them with Han immigrants. Tibetans are already a minority in Lhasa, Tibet's capital city, as a result of Chinese immigration. Han now constitute 92 percent of the 1.3 billion population of the People's Republic of China, making them the most numerous ethnic group in the world.

This section of an early 12th-century panoramic painting, Going Upriver at the Qingming Festival *by the Song dynasty artist Zhang Zeduan (1085– 1145), shows Chinese peasants using a variety of modes of transport.*

Forced out by poverty and war

The earliest significant overseas migration of Chinese was to Taiwan, during the Song dynasty period (960–1279). After the Mongols conquered China and overthrew the Song dynasty in 1279 Chinese refugees settled in Japan, Cambodia and Vietnam. Emigration continued during the period of Mongol rule (1277–1368) and new Chinese communities were established in Thailand, Sumatra, Java and Singapore. After the emperor Hongwu, the founder of the Ming dynasty (1368–1644), expelled the Mongols from China, the imperial government attempted to exclude foreign influences and in 1371 it banned the Chinese from travelling abroad. The ban could not be enforced and

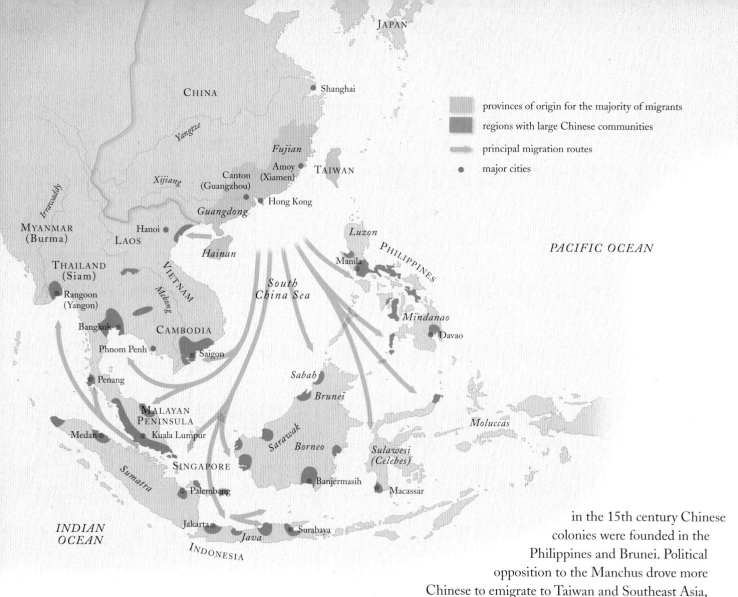

*Chinese migration in
Southeast Asia from the
14th to 19th centuries.*

in the 15th century Chinese colonies were founded in the Philippines and Brunei. Political opposition to the Manchus drove more Chinese to emigrate to Taiwan and Southeast Asia, where they often formed anti-Manchu secret societies. By the 19th century there were some 2.2 million Chinese living throughout Southeast Asia.

A new phase of emigration began after China's defeat by Britain in the first Opium War (1840–2). China was forced to cede Hong Kong to Britain and open a number of 'treaty' ports to foreign trade. It now became far easier for the Chinese to emigrate because they could do so in foreign ships. In 1860, the government repealed its ban on emigration. Between 1845 and 1900 about 2.3 million Chinese emigrated. Most were from peasant backgrounds and men far outnumbered women. For instance, of the 71,000 Chinese immigrants in the USA in 1910 less than 5000 were women. The majority came from the Guangdong province, the hinterland of the major ports of Guangzhou and Hong Kong. Most emigrants did not plan to leave China permanently – they hoped to return with savings to buy land or a business. However, rates of return from areas such as Southeast Asia, where there were old established Chinese communities, were very low.

Indentured labour around the world

Approximately 375,000 Chinese emigrants went to countries in the British empire. The abolition of slavery in 1834 had created a demand for cheap labour and the British actively recruited in China, going so far as to set up emigration bureaus in Guangzhou.

Although some emigrants paid their own way, most of them were indentured labourers. Typically, an indentured labourer was contracted to work for five years in return for his passage overseas. Indentured labourers were paid a wage of US $3 a month, less a 50 cent deduction to reimburse the cost of passage, plus a food ration of one pound of sugar, ten pounds of rice, eight pounds of meat and two ounces of tea. The main destinations were Malaya, to work in tin mines and on rubber plantations, South Africa, to work in gold mines, Australia and New Zealand, to work on farms and plantations, and Canada, to work in construction. Chinese labour played an important part in the construction of the Transcontinental railroad in the United States in the 1860s and the Canadian-Pacific railroad in the 1880s. Chinese labourers were also recruited to work on plantations in the West Indies. As a result of immigration encouraged by the British, Chinese now make up 33 percent of Malaysia's population and Singapore is a predominantly Chinese city. Britain's own Chinese community was founded by free emigrants, many of whom had signed on as crew on British merchant ships.

Several other European and American countries recruited Chinese indentured labour in the 19th century. Spain sent about 120,000 labourers to Cuba, the Peruvian government recruited about 120,000 to work in mining, and over 200,000 Chinese labourers went to the USA, many to work on railroad construction and mines. There was also large-scale emigration of Chinese labour to Thailand, and the French and Dutch colonies in Southeast Asia. To try to ensure the welfare of emigrants the Chinese government signed a number of emigration treaties with the recruiting nations, including Great Britain (1860), France (1860), Spain (1864), Peru (1868) and the USA (1880). In practice, abuses, including kidnapping, were common. Conditions on emigrant ships were often awful and death rates on the longer passages, such as the 150–160 day passage from China to Cuba, exceeded 10 percent. In Peru and Cuba, indentured labourers often found themselves put up for auction after landing. In both countries most Chinese re-emigrated to the USA after their indentures expired.

The willingness of the Chinese to work extremely hard for low wages led to a hostile reaction in many of the countries to which they emigrated. After anti-Chinese rioting erupted in Denver, Colorado, the US government passed the Chinese Exclusion Act of 1882, suspending immigration from China for ten years. This legislation was renewed for another ten years in 1892 and again, this time indefinitely, in 1902. Recent Irish immigrants were especially hostile to the Chinese because they were competing for the same low-paid, unskilled jobs. After 1885 Chinese immigration to Britain's 'white' colonies was also restricted. Although almost all Chinese emigrants came from rural backgrounds and went to work in rural locations overseas, their descendants had, within one or two generations, drifted to towns to work in commerce and Chinese communities overseas are now almost exclusively urban and generally very prosperous.

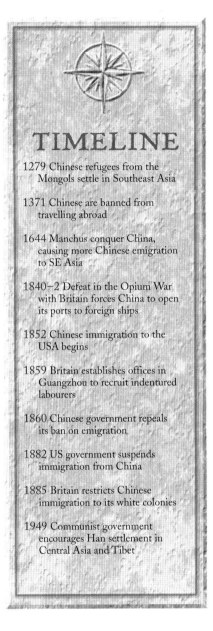

TIMELINE

1279 Chinese refugees from the Mongols settle in Southeast Asia

1371 Chinese are banned from travelling abroad

1644 Manchus conquer China, causing more Chinese emigration to SE Asia

1840–2 Defeat in the Opium War with Britain forces China to open its ports to foreign ships

1852 Chinese immigration to the USA begins

1859 Britain establishes offices in Guangzhou to recruit indentured labourers

1860 Chinese government repeals its ban on emigration

1882 US government suspends immigration from China

1885 Britain restricts Chinese immigration to its white colonies

1949 Communist government encourages Han settlement in Central Asia and Tibet

Transportation to Australia
1787–1868

Many governments have seen colonies as useful places of exile where petty criminals and other social undesirables could make new lives for themselves. Probably none has enjoyed more success in this respect than the British government which used transported convicts to begin the colonization of Australia in 1787.

After the ancestors of the Aborigines reached Australia some 50,000 years ago they remained almost completely isolated from the rest of the world until the 18th century (see pages 22–25). Seafarers in Indonesia and New Guinea certainly knew about Australia for hundreds, even thousands, of years before the first European, the Dutch navigator Willem Janszoon (c.1570–1630), sighted the continent's north coast in 1606. Through these contacts dogs, the Aborigines' only domesticated animal, were introduced to Australia. Other developments in the outside world, such as metalworking, pottery and farming remained unknown. Other Dutch navigators subsequently charted much of the north and west coasts of Australia, found them inhospitable and no attempts were made to settle. In 1770 the British captain James Cook (1728–79) explored the green and fertile east coast of Australia and discovered the harbour of Botany Bay. Cook thought it seemed a promising place to found a settlement and claimed it for Great Britain.

Colonization by convicts

Soon after Cook returned home to announce his discoveries, Britain's North American colonies rebelled and gained independence by 1783. The British government had been in the habit of transporting convicted criminals to America. Now that this could no longer be done, Britain's prisons started to overflow. In 1787 the government decided to send a fleet of 11 ships, with 548 male and 188 female prisoners and 294 guards to found the colony of New South Wales at Botany Bay. This expedition has gone down in Australian history as the 'First Fleet'. Botany Bay turned out to be too exposed, but just round the coast the colonists found the magnificent Sydney Harbour and built the settlement there. Over the next 60 years 162,000 men, women and children would be sentenced to be transported to Australia, often for offences as minor as stealing a loaf of bread. One such was Elizabeth Powley, an unemployed 22-year-old woman who was transported with the First Fleet, who had originally been sentenced to hang for stealing two shillings' worth of bacon and butter. Social activists were also transported, such as the Tolpuddle Martyrs, a group of Dorset farm labourers who founded the world's first trade union.

The early years were difficult, but under the direction of the governor Arthur Philip (1738–1814), the colony soon became self-sufficient in food. Life for the convict settlers was tough. Convicts were harnessed to ploughs like horses and they pulled the trucks on Australia's first railroad. Convicts sometimes rebelled to try to get better conditions but any resistance was punished by a severe flogging or worse. When a group of Irish convicts rebelled at Castle Hill in 1804, 20 were shot on the spot, eight were hanged later and dozens flogged. 'Incorrigible' convicts were sent to punishment centres in Tasmania and remote Norfolk Island. Few convicts tried to escape. Most of those that did were killed by the Aborigines or starved to death because they did not know how to survive in the bush. Some escapees survived for a time as bushrangers (bandits), stealing food, horses and weapons from the settlements.

The First Fleet was a well managed expedition; only 3 percent of the convicts died on the six months' voyage to Australia. Those who came after were less fortunate, as the ships' captains were more interested in making a profit than in the welfare of the convicts. Death rates were far higher for men (1 in 8 died on average) than for women

Britain's first tentative steps on Australian soil, depicted in the illustration The Founding of the Settlement of Port Jackson at Botany Bay *(1799) by Thomas Gosse.*

Map showing the penal settlement of Australia by Great Britain up to 1868.

(only 1 in 28 died), because the women could get better food by having sex with the sailors. One of the worst voyages was that of the Second Fleet. Sixteen people died before the fleet even left port and of the 1006 convicts who sailed, 267 died at sea and dozens more bodies were found in the ship when it landed. Convicts were kept locked in cages below decks for the whole voyage, often chained together, with no hygiene facilities. Meagre food rations of salted beef, hardtack and water left the transportees prey to scurvy. In the end the government had to offer captains a bonus of £4 a head (on top of the £18 a head for transporting them) for every convict who got there alive to reduce the terrible death rates.

A prosperous Australia – at a price

As word got about that there was good pasture in Australia, British settlers started emigrating to Australia voluntarily to start sheep farms. They were further encouraged by generous government land grants, subsidised passages and unpaid convict labour. Wool became a major export and the colony began to prosper. Because of its fine harbour, Sydney quickly developed into an important port and base for whaling and exploration of the southern oceans. Some convicts were sentenced to transportation for life but most were deported for lesser periods. However, few of them took the opportunity to return home. Most transportees had turned to crime only because they were destitute and had nothing to go home to. Members of the garrison, such as John Macarthur (1766–1834) who led the development of the colony's wool trade, decided to stay too. By 1815 the British population of Australia had reached 15,000. In the 1820s and 1830s new colonies were founded in Tasmania, Victoria, South Australia and Western Australia, and settlement also began to expand away from the coast into the interior. By 1851, when the population reached 400,000, free settlers far outnumbered convicts. The government finally stopped transporting convicts in 1868, partly because the free settlers complained about their colonies being used as a dumping ground for British criminals.

An 1864 cartoon entitled 'Colonists and Convicts' shows a rugged, hard-working free settler objecting to the British authorities sending any more convicts to Australia.

The negative impact of British settlement on Australia was considerable. Relations with the Aborigines were poor from the start. The local Aborigines shouted 'warra warra' at the British as they rowed ashore in January 1788. The British thought it was a welcome, it really meant 'go away!' The idea that the Aborigines had a prior claim to Australia never occurred to the British. Because they had no permanent buildings, used only simple technology and had no rulers or government institutions, the British considered the Aborigines to be living in a state of nature, that is they were seen as being little better than animals. Therefore, the British decided, Australia was *terra nullius*, or 'no man's land'. No attempt was made to consider Aboriginal land claims or to negotiate with them. Aborigines retaliated against the

WESTERN
AUSTRALI

Perth
Fremantle

Albany

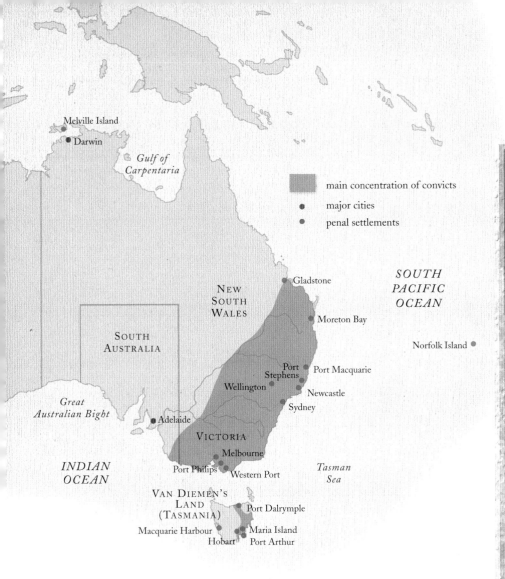

main concentration of convicts

major cities

penal settlements

TIMELINE

1606 Willem Janszoon becomes the first European to sight Australia

1707 James Cook claims Australia for Great Britain

1787 The 'First Fleet' leaves Britain for Australia with 1000 convicts and guards

1788 Sydney is founded as the first penal colony in Australia

1790 Pemulwy leads Aboriginal resistance to the British

1794 Sheep rearing for wool begins in Australia

1803 Penal colony founded on Van Diemen's Land (Tasmania)

1804 Castle Hill convict rebellion suppressed

1827 Penal colony founded at Perth, Western Australia

1851 Flood of free immigrants after gold is discovered in New South Wales

1868 Britain ends transportation of convicts to Australia

British settlers by stealing their livestock and burning crops and property. The settlers responded by organising 'nigger drives' to hunt down the Aborigines and massacre them. In Tasmania, settlers completely exterminated the Aborigines. Aboriginal numbers were also depleted by epidemics of European diseases. Major environmental changes also resulted from the introduction of agriculture. Overgrazing by millions of introduced sheep, cattle and rabbits turned vast areas of grassland into semi-desert.

Until the early 20th century Australians considered themselves to be essentially transplanted British. Though adapted to a warmer and sunnier climate, their way of life and culture remained fundamentally British. However, the convict and working class origins of so many of the original settlers led to social egalitarianism and a lack of deference to authority. The experience of pioneer life has also contributed to a culture that celebrates masculinity and comradeship, known as 'mateship'; ironically Australians are now among the most urbanized people in the world. In 1901 Britain united its Australian colonies to form the self-governing Commonwealth of Australia (fully independent 1931), but the defining event in the creation of a true Australian national identity was the First World War (1914–18), when heavy casualties incurred in the course of futile offensives such as the Gallipoli landings led to a lessening of respect for Britain and its institutions.

The Highland Clearances
1745–1886

The Highlands of Scotland are today a magnet for lovers of wild and unpopulated landscapes. Few modern visitors realize, however, that the 'natural' wilderness that so enthralls them is the product of a mass emigration less than 200 years ago known as the Clearances, which saw whole communities uprooted in the name of agricultural modernization.

Before the Act of Union with England in 1707 emigration from Scotland was limited. The most popular destinations for Scots emigrants were the Baltic, for its commercial opportunities, and Ulster (Northern Ireland), for land. Scotland's own attempts at founding colonies, in Nova Scotia in the early 17th century and at Darien in Panama in 1698–9, were failures. Scots then, as now, had mixed feelings about the union, but they welcomed the free access it gave them to England's growing colonial empire and emigration began to increase.

The changing face of the Highlands

At first, there were few Highlanders among the emigrants. In the early 18th century, the Highlands was an area where government authority was weak. The area was dominated by semi-autonomous clan chieftains, who had rights of private jurisdiction over their lands and maintained private armies, which they used to wage war on rival clans. Clans were cohesive societies, united by loyalty to the chief and common ancestry. There was little pressure on Highlanders to emigrate. Junior clan members were tenants of the chiefs and owed them military service. Clan chiefs thus had every interest in maximizing the number of their tenants because the more they had, the larger the clan's army, and the more influential and powerful the chief. For this reason, many chiefs actively recruited landless men, who adopted the clan surname to maintain the fiction of shared descent. In 1745 the clan chiefs supported the exiled prince Charles Edward Stuart ('Bonnie Prince Charlie'; 1720–88) in a doomed attempt to overthrow the reigning Hanoverian dynasty and put his father James (1688–1766) on the British throne. After the rising was crushed at the Battle of Culloden in 1746 the government suppressed the clan system.

The Battle of Culloden on 16 April 1746 snuffed out all hopes of a Jacobite restoration and precipitated the suppression of the Highland clans, culminating in the Clearances.

It was this defeat that led directly to the Clearances. The Clearances were actually part of a wider process of commercialization that transformed agriculture throughout western Europe in the early modern period, and resulted in millions of peasants being forced off the land. Highland landowners were well aware of these developments but the social and political circumstances of the Highlands did not favour their adoption until after 1745. Deprived of their autonomy, clan chiefs rejected their traditional responsibilities to junior clan members and became simply ordinary landowners, determined to raise the maximum possible income from their estates. The first tenants to go were the tacksmen.

Thurso

Wick

DURNESS 1841

STRATHNAVER 1814

Stornoway

SUTHERLAND 1812–15, 1819–20

KILDONAN 1813

LEWIS 1827, 1841, 1851–61

Golspie

STRATHCARRON 1841–5

HARRIS 1839

Kildermorie

STRATHCONON 1840–8

Elgin

NORTH UIST 1838, 1849–81

Inverness

SKYE 1790, 1794, 1825, 1840–83

STRATHGLASS 1790, 1803

SOUTH UIST 1793, 1802–03, 1849

Aberdeen

Kingussie

GLENELG 1849

BARRA 1851

RUM 1826–28

KNOYDART 1783

Fort William

RANNOCH 1831–81

COLL 1841–81

ARDNAMURCHAN 1828–86

N. BALLACHULISH 1804–62

BREADALBANE 1831–41

TIREE 1841–81

MULL 1821, 1826, 1840

GLEN ORCHY 1831–41

Oban

Perth

Inverary

ARGYLL 1831–81

Dumbarton

Edinburgh

ISLAY 1804–62

KINTYRE 1804–62

Glasgow

ARRAN 1828–86

Campbeltown

over 50 percent Gaelic-speaking in 1881

area of the Highland Land War 1882–8

TIREE 1841–81 major clearance with date

Map showing the major Highland Clearances during the 18th and 19th centuries.

Tacksmen were clan gentry who acted as the chieftain's military lieutenants, leasing land (tacks) from the chief and subletting it at a higher rate to peasant farmers who served under him in wartime. Now the days of private warfare were over, tacksmen could be dispensed with as unnecessary middlemen and were forced out by steep rent rises. Many emigrated to the North American colonies and often persuaded their tenants to go with them by offering freehold land for all. North Carolina, which had a Scots governor, was the most popular destination for Highlanders before the American Revolution broke out in 1776. This wholesale emigration was not encouraged either by landowners, who resented the loss of rents, or the government, which feared the loss of Highland recruits for the army. After American independence, the government changed its mind and began to encourage emigration to Canada, whose sparse population made it vulnerable to American attack. This paid off during the War of 1812, when local forces decisively defeated the American attempt to conquer Canada.

The introduction of the Cheviot, a specialized breed of sheep with high quality wool, to the Highlands in 1765 provided a further stimulus to emigration. In the later years of the 18th century landowners began to restructure their estates to create large single tenant sheep farms. This led to the widespread eviction of farming tenants and their resettlement in planned villages, mostly on the coast, where they were expected to make a living from crofting, fishing and kelping (making fertilizer from potassium-rich seaweed). George Granville Leveson-Gower, 1st Duke of Sutherland (1758–1833), became the most reviled figure of the Clearances when he removed almost the entire population of eastern Sutherland, some 10,000 people, to villages on the coast between 1812 and 1820, leaving the interior of the county a depopulated wilderness for sheep. Landlords faced frequent resistance from tenants. A celebrated incident, 'the Year of the Sheep' in 1792, saw troops deployed to Kildermorie in Easter Ross to stop tenants driving the landowner's sheep off the hills. Widespread discontent with the new arrangements meant that the flow of emigrants continued. Those who could not afford to emigrate began to migrate instead to the Lowlands to find work in the growing industrial towns.

The landlord-driven emigration that has made the Clearances so notorious in Highland folk memory began only after the end of the Napoleonic Wars in 1815. Imports of cheaper fertilizers from Chile made kelping uneconomic. Wool prices began to fall because of competition from Australia. As they watched their rental income dwindle, Highland landowners decided that emigration might not be such a bad thing after all. Landlords and colonial organizations introduced various schemes to help surplus tenants to emigrate. Varying degrees of compulsion were used: tenants were often burned out of their homes. In the 1860s a new wave of Clearances began as landlords cashed in on the fashion for deer-stalking. After popular protests, known as the Highland Land War, the government introduced reforms to give crofters greater security of tenure in 1886 but it was the 1920s before the tide of emigration finally began to slacken. The exact number of emigrants from the Highlands is hard to determine. Over 20,000 are believed to have left before 1815 and Highlanders formed a high proportion of the 1.8 million Scots who emigrated in the following century.

Scottish emigration to Australia and Canada

The main destinations for Highland emigrants were Australia and Canada. From the late 1830s land sales in Australia were used to fund the emigration of 5000 Highlanders to New South Wales. The passage of another 5000 to South Australia, Victoria and Tasmania was funded by the Highland and Island Emigration Society in the 1850s. Highlanders emigrated in family- or community-based groups hoping to transplant their communal way of life to a new country. Emigration schemes usually allowed families and communities to emigrate together; persuading Highlanders to emigrate would have been difficult otherwise, but when they arrived in Australia settlement agencies made no attempt to keep communities together by making collective land grants. Instead, Highland settlers were widely dispersed and, lacking supportive communities, their Gaelic culture and language did not long survive.

Because it was accessible and relatively inexpensive to reach, Canada was the most important destination for Highland emigrants after the American colonies won independence. The largest settlements were in southern Ontario, especially Glengarry County, Prince Edward Island, and on Cape Breton Island and around Pictou and Antigonish in Nova Scotia. The Highlanders struggled with the harsh Canadian winters and had many difficult years before their settlements began to prosper. Because Highlanders who emigrated to Canada settled in community groups and later helped finance the emigration of family members who had been left behind (a process known as chain migration), they formed enduring Gaelic-speaking communities there. Even today it is claimed that there are more speakers of Gaelic in Canada than in Scotland itself, though none speak it as a first language. Though Gaelic was in decline in Ontario by the 1880s and Cape Breton by the 1930s, Gaelic musical traditions remain strong, as do other manifestations of the modern Scottish Highland identity, such as Highland games.

TIMELINE

1745–6 Highland clans support Charles Edward Stuart's Jacobite rising

1752 Earliest Clearances for sheep farming, in SW Highlands

1765 Cheviot sheep introduced to the Highlands

1772 First emigrant ships leave West Highlands for America

1792 The 'Year of the Sheep': popular resistance to the Clearances in Easter Ross

1812–20 Duke of Sutherland evicts 10,0000 tenants

1825 Kelping industry collapses

1837 Emigration societies finance Highland emigration to Australia

1848–9 Potato blight causes famine in the Highlands

1860s Fashion for deer-stalking leads to more Clearances

1882–8 The Highland Land War: popular protests lead to the end of the Clearances

A bronze statue in Sutherland, cast in 2003, commemorates the many people of this region who were forced to emigrate.

The *Mfecane*
1816–28

The rise of the Zulu empire under its warlike king Shaka (r.1816–28) sent shock waves throughout southern Africa, triggering mass migrations of refugee peoples. Known as the *Mfecane* ('to be weak from hunger'), these upheavals completely rearranged the pattern of settlement in southern Africa and left vast areas depopulated.

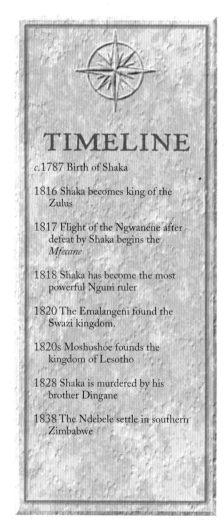

TIMELINE

*c.*1787 Birth of Shaka

1816 Shaka becomes king of the Zulus

1817 Flight of the Ngwanene after defeat by Shaka begins the *Mfecane*

1818 Shaka has become the most powerful Nguni ruler

1820 The Emalangeni found the Swazi kingdom.

1820s Moshoshoe founds the kingdom of Lesotho

1828 Shaka is murdered by his brother Dingane

1838 The Ndebele settle in southern Zimbabwe

The Zulu belong to the Nguni, the most southerly branch of the Bantu-speaking peoples. As a result of the *Mfecane* the Nguni are now widespread throughout southern Africa, inhabiting Zimbabwe, Malawi, Mozambique, Swaziland, Zambia, Tanzania and South Africa. However, in the late 18th century their homeland lay between the Drakensberg Mountains and the Indian Ocean in the KwaZulu–Natal and Eastern Cape provinces of South Africa. Cattle-herding pastoralists, the Nguni were divided into dozens of clans, one of which was the Zulu. The Zulu originated in the late 17th century under a chieftain called Mandalela, who settled with a small band of followers on lands along the White Umfolozi River in northern Natal. The Zulu took their name – in their own language amaZulu, meaning 'People of the Heavens' – from Zulu, their second chief.

Towards the end of the 18th century, the Zulu came under the domination of Dingiswayo (*c.*1780–1818), the chief of the powerful Mthethwa clan. Dingiswayo had built up the power of his clan by attacking neighbouring clans and forcing them to pay tribute in the form of cattle, as well as obliging them to send an annual levy of warriors to fight in his army. It was as a conscript soldier in Dingiswayo's army that Shaka first came to prominence. Born around 1787, Shaka was the illegitimate son of the Zulu chief Senzangakona ka Jama (*c.*1762–1816). After an unpromising childhood, Shaka grew up to be a tall, powerfully built man with a genuine love of battle. Impressed by his abilities, Dingiswayo appointed him chief of the Zulus in 1816, following the death of his father. Dingiswayo gave Shaka free rein to assert his authority over neighbouring clans provided he got a cut of the spoils. Within a year Shaka had increased the size of the Zulu army from 350 to 2000. When Dingiswayo was killed by the rival Ndwandwe clan in 1818, Shaka took over leadership of the Mthethwa. The following year he defeated the Ndwandwe and extended his rule over most of northern Natal. The size of Shaka's army increased tenfold as warriors flocked to share in his success.

A different mode of warfare

The secret of Shaka's success was a new style of fighting. Traditionally, the Bantu peoples fought at long range using throwing assegais and had little formal military organization. Shaka developed new and deadly close-quarters fighting techniques using stabbing assegais. Fierce discipline and drill were used to train warriors to use devastatingly effective encircling tactics. He also introduced a regimental system to act as a focus for his warriors' loyalty and fighting spirit. Shaka also brought a new ruthlessness to warfare. Not content with submission and tribute, Shaka set out to destroy his enemies and victory in battle was followed by the massacre of men, women and children alike. It was an approach to war that was calculated to spread terror. Many clans rushed to submit to Shaka before he attacked them, while those that resisted and lost had to flee for their lives. However, southern Africa was densely populated so that one clan could not move without first dislodging another. Refugee Nguni clans migrated north and west (the British Cape Colony blocked clans fleeing south), setting the neighbouring Sotho and

An attacking Zulu formation, of the kind devised by Shaka, just before the Battle of Isandlwana in 1879, in which the Zulu inflicted a shock defeat on the British.

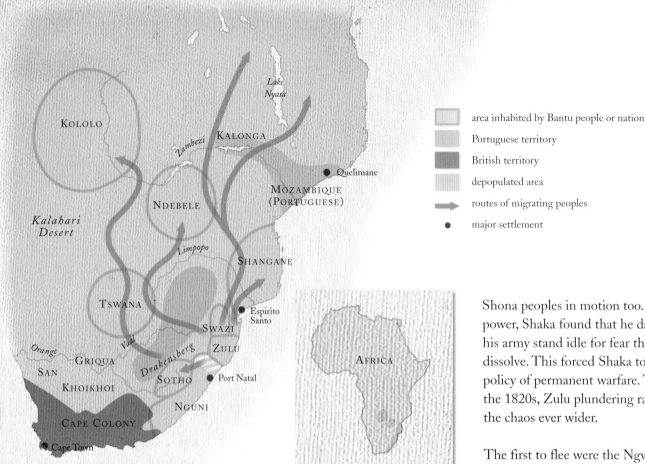

The displacement of southern African peoples and the kingdoms that emerged as a result of the Mfecane *from around 1816 onwards.*

Shona peoples in motion too. Having won power, Shaka found that he dared not let his army stand idle for fear that it would dissolve. This forced Shaka to adopt a policy of permanent warfare. Throughout the 1820s, Zulu plundering raids spread the chaos ever wider.

The first to flee were the Ngwanene. Weakened after a defeat by the Zulu in 1817, they were evicted from their lands by the Ndwandwes. The homeless Ngwanene attacked their neighbours, the Hlubi who in their turn fled across the Drakensbergs and descended on the unsuspecting Sotho peoples in the basin of the Vaal river. The Ngwanene had no chance to settle on the lands of the Hlubi before Shaka attacked them again, forcing them too to flee across the Drakensbergs. The displaced Nguni clans plundered their way through the Sotho lands, scattering clans in all directions, leaving their own trails of death and destruction behind them as they sought new homelands.

New chiefdoms emerge

Many of these refugee clans united under the leadership of a formidable woman chieftain called Mantatisi. By 1823 she had accumulated a disorganized horde of 50,000 followers. Moving constantly to find grazing for its thousands of cattle, the horde migrated aimlessly southwest towards the Cape Colony. Hundreds of refugees died daily from a lack of food and water. Mantatisi's horde was finally turned back by the Griquas (or Bastaards), a mixed-race people descended from Afrikaner settlers and the Khoikhoi. As the horde retreated north, it gradually broke up as more and more refugees died or fell behind out of exhaustion. Around the same time the Hlubi and Ngwanene accidentally blundered into one another, and in a five-day battle the Hlubi were annihilated. The Ngwanene then headed southeast, close to the borders of Cape Colony, where a British force destroyed them in 1828 after mistaking them for an invading Zulu army.

By the late 1820s the survivors of the *Mfecane* were beginning to coalesce to form new clans and chiefdoms. The most successful of these was created by a minor Sotho chief called Moshoeshoe (1786–1870). Displaced by Mantatisi's horde, Moshoeshoe led his clan to safety at Thaba Bosiu ('the Mountain of the Night'), an easily defended plateau in the Drakensberg Mountains. Other refugees from the *Mfecane* followed, seeking Moshoeshoe's protection. By copying their military tactics Moshoeshoe was able to defeat attacks by the Zulus and expand his territories in the Drakensbergs to create the kingdom of Lesotho. Faced with Boer aggression, Moshoeshoe agreed to his kingdom becoming a British protectorate in 1869: it regained its independence in 1966. A second kingdom to emerge from the chaos of the *Mfecane* was Swaziland, founded in 1820 by the Emalengeni people who migrated out of Natal to escape from Shaka. Their chief, Sobhuza (*c.*1780–1836), fended off Zulu attacks by adopting their military system, which also allowed him to extend his rule over neighbouring Nguni and Sotho clans.

Another nation created at this time was the Shangane (also known as the Gaza empire). This was founded by Soshangane, one of the few Ndwandwe leaders to escape Shaka's vengeance, who migrated north with a small band of followers and conquered the Tonga people of southern Mozambique. Towards the end of his reign Shaka quarrelled with one of his generals, Mzilikaze (1790–1868), who took his regiment north into Transvaal, founding the Ndebele nation. Driven out of Transvaal by the Afrikaners, the Ndebele headed further north, crossing the Limpopo River into southern Zimbabwe in 1838, where they destroyed the kingdom of the Rozwi, a Shona people. The region where the Ndebele finally settled is known as Matabeleland, and they remain the largest ethnic group in Zimbabwe after the Shona. A Sotho clan, the Kololo, migrated even further north, conquering the Lozi of Zambia around 1840.

Shaka eventually alienated the Zulu by his increasingly tyrannical rule and in 1828 he was murdered by his half-brother Dingane (*c.*1795–1840), who ended the constant warfare. By this time anything up to two million people had died from the ravages of war and starvation. In Natal, the land was empty of human habitation for over 100 miles (160 km) south of the Zulu border on the Tugela River. Across the Drakensberg Mountains, the devastation was even more complete. Thousands of square miles from the Orange River to the Limpopo River 600 miles (960 km) to the northeast were almost completely depopulated. This created a vacuum that opened the way for Europeans to extend their domination throughout the whole of southern Africa from the 1840s onwards (see pages 204–207).

An image of Shaka from a European traveller's account of his journeys in southern Africa, published shortly after the renowned Zulu king's death.

The Great Trek of the Boers 1835–40

Until the advent of black majority rule in 1994, South Africa was dominated by the Boers, or Afrikaners, white Europeans of mainly Dutch descent. Arriving at the Cape of Good Hope in the 17th century, the Boers colonized southern Africa in a series of migrations culminating in the Great Trek (1835–40).

The greatest threat faced by seafarers in the age of sail was not shipwreck or piracy but scurvy, a debilitating and ultimately fatal disease caused by vitamin C deficiency due to a lack of fresh fruit and vegetables. On the long six to eight months' voyages from Europe to the spice islands in the East Indies, scurvy frequently accounted for half of a ship's crew. In 1652 the Dutch East India Company sent Jan van Riebeeck (1619–77) to found the colony of Cape Town at Table Bay, near the Cape of Good Hope, to act as a staging post where its ships could take on fresh supplies. After initial conflict, the local Khoikhoi ('Hottentot') pastoralists submitted to the sovereignty of the East India Company in 1659.

The first settlers were employees of the East India Company, but in 1679 the first free Dutch settlers arrived and began farming wheat and livestock as private citizens. There was a shortage of women in the early years, so many Dutch men married Khoikhoi women. Because of their African blood, the descendants of these marriages, known as Bastaards, were shunned by later settlers. Local Khoikhoi were also employed as labourers and farmhands and large numbers of slaves were imported from other parts of Africa. Most Dutch settlers belonged to the Calvinist Reformed Church. Isolated from the European cultural mainstream, education rarely extended beyond basic literacy and Bible study. The settlers developed a narrow religiosity, which used the Bible to justify racial segregation and the superiority of the white man over the black. By 1795 the colony had a population of 15,000 Europeans, and as many slaves, and had expanded inland to encompass over 100,000 square miles (259,000 sq km). Dutch born in the colony had by this time begun calling themselves 'Afrikaners' (Africans): the alternative name for Dutch South Africans, Boers, is derived from the Dutch word for 'farmer'.

The Landing of Jan van Riebeeck, 6th April 1652 *by Charles Bell (1852) records the moment that white settlers first set foot on the Cape of Good Hope.*

Trekboers venture into the interior

The expansion of the colony inland was ~~accomplished by pioneers known~~ as *trekboers* ('migrating farmers'). Dutch law required the equal division of farms between male heirs.

Because Boer families were large, this would have resulted in uneconomic smallholdings so it was usual for the elder brother to buy out the others to keep the family farm intact. The typical *trekboer* was a younger son who had kitted himself out with wagon, a team of oxen, a bull, a flock of sheep and, hopefully, a wife, and headed for the frontier to find a site to set up his own farm. Local Khoikhoi would provide his labour force and cattle. Title to land was easily acquired. A *trekboer* could claim a farm of up to 6000 acres (2428 ha) on payment of a small annual fee in recognition of the East India Company's sovereignty. The cheapness of land did not encourage good husbandry. If an area became overgrazed, it was easy for a *trekboer* to move on. This led to an insatiable land hunger.

Frontier life had its risks. Hyenas, leopards and wild dogs took many sheep and cattle; so too did San (Bushman) and Bantu raiders. Apart from providing magistrates and pastors, the Company took little interest in the Boers, who therefore had to organize their own defences. The able-bodied men of a district formed mounted columns called commandos to carry out reprisal raids across the frontier. Religion and the need for communal defence made Boer society cohesive, self-reliant and independent-minded. Also prominent on the frontier were the Bastaards (or Basters), who did not fit in with the race-conscious society of the settled areas. The Bastaards lived a lawless existence, raiding white settlements on one side of the frontier and the Bantu on the other. In around 1800 the Bastaards changed their name to Griqua at the request of embarrassed missionaries.

A print of 1818 showing trekboers journeying through mountainous terrain near Plettenberg Bay in the eastern Cape.

In 1794, the Netherlands was occupied by revolutionary France, prompting the British to occupy Cape Town to prevent its use by the French navy. Britain acquired formal

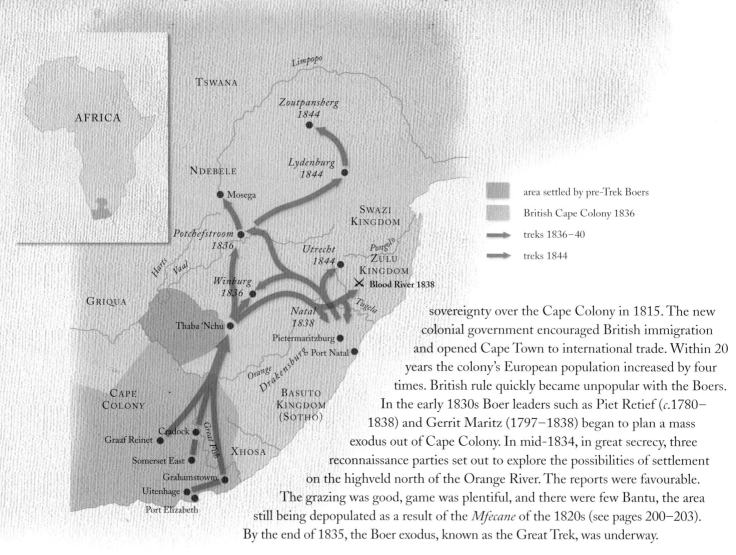

sovereignty over the Cape Colony in 1815. The new colonial government encouraged British immigration and opened Cape Town to international trade. Within 20 years the colony's European population increased by four times. British rule quickly became unpopular with the Boers. In the early 1830s Boer leaders such as Piet Retief (c.1780–1838) and Gerrit Maritz (1797–1838) began to plan a mass exodus out of Cape Colony. In mid-1834, in great secrecy, three reconnaissance parties set out to explore the possibilities of settlement on the highveld north of the Orange River. The reports were favourable. The grazing was good, game was plentiful, and there were few Bantu, the area still being depopulated as a result of the *Mfecane* of the 1820s (see pages 200–203). By the end of 1835, the Boer exodus, known as the Great Trek, was underway.

Map showing the treks undertaken by the Afrikaners of Cape Colony, and the resulting Boer republics (with their date of foundation).

A hard road to shortlived independence

It is often claimed that the British abolition of slavery throughout their empire in 1834 was the main cause of the Great Trek, but this was only one among an accumulation of grievances. Boers did not like the British administration's liberal attitude to the Khoikhoi, or its encouragement of missionaries who taught Africans that they were equal with Europeans in God's eyes. They also realized that the administration's commitment to achieving peaceful and stable borders with the Bantu would threaten their freedom to expand. New laws of land tenure also made what land was available more expensive to acquire. These measures gradually convinced the Boers that their accustomed independence was doomed.

A permanent wagon laager memorial was set up at the site of the Battle of Blood River to commemorate the Boer victory over the Zulu.

Most of the trekkers came from the eastern Cape districts of Uitenhage, Somerset East, Cradock, Graaf Reinet and Albany. In all about 15,000 Boers and several thousand free black servants left Cape Colony between 1835 and 1840. The Great Trek was not a single column of wagons. Trekkers left in small groups, every family with a handful of covered wagons full of provisions, tools, gunpowder, clothes and furniture, accompanied by the flocks of sheep and herds of cattle, which were their most valuable possessions. Sometimes parties joined up to form trains of 50–200 wagons, but the need to find sufficient grazing for their livestock meant that trekkers soon went their own ways again. For security livestock was penned for the night in a wagon laager, which was often reinforced with thorn bushes.

The trekkers rendezvoused at Thaba 'Nchu, on the highveld about 100 miles (160 km) north of the Orange River. Yet political disagreements caused the trekkers to split up again. Some groups settled the highveld between the Orange River and the Vaal River, while others continued and settled north of the Vaal or crossed the Drakensberg Mountains into Natal. Three Boer republics were founded: the Orange Free State, Transvaal, and Natalia. The Boer trekkers met with fierce resistance from the Ndebele in Transvaal and the Zulu in Natal. The Ndebele were quickly expelled from Transvaal with little loss to the Boers. The Zulu king Dingane lured Piet Retief, the leader of the Boer trekkers, to Natal for negotiations, then murdered him and his party in February 1838. Dingane then proceeded to attack Boer settlements in Natal, killing over 300 Boers and 200 of their African servants. The Boer position was saved when a commando of 470 men under Andries Pretorius (1798–1853) defeated the Zulu at the Battle of Blood River in December 1838. Boer firepower won the day after the Zulu attacked Pretorius' wagon laager: over 3000 Zulu were killed. The Boers suffered no fatalities.

This victory did not win the Boers freedom from the British, however. In 1843 the British annexed Natal and many of the Boers fled to Transvaal. The British at first recognized the independence of the Orange Free State and Transvaal. The discovery of great mineral wealth and the strategic need to forestall German colonial ambitions led the British to conquer the Boer republics in 1899–1902 and incorporate them, with Cape Colony and Natal, in the Union of South Africa. British peace terms were generous, allowing the Boers to dominate South Africa and, after independence (1931), impose the apartheid system of racial segregation in 1948.

TIMELINE

1652 The Dutch East India Company found Cape Town

1795 Cape Town occupied by British

1815 Britain acquires sovereignty over the Cape

1834 Slavery is abolished in the British empire

1835–40 The Great Trek. Boer republics founded in Natal, Transvaal and Orange Free State

1838 Zulus defeated by the Boers at the Battle of Blood River

1843 Britain annexes Natal

1899–1902 Anglo-Boer War: Britain conquers the Boer republics

1931 South Africa becomes independent of Britain

1948 Apartheid system introduced

The Trail of Tears
1830–42

The expansion of the United States across the North American continent was accompanied by the wholesale displacement of the native Indian nations from their homelands. One of the most notorious incidents was the 'Trail of Tears', the forcible removal under conditions of great hardship of the so-called Five Civilized Tribes of the south in 1832–42.

One of the grievances contributing to the outbreak of the American Revolution had been the British Proclamation Line of 1763, a notional western boundary just on the far side of the Appalachian Mountains, beyond which white settlement was forbidden in the interests of maintaining peaceful relations with the Indians. Even during the colonial period, this demarcation line was largely ignored in practice, in favour of an open frontier policy. After the war, settlers began to push across the mountains, causing new wars with the Indians as they tried to defend their territories. The US government sought to resolve these conflicts, and appease settler opinion, by using a mixture of force, bribery and negotiation to persuade Indian nations to make land cession treaties. To give legality to these coercive treaties, the US government formally recognized the sovereignty of Indian nations over their lands. Unfortunately, the land hunger of settlers and speculators was insatiable and no treaty was honoured for very long before the Indians would be coerced into ceding yet more land.

A contemporary engraving showing distribution of rations to columns of destitute Indians during one of the forcible resettlements of the 1830s.

Alongside the policy of forcing the Indians to cede their lands was a humanitarian policy of 'civilizing' the Indians in preparation for what was considered to be their inevitable assimilation into American society. These efforts were especially successful among the southern Cherokee, Choctaw, Chickasaw, Creek and Seminole nations, known as the 'Five Civilized Tribes'. The Cherokee went the furthest in adopting the white man's ways, believing that this would earn them respect as a civilized nation and protect them against further encroachment by white settlers. The Cherokee adopted European farming methods, set up grist and timber mills, lived in European style houses, wore European clothing, and converted to Christianity. The Cherokee even devised their own alphabet. In 1827 they adopted a written constitution modelled on the Constitution of the United States. This proclaimed the Cherokee an independent nation with sovereignty over its peoples' lands in North Carolina, Georgia, Alabama and Tennessee. The federal government had 'solemnly guaranteed' the Cherokee their remaining lands in 1798, but this conflicted with a promise made to Georgia in 1802 to extinguish all remaining Indian land titles in the state in return for it giving up land claims in the west.

Removal to 'Indian territory'

There was considerable resentment in Georgia that the government had not fulfilled its promise. Arguing that the Cherokee constitution would create a state within a state, Georgia's state legislature announced in 1828 that all Indians within its borders would be brought under its jurisdiction and it demanded the government remove them. Other southern states quickly made similar declarations. To prevent a constitutional crisis, President Andrew

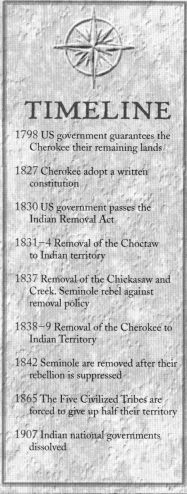

TIMELINE

1798 US government guarantees the Cherokee their remaining lands

1827 Cherokee adopt a written constitution

1830 US government passes the Indian Removal Act

1831–4 Removal of the Choctaw to Indian territory

1837 Removal of the Chickasaw and Creek. Seminole rebel against removal policy

1838–9 Removal of the Cherokee to Indian Territory

1842 Seminole are removed after their rebellion is suppressed

1865 The Five Civilized Tribes are forced to give up half their territory

1907 Indian national governments dissolved

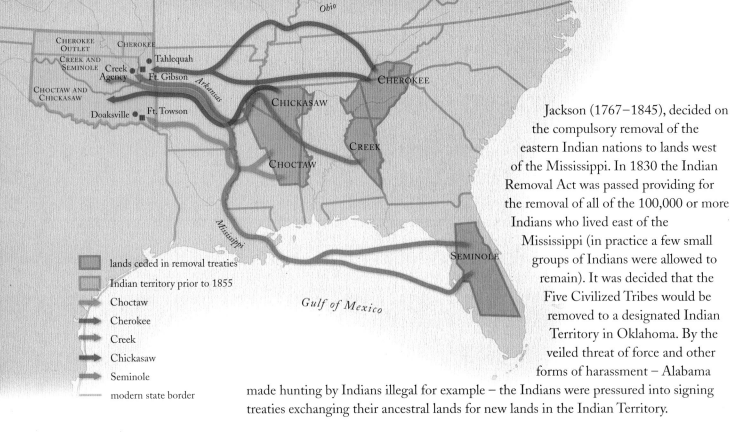

Map labels:
CHEROKEE OUTLET
CHEROKEE
CREEK AND SEMINOLE
Creek Agency
CHOCTAW AND CHICKASAW
Tahlequah
Ft. Gibson
Doaksville
Ft. Towson
Ohio
Arkansas
CHEROKEE
CHICKASAW
CREEK
CHOCTAW
Mississippi
SEMINOLE
Gulf of Mexico

Legend:
■ lands ceded in removal treaties
□ Indian territory prior to 1855
→ Choctaw
→ Cherokee
→ Creek
→ Chickasaw
→ Seminole
---- modern state border

Indian removals from the southeast and Indian Territory, 1830–55.

Jackson (1767–1845), decided on the compulsory removal of the eastern Indian nations to lands west of the Mississippi. In 1830 the Indian Removal Act was passed providing for the removal of all of the 100,000 or more Indians who lived east of the Mississippi (in practice a few small groups of Indians were allowed to remain). It was decided that the Five Civilized Tribes would be removed to a designated Indian Territory in Oklahoma. By the veiled threat of force and other forms of harassment – Alabama made hunting by Indians illegal for example – the Indians were pressured into signing treaties exchanging their ancestral lands for new lands in the Indian Territory.

As part of the treaties, the government agreed to give the Indians financial compensation and undertook to transport and supply them until they were established in their new homes. Small groups of Choctaw, Cherokee and other eastern Indians had already emigrated voluntarily to the Indian Territory and their resettlement had gone well. This was not to be the case with the compulsory removals. The greater numbers involved – about 70,000 – caused confusion: compounded by incompetence and fraud, the Indians suffered great hardship and mortality during their forced migrations.

The first nation to be removed were the Choctaw, migrating the 550 miles (880 km) east in three parties between 1831 and 1834. Travelling by wagon train, the first party left late in the year and 2500 Indians died in severe winter weather. After this experience about 2000 Choctaw refused to leave under any circumstances: their descendants still live in Mississippi. The Chickasaw negotiated a good deal, sold their lands at good prices, invested the proceeds in cattle and slaves, and migrated to Indian Territory in summer 1837, where they settled among the Choctaw. After four years of increasing harassment, the Creek were removed in winter 1837. Some discontented warriors, who had rebelled against their treatment, had captured and burned a riverboat on the Chattahoochee River. This gave President Jackson the excuse to send in troops and remove the Creek without paying them compensation. The destitute Creek arrived in Indian Territory in the middle of one of the coldest winters on record, causing many deaths. Shortly before their removal was due to begin in January 1837, the Seminole rebelled and were only finally suppressed in 1842 after thousands of lives were lost on both sides. Removal took place steadily while the war continued. As groups of Seminole surrendered, they were transported by ship to New Orleans and transferred to river boats for the journey up the Mississippi and Arkansas rivers to the Indian Territory. About 500 evaded capture and remained in Florida.

While the Seminole fought removal in the swamps, the Cherokee successfully challenged the legality of the policy in the US Supreme Court. However, the court's verdict was not enforced, and the removal of the Cherokee was scheduled for June 1838. About 6000 sold up at good prices and left before the deadline, but the majority, about 16,000, adopted a policy of passive resistance and made no preparations to migrate. Troops and militia were sent in and the Cherokee were rounded up at gunpoint and imprisoned in stockades while sufficient wagons were obtained to transport them west. Some Cherokee evaded the round-up and fled to the Great Smoky Mountains in North Carolina, where they were later given a reservation. Food was short and conditions in the crowded stockades were unhygienic. Epidemics of measles, whooping cough and cholera had killed 2500 Cherokee even before they began their 600-mile (960-km) journey to the Indian Territory in the winter of 1838–9. Conditions were so dreadful that the Cherokee described the journey as the 'trail where we cried', now better known as the 'Trail of Tears'. After provisions and personal belongings had been loaded onto the wagons, there was room only for infants and the sick to ride. A few had horses, everyone else had to walk. The journey was made worse by White settlers along the route who overcharged for supplies and often robbed the reluctant migrants. By the time the Cherokee reached their new homes in March, about 1500 had succumbed to disease and exposure.

Further displacement

In the Indian Territory, the Five Civilized Tribes organized national governments modelled on the US federal government. Schools, churches and law courts were built and written law codes were introduced. Literacy, using the alphabet earlier devised by the Cherokee, became widespread. The prairie environment of the Indian Territory was quite different from the woodlands of the east, but the land was good and the Indians established a flourishing agricultural economy and many prosperous small towns grew up as a result.

A late 19th-century political cartoon depicts the proud Cherokee nation as a Gulliver-like figure, tied down and tormented by the Lilliputian hordes of white settlers swarming over its former territory.

The Five Civilized Tribes had been promised their new lands in perpetuity, but by the beginning of the 20th century they had been almost entirely dispossessed. Sandwiched between Union and Confederate states, the Indian Territory was unavoidably drawn into the Civil War. After the war, the federal government declared the Five Civilized Tribes to have been allies of the Confederacy and forced them to give up half of their territory, which was divided up to form reservations for displaced Plains Indians. The Indian Territory was progressively opened up to white settlement and the Indians' national governments were dissolved in 1907 when they were brought under the authority of the newly created state of Oklahoma.

Survivors of the Great Famine
c.1830–1914

Despite the great contribution of Protestant Irish to the foundation of the USA, today's Irish-American identity is overwhelmingly a Catholic one. This is the consequence of mass immigration of Catholic Irish in the 19th century. Irish-American tradition sees these immigrants as victims, refugees from starvation and British oppression, but does this really stand up to examination?

Early emigration from Ireland was certainly mainly motivated by political and religious reasons. The wars and rebellions of the 16th and 17th centuries produced a steady stream of Catholic exiles. Most of them were young men who wanted to continue the fight against England by joining the French and Spanish armies. These Irish soldiers distinguished themselves in several battles. However, in the 18th century, Catholic emigrants were outnumbered by Presbyterian Ulster Scots. Disillusioned with the Anglican establishment and high rents, around 250,000 of them left for Britain's North American colonies.

Despite emigration, Ireland's population grew rapidly thanks to the spread of potato cultivation. In the 50 years before 1841 Ireland's population more than doubled, from around four million to 8.2 million (representing some 20 percent of the total population of the United Kingdom). The potato's high nutritional content and ability to thrive even in wet infertile soils made it an ideal staple crop for poor peasant farmers, who could support a family on the produce of tiny plots. While landowners devoted their best land to grain production and stock rearing, they encouraged peasant farmers to take out tenancies on more and more marginal land. By the 1830s one third of Ireland's population relied on potatoes for 90 percent of their calorie intake.

The scourge of potato blight

In June 1845 potato blight – a fungal infection that causes tubers in the ground to rot – broke out in Belgium and quickly spread across Europe: it reached Ireland in September of that year. The blight caused hardship across Europe but nowhere was so dependent on the potato crop as Ireland. Hunger quickly turned to starvation for millions. In the six years before the potato crop recovered, between 500,000 and one million Irish people died of hunger

TIMELINE

1845 Blight destroys the Irish potato crop

1846 Failure of the potato crop for a second year brings famine to Ireland

1847 British government sets up soup kitchens for famine victims

1848 By this date, emigration and death by famine has reduced the Irish population by over 2 million

1852 The Irish potato crop recovers from the blight

or disease. Wedded to the ideologies of Malthusianism – the theories of the economist Thomas Malthus (1766–1834), who claimed that unchecked population growth would outstrip the food supply – and *laissez-faire* capitalism, the British government did little to save the Irish from starvation. The government believed that overpopulation was the main cause of Ireland's poverty so the famine was seen as a necessary corrective that would lead to a more prosperous country once the population had fallen to a sustainable level. Food aid and a ban on food exports were opposed on free trade grounds, as it was feared that these would undermine prices and put Irish farmers unaffected by the blight out of business and so reduce the country's food production even more.

The famine caused a scramble to emigrate to Britain and America. It was not only starving peasant farmers who left. British poor relief laws made every parish responsible for its own poor. Rather than face financial ruin, many people of modest means working in trade or crafts emigrated. Most emigrants first made their way to Liverpool, the main British west coast port, and sailed from there. The poorer emigrants were exploited by unscrupulous captains who crammed three or four times the numbers of passengers considered safe for an Atlantic voyage into decrepit 'coffin ships'. Many passengers were already malnourished and the poor hygiene and inadequate rations on the worst of these

Irish emigrants arriving in America in the early 1850s, just after the end of the Great Famine, from the painting The Bay and Harbour of New York *(1853–6) by Samuel B. Waugh.*

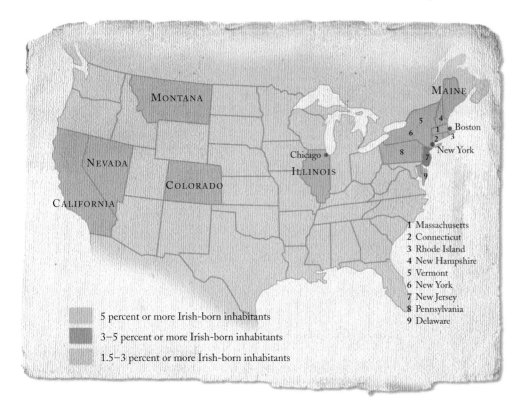

1 Massachusetts
2 Connecticut
3 Rhode Island
4 New Hampshire
5 Vermont
6 New York
7 New Jersey
8 Pennsylvania
9 Delaware

5 percent or more Irish-born inhabitants

3–5 percent or more Irish-born inhabitants

1.5–3 percent or more Irish-born inhabitants

Proportion of settlers of Irish origin in the USA in 1910, by state.

vessels proved too much for some of them. Nearly 2000 emigrants died crossing the Atlantic in 1847 alone. The coffin ships caused a political scandal and after the famine better regulation led to great improvements in conditions on emigrant ships.

If Irish emigrants expected a warm welcome in the land of boundless opportunity, they were to be sorely disappointed. In the 1840s, the USA was still an overwhelmingly Protestant country and there was considerable prejudice against the mainly Catholic immigrants. It is this early sense of exclusion that has made the Irish-American identity primarily a Catholic one –

Protestant Irish immigrants were able to integrate into American society much more easily. Catholic Irish immigrants also found prosperity hard to achieve. While most English, Scots and Protestant Irish immigrants brought capital and professional or industrial skills with them, most Catholic Irish were destitute and unskilled. The great majority of Catholic Irish settlement was concentrated in the industrial cities of New York, Pennsylvania, New Jersey and Massachusetts where there was demand for unskilled labour in factories and construction. The precariousness of their economic position was only too obvious during the American Civil War (1861–5). The Catholic Irish strongly opposed the abolition of slavery and rioted against attempts to conscript them into the Union army, fearing that free blacks would migrate to northern cities and flood the labour market. Because of the need for mutual support, the immigrant community was close knit. This unity eventually gave Irish-Americans considerable political influence in cities where they were numerous, such as New York and Chicago, making them the first immigrant group seriously to challenge 'Anglo-Saxon' Protestant dominance in the USA.

Enforced exiles or economic migrants?

In Irish and, especially, Irish-American tradition the Great Famine has come to be seen as the main cause of the mass emigration and depopulation that Ireland experienced in the 19th century. The immediate demographic impact of the famine was certainly dramatic. Between 1841 and 1851 the Irish population dropped by about 20 percent and in the seven years that the potato blight continued (1845–52) around one and a half million people emigrated from Ireland. Yet mass emigration continued right up until the outbreak of the First World War in 1914 by which time Ireland's population was only 4.4 million. Clearly, the millions of Irish who emigrated after the early 1850s cannot have been refugees from the famine. In fact emigration was already increasing before the famine because the Irish rural textile industry collapsed due to competition from textile manufacturing towns in northern England and Ulster. The impact in terms of lost employment opportunities was considerable. It is also relevant that while Ireland's population as a whole declined, that of the poorest west coast districts actually increased in the 30 years after the famine. Emigration was higher from the fertile east because land there was scarce. By contrast, in the west, because of the mass evictions of destitute tenants during the famine, land was plentiful. By the 1880s land had become more difficult to obtain in the west and emigration increased from that area too. It was, therefore, lack of opportunities in industry and agriculture that were the real reasons for sustained Irish emigration in the 19th century.

There is also the question why such a high proportion of Irish emigrants went to the USA. It seems obvious at first sight that there was a strong desire to escape British oppression: British rule often was harsh and was rarely better than neglectful. Although the famine became a great stimulant to Irish nationalism, a political motive for the majority of emigrants seems unlikely. Both before the famine and throughout the 20th century Britain was the most popular destination for Irish emigrants and even in the second half of the 19th century it was second in popularity only to the USA.

In the 1840s Britain was suffering from a major industrial recession and it was this, more than anything else, that encouraged emigrants to go to America, where employment opportunities were better. Money sent back home by emigrants to their relatives then funded a self-sustaining chain of emigration that continued for the rest of the 19th century.

Though emigration did eventually furnish them with a much improved standard of living, historically many Irish-Americans have interpreted the experience of emigration as involuntary exile, rather than a search for better opportunities. While those who emigrated during the famine had little choice, this is not true of the majority of Irish who emigrated during the 19th century. For most people, emigration is emotionally traumatic; it involves severing close relationships and abandoning elderly relatives to loneliness and poverty. By seeing their experience as a continuation of the earlier tradition of going into exile for political reasons and blaming the British for forcing their decisions on them, Irish emigrants were more easily able to come to terms with intense feelings of guilt and loss.

An 1878 cartoon from the American satirical magazine Puck *highlights the essential difference between immigrants from China, who intended staying only temporarily, and those from Ireland, who meant to put down roots in the United States.*

The Oregon Trail
1832–83

The Oregon Trail, the most famous of the wagon trails of the American West, was pioneered in the 1840s and played a decisive role in the acquisition of the Oregon country for the USA. Though it was not the first of the wagon trails of the West – that was the Santa Fe Trail, opened in 1821 – it was the first to be used for the mass migration of settlers.

The Oregon country lay between the continental divide and the Pacific Ocean, stretching from the northern border of California to the southern border of Russian Alaska at 54°40' north. In the early 19th century the territory was claimed by Russia (until 1824), Great Britain and the USA, but settlement was limited to a few fur trading posts. The 'Oregon Question', as it became known, remained unresolved, but it was agreed that the country would be open for settlers from both nations. This meant that whichever nation succeeded in settling the territory first was likely to establish the best claim to it. The long sea routes from the east coast of the USA and Britain were prohibitively expensive, so settlers were going to have to journey to the Oregon country overland.

Although the pioneer explorers Meriwether Lewis (1774–1809) and William Clark (1770–1838) had passed through in 1806 on their epic transcontinental journey, the British were initially most active in exploring and mapping the area. By the 1820s British and Canadian fur trappers working for the Hudson's Bay Company had established an extensive network of trading posts throughout the Oregon country. American trappers and mountain men were active mainly south of the Columbia River. There were still only a few hundred Europeans, nearly all of them male, living in the vast Oregon country.

'Oregon fever' takes hold

This situation began to change after the US government sent Captain Benjamin Bonneville (1796–1878) to scout for trails in the northwest in 1832–4 under cover of a fur-trapping expedition. Bonneville reached Walla Walla (Washington), near the Columbia River before being turned back by the British, but he had proved that it was possible for a wagon train to cross the continental divide. In 1834 Jason Lee (1803–45), a Methodist minister, founded a mission among the Flathead Indians in the fertile Willamette River Valley (now in Oregon State). Two years later, Marcus Whitman (1802–47) founded a mission among the Cayuse Indians south of Walla Walla. Other missionaries followed. Reports from these missions about the great potential of the Oregon country for farming settlement, and its mild healthy climate, led to the outbreak of 'Oregon Fever' back east. In spring 1843 the first party of around 1000 settlers gathered with 120 wagons and 1800 cattle at Independence, Missouri, for the five

months' trek to the Willamette Valley. The party was guided by Marcus Whitman. The first settlers set up a provisional government and introduced a system of donation land claims, which allowed a married man to claim up to 640 acres (259 ha) of land. By 1846, nearly 7000 people had used the Oregon Trail. Oregon City, founded in 1843, had grown from nothing to a town of 1000 inhabitants in less than three years, and nearby Portland was a village of 100 people. Wagon trains of settlers continued to travel the Oregon Trail until 1883, when the railroad reached Portland, by which time at least 80,000 people had made the journey.

This flood of American settlers increased pressure for a settlement of the Oregon Question. The British wanted to divide the country along the Columbia River. President James Polk (1795–1849) famously threatened '54°40' or fight', which would have cut Canada off from the Pacific Ocean. There was strong talk of America's 'manifest destiny' and sabres were rattled, but without much conviction on either side. The fur trade was in decline and the fast-growing American settlements convinced the British that their position was untenable. In 1846 a compromise was reached that divided the Oregon

In this romanticized scene from a mid-19th century print, a Westward-bound wagon train is shown making the arduous journey through the Rocky Mountains.

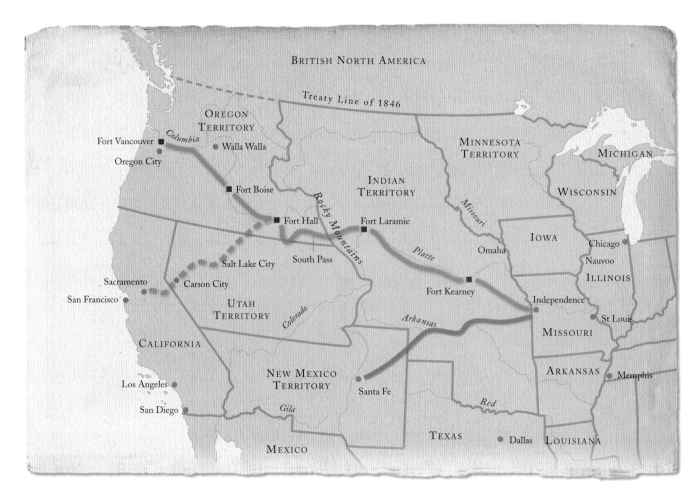

BRITISH NORTH AMERICA

Map showing the route taken by the Oregon, Santa Fe and California trails, which opened up the American West to white settlement.

▬▬▬	Oregon Trail
▪ ▪ ▪	California Trail
▬▬▬	Santa Fe Trail
-------	state/territory borders

country along the 49th parallel. In 1848, the USA formally organized its newly acquired lands into the Oregon Territory, later to be divided into the states of Washington, Oregon and Idaho. The British share would become the Canadian province of British Columbia.

The trail and its hardships

The Oregon Trail began at Independence, which migrants could reach by riverboat along the Missouri River, headed northwest to Fort Kearney (Nebraska), then west along the south bank of the Platte and North Platte Rivers to Fort Laramie (Wyoming). The Rockies were crossed by South Pass, after which the trail headed northwest to Fort Hall (Idaho) and followed the Snake River to Fort Boise, then northwest again to the Columbia River. The last stretch of the trail, along the Columbia River to Fort Vancouver, a former Hudson's Bay Company post, was usually rafted. The total distance was about 2020 miles (3232 km). In a dry year the trail could be done by wagon in four months, in a wet year, more than five months. After a brief rest at Fort Vancouver, the migrants were ferried across the Columbia River and up the Willamette River to Oregon City. Here they would spend the winter before moving up the Willamette Valley in early spring to stake their land claims.

Few of the settlers who used the Oregon Trail in the early days were landless immigrants; most were farming families from the Midwest who already owned farms there. There was, however, much dissatisfaction in the Midwest. There was a severe agricultural recession, wheat prices were low and the value of improved farmland had fallen by 80 percent. Cholera, malaria and other serious diseases were endemic. Selling up and moving on to start again in the fertile and healthy Oregon country had great appeal to many. There was a minor publishing boom in guide books giving advice (not all of it good) to migrants. A typical migrant family would have two 'prairie schooners' (covered wagons), draught oxen, tools and cooking utensils, clothing, food supplies for about 18 months to see them through the journey and the time taken to establish a new farm, and as many head of cattle as they could afford. If the wagons and teams were sold at the end of the trail, the total cost of migration for four was estimated at around $220.

Life on the Oregon Trail was tough and sometimes dangerous. Covered wagons provided shelter from bad weather, but they did not have springs and gave a bone-jarring ride. Fatigue was something everyone had to endure. Progress had to be maintained whatever the weather if the wagon train was to reach its destination before winter closed the Rocky Mountain passes. Thirst too was a problem on the arid middle section of the trail. Of the estimated 10,000 migrants who died on the trail some 95 percent were victims of disease. The trail had recognized stages and camping sites. Unfortunately, the migrants, knowing that they would not be returning, were careless about hygiene. Latrines were dug next to wells, or were not dug at all. A day or two after one wagon train had departed another would arrive and camp on the fouled site, so infections easily passed from one party to another. Cholera was the greatest killer, with children being especially vulnerable. Accidents took their toll, as did lightning, grass fires, river crossings and floods. Parties that started late in the year risked getting snowed up in the Rockies if they were still on the trail come October, and that brought the risks of death from exposure or starvation as supplies began to run out. The most overstated danger was Indian attack. Migrants were advised to take a rifle and a shotgun each, but these were much more likely to be used against game than Indians. Wagons were circled at night for security and sentries were posted but the main dangers from the Indians were robbery and horse theft. Parties of 20 wagons or more were generally considered to be secure and migrants were rarely killed before the 1860s, by which time it had become all too clear to the Indians that the white man meant to despoil them of all their lands if he could.

An emigrant family pictured crossing Nebraska in the 1880s, at the end of the heyday of the Oregon Trail.

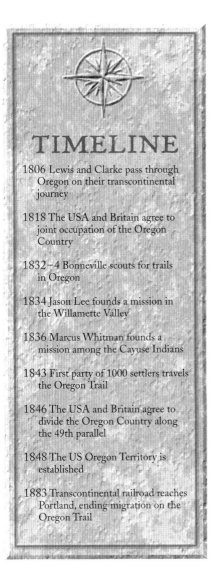

TIMELINE

1806 Lewis and Clarke pass through Oregon on their transcontinental journey

1818 The USA and Britain agree to joint occupation of the Oregon Country

1832–4 Bonneville scouts for trails in Oregon

1834 Jason Lee founds a mission in the Willamette Valley

1836 Marcus Whitman founds a mission among the Cayuse Indians

1843 First party of 1000 settlers travels the Oregon Trail

1846 The USA and Britain agree to divide the Oregon Country along the 49th parallel

1848 The US Oregon Territory is established

1883 Transcontinental railroad reaches Portland, ending migration on the Oregon Trail

Indian Migration in the British Empire
1834–1947

The abolition of slavery in the British empire in 1834 created a shortage of cheap labour in Britain's tropical colonies because most freed slaves chose to become smallholders rather than work for their former owners. The British solved this problem by recruiting indentured labour in the Indian subcontinent to work on plantations and construction projects throughout the empire. The result was a diaspora of Indians – Hindus, Muslims and Sikhs alike – to every continent.

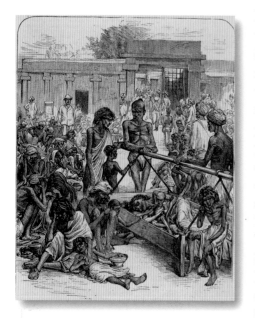

Above: Famine victims in India. Hardship drove many Indians to become indentured labourers.

Right: Muslim refugees during the upheavals that followed Partition in 1947.

Before the 19th century the Indian subcontinent was a place people migrated to, rather than from. The lack of emigration was the result of many factors, including the custom of partible inheritance, which guaranteed land to all the male children of peasant families, close family structures, and the caste system, which stifled social mobility. The same factors also meant that there was little internal migration before British rule in the 18th century. The British actively promoted labour mobility using the indenture system to recruit workers for plantations and factories within India and for sugar and rubber plantations, construction sites and mines in British colonies overseas. Labourers were contracted for periods of three to five years, in return for free travel, housing and a small wage. On termination of the contract the labourer was given free passage home, or was free to renew his contract for another term or to remain as a settler. While whole families were often recruited to work within India, most overseas indentured labourers were single, with men outnumbering women by about 3:2. Because of the shortage of wives, women frequently found themselves victims of sexual abuse and forced marriage. The most important recruiting grounds for indentured labour were the densely populated, famine-prone areas of the Ganges plain and Bengal, which had good communications with the port of Calcutta (Kolkata), and the hinterlands of the ports of Bombay (Mumbai) and Madras (Chennai).

Workers for the empire

The majority of Indian labour went to British colonies around the Indian Ocean. Between 1834 and 1837 about 7000 labourers were recruited in Calcutta and sent to work on plantations on the island of Mauritius. By 1910 this had risen to over 455,000. In the second half of the 19th century 1.75 million Indians went to Malaya, 1.16 million to Burma and 2.3 million to Ceylon (now Sri Lanka). Most Indian emigrants to Ceylon were Hindu Tamils from Madras. Smaller numbers went to East Africa (40,000) and Natal in South Africa (153,000). Away from the Indian Ocean, 440,000 Indians were sent to work in the Caribbean, especially Trinidad and British Guiana (now Guyana), and about 60,000 went to Fiji in the Pacific. The indenture system was finally abandoned in 1920 following protests led by the nationalist leader Mohandas K. Gandhi (Mahatma Gandhi; 1869–1948), who had been radicalized by the racism faced by Indian labourers while working as a lawyer in South Africa in 1910–14.

Within one or two generations, the descendants of Indian indentured labourers had moved into commerce and the professions and became prosperous. As a result, Indians often faced a backlash from the native population when Britain decolonized in the 20th century. Burma expelled all Indians in the 1960s, as did Kenya and Tanzania – Uganda's Indians followed in the 1970s. Most East African Indians were allowed to settle in Britain. In Sri Lanka tension between the native Buddhist Sinhalese and the Hindu Tamils has led to a long-running civil war. Since its independence in 1970 Fiji

CANADA

British empire

migration routes of Indian labourers

JAMAICA

TRINIDAD

BRITISH GUIANA

has experienced political instability as a result of conflict between the native Melanesians and the Indians. In South Africa, Indians, classed as 'coloureds', were subjected to the racist segregationalist laws from 1910 and the apartheid system from 1948 to 1993.

The pain of partition

The last great migration of the British empire began as India moved towards independence. Modern Indian nationalism began with the foundation of the Indian National Congress party in 1885. Congress at first campaigned for home rule but after Gandhi became party leader in 1920 it began to demand full independence. Congress' ideal was the creation of a secular unitary state comprising all of British India. This was problematic, as the subcontinent had an ethnically diverse population that had never had a common national identity or even a common language. India was split principally along religious lines, between the Hindu majority and the large Muslim minority. For many Muslims the idea of sharing a nationality with Hindus was anathema and so in the 1930s the Muslim League began agitating for the creation of a separate Muslim state. The British were finally forced to promise India its independence in 1942 as the price of securing continuing Indian support in the Second World War (1939–45). In 1946 the British proposed making India independent as a unitary state but, as a concession to Muslims, with a high degree of regional autonomy, which would allow them to run their own domestic affairs in the areas where they were a majority. This compromise was acceptable neither to Congress nor to the Muslim League. After Muslims in Calcutta massacred 5000 Hindus in August 1946 sectarian violence quickly spread across the subcontinent. The worst unrest was in Bengal, which was split almost equally between Hindus and Muslims, and Punjab, which had a mixed population of Muslims, Hindus and Sikhs.

The only solution was partition of India along religious lines, with those areas with Muslim majorities becoming independent as Pakistan ('the land of the pure'). Because the Muslim population was concentrated in the northwest and in eastern Bengal, in the north-east, Pakistan would consist of two widely separated parts (West and East Pakistan), which had little in common apart from their Muslim religion (East Pakistan eventually became independent as Bangladesh in 1971). A boundary commission

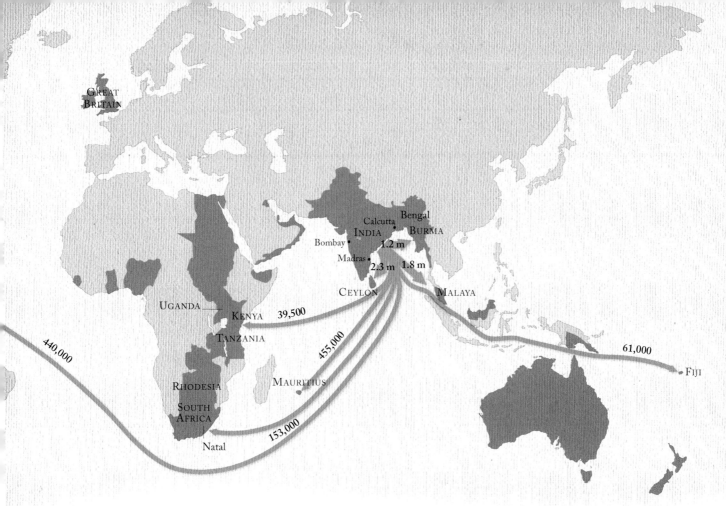

hurriedly set to work in June 1947 drawing the boundaries of India and Pakistan, and independence was proclaimed at midnight on 14–15 August 1947. The boundaries left 18 million Hindus in Pakistan and 40 million Muslims in India. Partition prompted the largest single mass migration of the 20th century. By the end of 1947 between six and seven million Hindus had fled Pakistan and almost equal numbers of Muslims had left India for Pakistan. One of the largest single refugee movements was the 45-mile (72-km)-long column of 800,000 terrified Hindus and Sikhs that fled West Pakistan for India in October 1947, impelled by rumoured and actual massacres, rapes and robberies. In the six weeks following independence between 500,000 and one million people were killed in intercommunal violence in both countries.

Refugees continued to flee India and Pakistan until the early 1950s. By this time almost the entire Hindu population of West Pakistan had been driven out, about eight million people in all. A substantial Hindu minority remained in East Pakistan, as did a sizeable Muslim minority in India. Numbering some 100 million, India's Muslim population is now the third largest in the world after Indonesia and Pakistan but, despite official secularism, religious tensions persist. The bloodshed of partition has made it difficult for India and Pakistan to establish normal relations. So too has the dispute over the Himalayan state of Kashmir, whose unresolved status has been the cause of three wars between India and Pakistan. Kashmir has a mainly Muslim population, but is currently divided along a 'line of control' between India and Pakistan; Indian Kashmir is the scene of much Pakistani-backed separatist terrorism. There has been significant emigration from Pakistan, Bangladesh and India since their independence, notably to Great Britain and, increasingly, to the USA.

Map showing the migration of Indian indentured labour within the British empire.

Mormons in Search of a Promised Land
1846–69

The Mormons have been described as the most systematic, organised, disciplined and successful pioneers in American history. For over 20 years they were one of the main forces driving the settlement of the American West. The Mormons were remarkable also in migrating as a whole community, unlike the individualists and opportunists who made up the majority of the settlers of the West.

A contemporary newspaper caricature of Brigham Young and his seven wives. From the outset, polygamy was a controversial tenet of the Mormon faith, and had to be renounced before Utah was permitted to join the Union in 1896.

The Mormons are members of the Church of Jesus Christ of Latter-day Saints, a church founded by Joseph Smith (1805–44) at Fayette in New York State in 1830. Smith attracted a small group of followers who settled at Kirtland, Ohio, and around Independence, Missouri. Because of conflicts with non-Mormons, the Mormons moved first to northern Missouri and then in 1839 to Nauvoo on the Illinois bank of the Mississippi. Persecution did the church no harm, merely enhancing the solidarity of its members. Smith preached the gathering of the faithful in one place and about 25,000 Mormons were soon living around Nauvoo and across the Mississippi in Iowa. Rumours about Smith's unorthodox teachings, which included polygamy, caused conflict with non-Mormons and he was murdered by a mob in June 1844.

The 'Great Migration' and after

After Smith's death, Brigham Young (1801–77) was chosen as leader of the church. A formidably gifted administrator, Young began to organize an exodus of Mormons to the west. His plan was to head for the Rockies and find a suitable valley where they could create a religious community free from the influence and persecution of non-Mormons. The Mormons saw themselves as Israelites and Brigham Young was their Moses. Between February and September 1846 the Mormons left Nauvoo, crossed the Mississippi into Iowa and began their 'Great Migration'. Pioneers set out first to blaze the trail, found temporary settlements along the route, and build a ferry on the Missouri at Council Bluffs. Parties began reaching the Missouri in late June and crossed into Nebraska. Young and about 3500 Mormons spent the winter in cabins at Winter Quarters in Nebraska. Another 10,000 Mormons were living in the temporary settlements along the trail and as many more were scattered elsewhere in the Midwest.

In April 1847 Young led the first party of 148 pioneers out of Winter Quarters for the Rockies. Their route followed the north bank of the Platte and North Platte rivers (the opposite bank to the Oregon Trail; see pages 210–213) as far as Fort Laramie. From there, the Mormons followed the Oregon Trail as far as Fort Bridger. Not wishing to settle near a migration route used by non-Mormons, Young left the Oregon Trail here and continued southwest for a further 100 miles (160 km) until arriving in the valley of the Great Salt Lake in Utah in late July. After a brief exploration, Young decreed that this was the place God meant them to settle and within days work had begun laying out Salt Lake City. The arid, mountain valley was unlike anything the Mormons had ever known, requiring them to learn completely new methods of farming, but it was a suitably biblical location, complete with its own Dead Sea. Following the pioneers was the Big Company of over 2000 migrants, which arrived in the valley in late September. Only six people had died of disease and one had been shot by Indians. Young and other leaders returned to Winter Quarters and in 1848 led another party of 2400 migrants to Utah.

Gathering the Mormons remained a priority for Young. In 1848, after a good harvest had set the Mormons on the path to prosperity, the Perpetual Emigrating Fund was set up to make interest free loans to poor Mormons to help them migrate to Utah. The fund was first used to help those Mormons who had remained in the Midwest at the time of the Great Migration. Some 3000 wagons travelled the trail blazed by Young between

More than a decade after the first 'Great Migration', a party of Mormons are shown encamped at a temporary site in Illinois before heading west in this engraving of 1858.

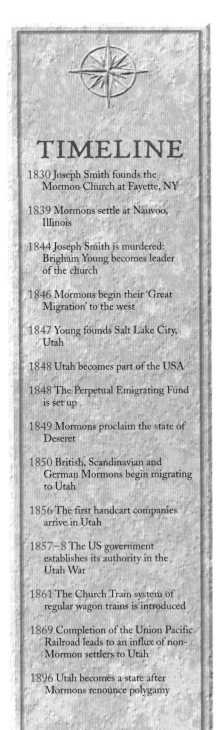

TIMELINE

1830 Joseph Smith founds the Mormon Church at Fayette, NY

1839 Mormons settle at Nauvoo, Illinois

1844 Joseph Smith is murdered: Brigham Young becomes leader of the church

1846 Mormons begin their 'Great Migration' to the west

1847 Young founds Salt Lake City, Utah

1848 Utah becomes part of the USA

1848 The Perpetual Emigrating Fund is set up

1849 Mormons proclaim the state of Deseret

1850 British, Scandinavian and German Mormons begin migrating to Utah

1856 The first handcart companies arrive in Utah

1857–8 The US government establishes its authority in the Utah War

1861 The Church Train system of regular wagon trains is introduced

1869 Completion of the Union Pacific Railroad leads to an influx of non-Mormon settlers to Utah

1896 Utah becomes a state after Mormons renounce polygamy

1849 and 1852, carrying over 20,000 people. Losses from disease were slight in comparison to those suffered on the less well organized non-Mormon wagon trains. Once the Nauvoo refugees had been brought to Utah, the resources of the Perpetual Emigrating Fund were directed to gathering the Mormon converts from overseas. Mormon missionaries had enjoyed great success winning converts among poor industrial workers, especially in the grimy mill towns of northern England, who were only too willing to emigrate if given the opportunity. By the end of 1854, 15,642 British, 1002 Scandinavian and 50 German Mormons had been shipped out of Liverpool to begin the long journey to Utah. Mormon emigrants sailed on specially chartered ships and throughout their journeys they were accompanied by Mormon agents, who imposed discipline, organized provisions and hygiene on board ship, helped them through immigration on landing in America, arranged their transport to the West, procured wagons and supplies and guided them on the trail to Utah where they would be settled into a supportive community. As a result of this network, Mormons suffered few of the trials and tribulations experienced by other immigrants to the USA.

When the Mormons arrived in Utah it was still part of Mexico. Following the end of the US-Mexican War (1846–8) a year later, Utah became part of the USA. In 1849 the Mormons proclaimed the State of Deseret and applied for recognition as a state of the Union. Deseret encompassed a vast area extending from the Oregon Territory in the north to the Mexican border in the south and from the continental divide in the east to the Pacific Ocean in the west. Congress refused to recognize Deseret and instead formed the smaller Utah Territory with Brigham Young as governor. Utah was only granted statehood in 1896, after the Mormons renounced polygamy.

A contemporary woodcut shows one of the Mormon handcart companies passing through Iowa on its way to Utah in the 1850s. Many hardships awaited these intrepid travellers.

Across the plains by handcart

The refusal of Congress to recognize Deseret left Young desperate to increase the number of Mormon settlers as quickly as possible to limit the influence of non-Mormons in Utah. A scheme to bring emigrants from Liverpool to Salt Lake City for

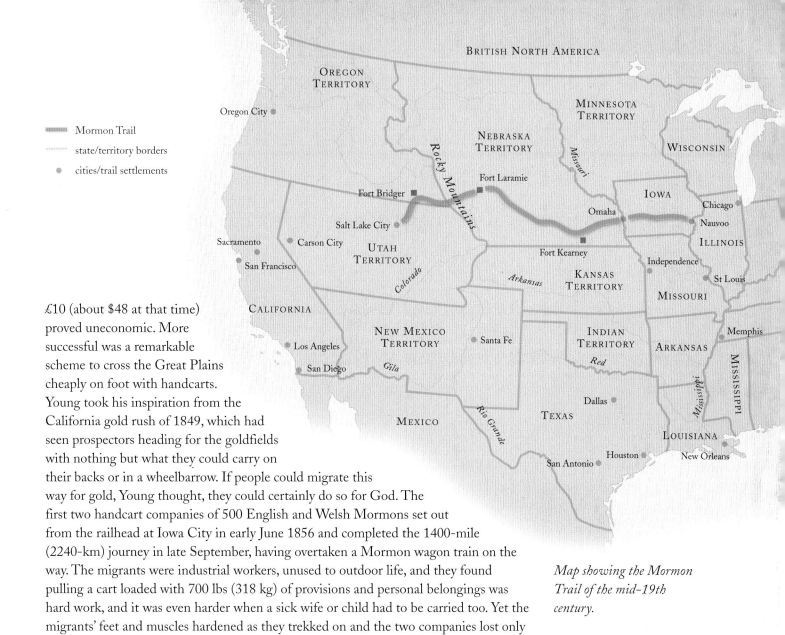

£10 (about $48 at that time) proved uneconomic. More successful was a remarkable scheme to cross the Great Plains cheaply on foot with handcarts. Young took his inspiration from the California gold rush of 1849, which had seen prospectors heading for the goldfields with nothing but what they could carry on their backs or in a wheelbarrow. If people could migrate this way for gold, Young thought, they could certainly do so for God. The first two handcart companies of 500 English and Welsh Mormons set out from the railhead at Iowa City in early June 1856 and completed the 1400-mile (2240-km) journey in late September, having overtaken a Mormon wagon train on the way. The migrants were industrial workers, unused to outdoor life, and they found pulling a cart loaded with 700 lbs (318 kg) of provisions and personal belongings was hard work, and it was even harder when a sick wife or child had to be carried too. Yet the migrants' feet and muscles hardened as they trekked on and the two companies lost only 21 people to disease, most of them children. Two more companies made uneventful journeys that summer, but the last two, which did not leave until late July, did not make it out of the mountains before winter set in. Of the 1000 migrants, over 200 died of hunger and exposure. The casualties would have been far higher but for a heroic rescue mission launched from Salt Lake City. Another five handcart companies made the journey successfully between 1857 and 1860. The last made the trip with no fatalities.

The final phase of the Mormon migration began in 1861, when the Church Trains were introduced to bring migrants to Utah cheaply. Instead of purchasing new wagons and draft animals for one-way trips from the Midwest, wagon trains loaded with grain were sent out from Salt Lake City in the early spring. Reaching Missouri in early summer, the grain was sold and the empty wagons returned loaded with migrants by the early autumn. The completion of the Union Pacific railroad in 1869 put the wagon trails out of business, but by that time the Church Trains had brought 23,000 migrants, most of whom were British, German and Scandinavian, to Utah. The railroad led to an influx of non-Mormon settlers into Utah, but Mormons still make up 70 percent of the state's population.

Map showing the Mormon Trail of the mid-19th century.

Gold Rush to California
1848–53

Gold rushes – an extreme form of economic migration – have played an important part in the exploration and settlement of many countries, including South Africa, Australia, New Zealand and Canada. However, none had a more dramatic impact than the California gold rush of 1849, which instantly drew around 100,000 settlers to the West.

The California gold rush began with the discovery on 24 January, 1848 of a gold nugget in a water channel by a foreman at John Sutter's sawmill at Coloma on a branch of the American River in the foothills of the Sierra Nevada mountains. Afraid that they would abandon their jobs, Sutter gave his employees permission to dig for gold in their spare time, at the same time begging them to keep the discovery secret. Inevitably, people gossiped and rumours leaked out. Three Mormons working at another of Sutter's mills prospected a second site, Mormon Diggings, and also found gold, proving that the first find had not been just a localized deposit. In May news of the gold strike finally broke in

Sutter's Mill, site of the first discovery of gold in California in 1848, which prompted the huge gold rush of the following year.

San Francisco and the city emptied as almost all its able-bodied inhabitants rushed to the American River. Ranchers abandoned their stock, taking their Indian farmhands with them. By the end of the year around 2000 whites and 4000 Indians were working the gold field. Early results were spectacular. Job Dye's party of seven whites and 50 Indians recovered 273 lb (124 kg) of gold in two months, valued at over US $90,000 at a time when $50 a month was considered a good wage. Meanwhile news of the gold strike was spreading around the world.

At the time of the gold strike, California was still officially part of Mexico. Just over a week later, on 2 February, it was transferred to the USA by the Treaty of Guadalupe Hidalgo, which concluded the US-Mexican War (1846–8). Americans had been settling in small numbers in California since the 1830s. At first there were just a few adventurous individuals, like Swiss-born John Sutter (1803–80) who planned to found a new Switzerland on the Sacramento River. In the event, the only Swiss immigrant Sutter attracted to 'New Helvetia' was one of his sons, but his private fort near Sacramento attracted many Americans. Small parties of families hoping to set up farms began to arrive in the central valley after the opening of the California Trail in 1841. Starting at Independence, Missouri it followed the same route as the Oregon Trail as far as Fort Hall on the Snake River, before heading southwest across the Great Basin deserts to Carson City and over the Sierra Nevada to Sacramento. There were shorter routes but these were tougher than the main route. One wagon train, the Donner-Reed Party, took the short-cut south of Great Salt Lake and got snowed in for the winter in the Sierra Nevada in 1845–6. Short of supplies, the party turned to cannibalism. Of 89 people in the party only 30 survived.

Arrival of the 'Fortyniners'

Most of these American settlers were regarded as illegal immigrants by the authorities because they would not accept Mexican citizenship. Tensions increased and in June 1846 the American settlers declared California an independent republic. Unbeknown to them, war between the USA and Mexico had broken out a few weeks earlier. On 7 July US naval forces captured Monterey and claimed California for the USA, bringing the short-lived republic to an end. American immigration continued during the war but in early 1848 there were still only three or four thousand American settlers, compared to 12,000 Californios (Mexican Californians) and 50,000 Indians. The gold rush would change this in a quite dramatic way, thoroughly Americanizing

California Prospectors *(1891) by Allen Carter Redwood. The sudden influx of settlers changed the face of the region for ever.*

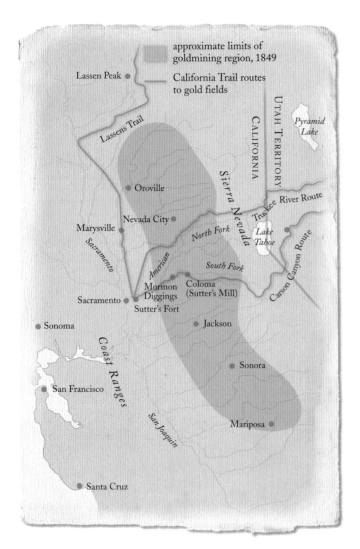

Map showing the area affected by the California gold rush of 1849–53.

California and driving it towards statehood in the space of just two years.

By the time heavy winter rains brought the mining season to an end in November 1848, $10 million worth of gold had been dug out of the Sierra Nevada. No effective territorial government had yet been set up to adjudicate claims and crime and violence had become endemic in the mining camps, where vigilante committees struggled to maintain a semblance of order and meted out rough justice. This was just a pale shadow of what was to happen in 1849.

In spring 1849 as many as 30,000 would-be gold miners set out for the five-month journey on the California Trail. Another 25,000 set sail from east coast ports. The shortest route was to sail to Panama, cross the isthmus to the Pacific by mule and pick up another ship to San Francisco. Taking only a month, this was the fastest route to California. It was also the most dangerous because of the risks of tropical diseases in the swamps of Panama. A cheaper and safer route was to sail steerage on the 15,000-mile (24,000-km) trip around Cape Horn. This usually took around three months, but if the weather was bad, it could easily last nine. Many a ship's captain must have regretted his decision to carry gold miners. As soon as they docked in San Francisco their crews jumped ship and headed to the gold fields with the passengers. By the early 1850s, San Francisco harbour was crammed with hundreds of rotting abandoned ships. Despite the hazards of disease, accident and Indian attack common to all wagon train travel, those who came overland fared best: they had become accustomed to active outdoor life on their journey. Those who arrived by sea were unfit and often in poor health after months in cramped, unhealthy accommodation on board ship. Gold fever was not confined to the USA. In 1849 alone 25,000 immigrants arrived in California from Britain, with smaller contingents from Mexico, France, Australia, Hawaii, Peru and Chile.

The typical 'Fortyniner' was young, male, white and from a moderately prosperous background with savings or property that could be mortgaged to raise the funds to go to California and set up as a miner. One party of hopefuls from Michigan included teachers, clerks, farmers, doctors, lawyers, artists, blacksmiths, carpenters and mechanics. There were, unfortunately, many career criminals as well, attracted by the lawless conditions. Although Mexican immigrants were likely to bring their wives and children with them, few others did so. In 1850 women made up only 7.5 percent of California's white population. Few of the Fortyniners had any experience of gold mining, or any conception of the social chaos they would face in the mining camps. They had just one aim in life, to strike it rich and then go home.

Fortunes won and lost

A few prospectors did indeed make a fortune. Antonio Coronel (1817–94), a Mexican schoolteacher, found over 12 lbs (5.5 kg) of gold in just three days. Investing the proceeds wisely, he was elected mayor of Los Angeles four years later and eventually became treasurer of the state of California. John Sullivan, an Irish teamster, dug up $26,000 worth of gold in the summer of 1848, bought real estate in San Francisco and founded a bank. However, most prospectors left little richer than they had arrived, having drunk and gambled their gold away, if they ever found any in the first place. The real winners were the traders, shopkeepers and saloon keepers who followed the prospectors and sold them, at grossly inflated prices, the necessities and luxuries of life.

A contemporary cartoonist created the figure of the destitute 'Used-up Man' to satirize gold prospectors' dreams of instant wealth.

The flood of immigrants continued into the early 1850s. California's white population exceeded 100,000 in 1850, more than justifying its admission as the 31st state of the Union. By 1852, the year that gold production peaked, it was 225,000, and by the year's end another 52,000 people had arrived overland, plus 67,000 by sea, including 20,000 from China. Not all of them were planning on digging for gold. The sudden influx of tens of millions of dollars worth of gold into the California economy had created an inflationary boom and labour shortages had driven wages well above levels in the rest of the USA and there was well-paid work for everyone servicing the needs of the miners. Gold production began to fall in 1853 and the flood of immigrants quickly dried up. Some miners sought their fortunes elsewhere, but most of the immigrants who had arrived at the peak of the gold rush stayed on, realizing that California had more to offer than gold mines.

TIMELINE

1821 California becomes part of newly independent Mexico

1841 California Trail opens, beginning American immigration to California

1846 (June) American settlers declare California an independent republic

1846 (July) US forces occupy California

1848 (January) Gold discovered at Sutter's Mill, Coloma

1848 (February) Treaty of Guadalupe-Hidalgo transfers California to the USA

1848 (May) News of the gold find reaches San Francisco, starting the gold rush

1849 Over 80,000 gold miners arrive in California

1850 California is admitted as 31st state of the Union

1853 The gold rush ends as production declines

The Armenian Diaspora
582–1922

The Armenians have an extremely turbulent history of migration, dispersion, persecution and statelessness that lasted for over 1500 years. Since 1991 and the collapse of the Soviet Union, Armenians once again have an independent homeland, but its population is far outnumbered by Armenians living abroad.

The Armenians first appear in the historical record in 521 BC when they were conquered by the Persians: they are believed to be descended from several different Indo-European-speaking peoples who migrated to the mountainous Lesser Caucasus region early in the second millennium BC. Since their conquest by the Persians, the Armenians have enjoyed only brief periods of independence and their country was frequently fought over by neighbouring powers. The Armenians were converted to Christianity in 294, and in 312 Armenia became the first state to adopt Christianity as its official religion. The Armenian Apostolic Church has remained autonomous throughout its history and remains an important element in the identity of Armenians, both in Armenia and in the diaspora.

Beginnings of the diaspora

The dispersal of Armenians from their homeland began when the Byzantine emperor Maurice (r.582–602) deported 12,000 of them to Bulgaria. Reinforced by further immigration in the 12th and 17th centuries, this community still survives today. Many Armenians served in the Byzantine army, some becoming generals, and four ninth-century emperors were of Armenian origin. The diaspora continued after Armenia was conquered by the Seljuk Turks in 1080. A refugee prince established the colony of Lesser Armenia in Cilicia, on the Mediterranean coast of southeast Anatolia, which retained its independence until it too fell to the Turks in 1375.

A political cartoon from the 19th century portrays Armenia (right) being threatened by a rapacious Ottoman Turk. England's John Bull looks on, unwilling to help Armenia for fear of losing trade.

At around the same time other Armenians sought refuge in the Crimea, Moldavia, Hungary and Poland, where L'viv became a major Armenian centre. In the 14th century, Armenians from L'viv settled in Romania and Lithuania. After Lesser Armenia was overrun, refugees went to join the established Armenian colonies in eastern Europe. Many Armenian exiles in Poland became involved in trade and in the 14th century they were granted many commercial privileges by the crown. After L'viv came under Russian rule in the 18th century, its importance as a trade centre declined and the Armenian community had dispersed by the 20th century. Smaller communities of Armenian traders and craftsmen were also established in Venice, Marseilles, Paris, Bruges and London.

In the 16th century, eastern Armenia passed from Turkish to Persian rule. Shah Abbas I (r.1588–1629) deported many thousands of Armenians to Isfahan (Iran), where they became deeply involved as middlemen in the silk trade. Armenian merchants from Isfahan spread out along the main Eurasian trade routes, founding small mercantile communities as staging posts in the main ports and trade centres throughout Europe, Egypt, the Middle East and India. There were even Armenian communities in Lhasa, the capital of Tibet, in China, the Philippines and East Africa. Armenians also settled in Pegu in Burma (Myanmar) and won a monopoly over the export trade in rubies. The Asian branch of this network went into decline in the 18th century because of competition from the British, but substantial Armenian communities survived in Alexandria, Madras, Calcutta, Singapore and Jakarta into the 20th century. Like the Greeks, the Armenians left Alexandria after the Second World War due to rising Egyptian nationalist hostility. The Armenian community in Iran has now almost vanished too. After declining slowly for decades, most Armenians left Iran to escape the persecution of religious minorities that followed the Islamic Revolution in 1979.

Northern Armenia came under Russian control in 1828. Armenians welcomed Russian rule as liberation from Muslim oppression. With the encouragement of Russia, an Armenian nationalist movement began to develop in the later 19th century, but this led to a catastrophic backlash against those Armenians who were still living under Turkish rule. The Ottomans had seen how nationalist movements had destroyed their empire in the Balkans so they became increasingly suspicious of the Armenians. In 1894–6 Sultan Abdülhamit II (r.1876–1909) encouraged massacres in which around 300,000

With their children and worldly possessions loaded on ox carts, Armenian refugees flee Turkish persecution in the 1920s.

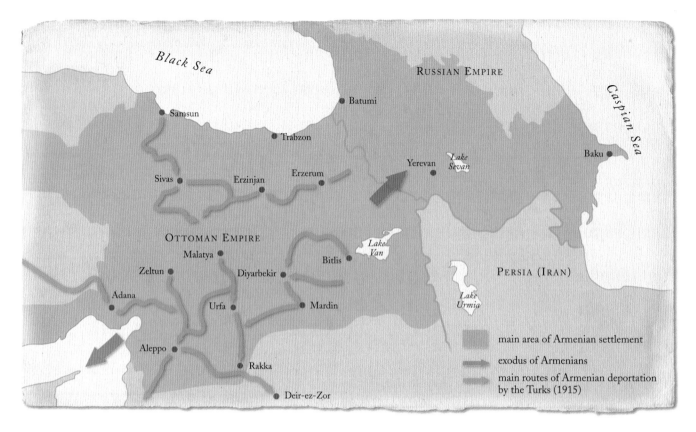

Map showing the area in Asia Minor and the Caucasus, straddling the Ottoman and Russian empires, occupied by the Armenians in the early 20th century.

Armenians were killed. This sparked the emigration of up to 80,000 Armenians to the USA. Most of the emigrants settled in New York, Boston, Philadelphia and California. Smaller numbers emigrated to Canada.

Systematic Ottoman genocide

A far more terrible fate awaited the Armenians in the First World War (1914–18), when the Ottoman empire allied with Germany and the Austro-Hungarian empire (a coalition known as the Central Powers) against France, Russia and Great Britain. In November 1914, the Russians invaded Ottoman Armenia. Suspecting them of aiding the Russians, in April 1915 the Ottoman government instigated a policy of ethnic cleansing and genocide against the Armenian population. At that time, there were approximately two million Armenians living in the Ottoman empire, concentrated in the area around Lake Van and Mount Ararat, eastern Anatolia and northern Syria. There were also substantial Armenian communities in Istanbul, Trabzon and Smyrna.

Estimates of the numbers of victims of the genocide range from around one million in 1915–16 and perhaps another 400,000 by 1922, by which time over 90 percent of the Armenian population of the Ottoman empire had been killed or had fled abroad. The genocide began with the arrest and summary execution of Armenian political, educational, intellectual and religious leaders, not only in Armenia but in all cities with Armenian populations, including Istanbul. Armenians serving in the Ottoman army were disarmed and executed. Over the summer of 1915 Armenian civilians were rounded up and massacred. In the worst slaughters, at Sivas and Mush, a total of 100,000 Armenians were killed. The survivors of the massacres were deported to Syria. Long columns of Armenians trudged hundreds of miles through an arid countryside with little food and water, constantly subjected to the casual brutality of their Kurdish guards. Tens of thousands died along the way: the survivors were settled in camps around Aleppo and Damascus in Syria and Beirut in Lebanon. The genocide is still officially denied by the Turkish government; in 2005, the Nobel Prize-winning author Orhan Pamuk (b.1952) was unsuccessfully charged with defaming the Turkish state for stating that the Armenian genocide had taken place.

20th-century Armenian migration

The success of the October Revolution that overthrew the Tsarist regime in Russia in 1917 led to the successor government of the Bolsheviks withdrawing from the war, in the Treaty of Brest-Litovsk. Most of the surviving Armenian population that remained in Ottoman Armenia, about 300,000, left with the retreating Russian armies and settled in Russian Armenia. After a failed bid for independence in the civil war that followed the revolution, Armenian identity and culture were severely repressed during the Soviet era. Thousands of Armenians migrated to other Soviet republics to work, notably neighbouring Georgia and Azerbaijan.

In 1988 and 1989, Armenians living in Azerbaijan faced pogroms perpetrated by the majority Muslim Azeri population. In the aftermath of these attacks about 250,000 Armenians fled Azerbaijan and resettled in Armenia. Similar numbers of Azeris, faced with revenge attacks in Armenia, went the other way. With the collapse of the Soviet Union in 1991, Armenia became an independent republic, though it comprises only a fraction of historical Armenia. The 1990s saw conflict with Azerbaijan over the Nagorno-Karabakh region, which has a mainly Armenian population. The war led to 20,000 deaths and left 600,000 Armenians and Azeris homeless. Economic hardship caused by the war led many more Armenians to join the diaspora.

At the end of the First World War, Syria and Lebanon became French League of Nations mandated territories. Many Armenian refugees there emigrated to France, which had a labour shortage because of its heavy war casualties, while others went to the USA, Argentina and Australia. Significant numbers of Armenians remained in Lebanon and Syria. The surviving Armenian population of Istanbul also emigrated in the immediate post-war period, many going to Greece. Their passports were stamped 'No Return Possible' as they left. Few Armenian emigrants spoke the languages of their host countries and found only unskilled work, on farms or in factories. Subsequent generations have moved into various forms of commerce and live almost exclusively in urban areas. The migrations that followed the genocide decisively altered the balance of the Armenian diaspora, shifting it away from the Middle East to France, which now has over 300,000 Armenians, and the USA, with over 800,000. The total of the overseas diaspora is estimated at over five million, compared to a home population of 3.6 million.

TIMELINE

521 BC Earliest historical records of the Armenian people

AD 312 Armenia adopts Christianity as state religion

c.600 Beginning of the Armenian diaspora: Byzantine emperor Maurice deports Armenians to Bulgaria

c.1080 Armenian colony founded in Cilicia

1300s Armenian refugees from the Turks spread throughout Europe

1600s Armenians deported to Iran by Shah Abbas I

1828 The Russians conquer northern Armenia

1894–6 80,000 Armenians emigrate to the USA following massacres in the Ottoman empire

1915–22 Ottoman Turk campaign of genocide against Armenians

1979 Armenians flee Iran after the Islamic Revolution

1991 Armenia becomes independent following the breakup of the Soviet Union

Back to Israel
1881–2007

Throughout the years of the Diaspora, Jews around the world kept alive the hope of a return to the biblical homeland of the Children of Israel through the establishment of a Jewish state in Palestine. In 1948, after persecution of the Jews in Europe had reached a terrible crescendo in the Holocaust, that hope was finally fulfilled with the declaration of the state of Israel.

It was never the case that the historic land of Israel was completely depopulated of Jews. Aliyah ('ascent to Zion'), emigration to Palestine, remained an important expression of the historical link between the Jews of the Diaspora and their ancestral home. Even in the Middle Ages there was a trickle of migrants returning to Palestine. Even so, in the early 19th century there were only about 6700 Jews living in Palestine, mainly in the cities of Jerusalem, Safed, Hebron and Tiberias. Thanks to the tolerant attitude of the Ottoman authorities, that number had increased to about 27,000 by 1880. Jewish emigration to Palestine increased dramatically in the 1880s. The assassination of Tsar Alexander II (r.1855–81) in 1881 was blamed on Jews and a wave of anti-semitic violence swept across Russia and eastern Europe. Between 1881 and 1891, hundreds of thousands of Jews emigrated to escape persecution. The majority went to the USA and western Europe, but over 30,000 idealistic Jews went to Palestine. These refugees became known as the First Aliyah.

Early Zionist settlement of Palestine

The Jews of the Diaspora were almost entirely urbanized. Most Jews of the First Aliyah therefore settled in towns, especially Jerusalem, Jaffa and Haifa, but significant numbers bought land from Palestinian Arabs and founded farming communities. The first of these was Petah Tikva ('Gateway of Hope'), founded by Eastern European Jews in 1878. These communities became symbolic of the Jews' commitment to the land but the settlers' lack of experience of agriculture meant that for many years their survival was dependent on the support of wealthy Jews overseas, such as the banker Edmond de Rothschild (1845–1934). Rural settlement increased during the Second Aliyah, which took place in the ten years before the outbreak of the First World War in 1914. This saw the immigration of another 40,000 Jews, most of them again from eastern Europe. Many immigrants had been inspired by the Zionist movement, which had developed in the 1880s and 1890s as a reaction to rising anti-Semitism in eastern Europe. Zionists argued that Jewish aspirations could only be fulfilled by the establishment of a Jewish national homeland in Palestine. The Second Aliyah saw the foundation of the first kibbutz, a farming commune run on socialist principles, at Deganya in Galilee in 1909. Dozens of kibbutzim were founded, greatly advancing Jewish settlement in rural Palestine.

The other major development of the Second Aliyah was the revival of Hebrew as a spoken language. Although it survived as a liturgical language, Hebrew had died out in everyday use in ancient times and Jews spoke several different languages. By giving the settlers a common language rooted in their shared historical identity, Hebrew became central to the creation of the Israeli national identity.

During the First World War (1914–18), British forces invaded Palestine from Egypt and drove the Ottomans out. On 2 November, 1917 the British foreign minister Arthur Balfour (1848–1930) committed his government to supporting the Zionist ambition to create a Jewish national homeland in Palestine, provided that the rights of the existing non-Jewish communities were protected. After the war, these aims were incorporated into the League of Nations Mandate for Palestine, which placed the territory under British rule. The British mandate period saw successive aliyot. Total Jewish immigration to Palestine between 1919 and 1939 was 250,000, around half of whom settled in Tel Aviv. Many immigrants were German Jews fleeing Nazi persecution. Jewish emigration agencies bought land for settlements and evicted Arab tenants to make room for Jews. This caused growing resentment among Palestinian Arabs and terrorist attacks on Jewish settlers became common. The Jews set up the Hagana, a highly disciplined self-defence militia. Faced with growing disorder, in 1939 the British attempted to limit Jewish

In the tense period between the end of the Second World War and the founding of the state of Israel, thousands of Jewish refugees from Europe crowded onto ships and made for Palestine, where the British authorities refused them entry. Here, two such ships are seen arriving at the port of Haifa in 1947.

North
Sea

DENMARK
Copenhagen

Baltic Sea

UNITED
KINGDOM

London

NETHERLANDS

Berlin

Warsaw

Vilna (Vilnius)

RUSSIA

Byelorussia

GERMANY

Poland

Kiev

Kharkov

BELGIUM   Cologne

Prague

AUSTRO-
HUNGARIAN
EMPIRE

Ukraine

Rostov

Paris

Vienna

FRANCE   Basel
SWITZERLAND

Budapest

Odessa

Constanta

Black Sea

ROMANIA

SERBIA

MONTENEGRO

BULGARIA

ITALY

Constantinople (Istanbul)

ALBANIA

OTTOMAN EMPIRE

GREECE

Mediterranean Sea

Immigrants from
Middle Eastern
countries

Beirut

Immigrants from Morocco

Acre

Jaffa

Jerusalem

the Pale of Settlement

Immigrants from
Yemen

Jewish immigration to Palestine before 1914

pogroms against the Jews following Tsar
Alexander II's assassination (1881)

*Map showing Jewish
migration to Palestine from
Europe and North Africa
prior to 1914.*

immigration to 10,000 a year. With
so many European Jews seeking refuge from the Nazis,
this severely strained relations between Zionists and the British authorities. Despite
British efforts to suppress it, illegal Jewish immigration continued throughout the
Second World War (1939–45). By 1945 there were 554,000 Jews living in Palestine
but 70 percent of the population were still Arabs (mostly Sunni Muslims with Christian
and Shiite minorities).

Aftermath of the Holocaust

In the Holocaust (Shoah), over six million Jews, roughly two-thirds of Europe's Jewish
population, died in Nazi extermination camps. The long-established Jewish communities
of central and eastern Europe, which had been the centre of the Jewish Diaspora, were
almost completely destroyed. At the end of the war, most of Europe's surviving Jews
were displaced and homeless refugees. Zionists demanded that the British admit them
to Palestine. Unable to control the escalating violence or Jewish immigration, the British
announced their intention to withdraw from Palestine by 15 May, 1948. The United
Nations drew up a plan for the partition of Palestine into a Jewish state (Israel) and an
Arab state (Palestine), provoking Arab attacks on Jews not only in Palestine but across
the Arab world. The Zionists accepted the UN plan but the Palestinian Arabs refused,
forming a guerrilla army to prevent partition by force. In heavy fighting in spring 1948,

the Hagana succeeded in winning control of the territory allocated to the Jewish state by the UN. On 14 May, 1948 a provisional national council declared the independence of the state of Israel. The next day forces from Egypt, Jordan, Iraq, Lebanon and Syria invaded with the intention of expelling the Jews from Palestine. Though outnumbered, the Israelis triumphed and by the ceasefire in January 1949 they had occupied large areas that had been allocated to the Palestinian state by the UN plan. Of Palestine, only Gaza and the West Bank remained under Arab control.

During the war and its immediate aftermath around 940,000 Palestinians became refugees. Some were driven out of their homes by Israeli forces, others, however, fled at the urging of Arab governments and expected their exile to be a short one. The continuing hostility of the Arab states made it inevitable that Israel would not permit these refugees to return after the war: no solution to their problems is yet in sight. The possibility of return was made more remote by the destruction of many abandoned Palestinian villages and the occupation of Palestinian land to make way for the Jewish settlers who now began to flood into Israel from all over the world. In the first three years of independence over 600,000 Jews emigrated to Israel. To encourage immigration, in 1950 Israel introduced the Law of Return, which gave the right to all Jews to immigrate to Israel and become an Israeli citizen. Immigration continued at a slower rate after 1951 but by 1967 the Jewish population of Israel had reached three million.

The origins of immigrants to Israel reflect to a considerable degree the economic and political conditions of their home countries. In the years immediately after the war, immigrants were mainly Holocaust survivors from eastern Europe and Germany. They were joined after independence by refugees from government-orchestrated anti-Semitic violence in Muslim countries in North Africa and the Middle East. Turkey, Morocco and Tunisia are the only Islamic countries now still to have significant Jewish communities. In 1985 the right of return was extended to the Falashas, Ethiopian Jews, who were airlifted to Israel from the midst of a famine. Relatively few immigrants came from the USA, Great Britain, France and other prosperous democratic countries where Jews had long enjoyed civic equality with non-Jews. The USA, which has the world's largest Jewish population, sees net Jewish immigration from Israel. Despite this, the support of the American Jewish community has been vitally important to Israel, particularly for its lobbying influence with the US government. Since the 1970s, the main source of immigrants has been Russia. During most of the Soviet period, Jews were prevented from emigrating. Since restrictions were relaxed in the 1970s, about 80 percent of Russia's two million Jews have emigrated, most of them to Israel. Russian Jews are highly secularized and have proved reluctant to learn Hebrew and assimilate with Israeli society.

TIMELINE

1878 Petah Tikva, a Jewish farming community, is founded in Palestine

1880s Anti-Jewish pogroms in Russia

1882–1903 The First Aliyah: 30,000 eastern Europe Jews migrate to Palestine

1904–13 The Second Aliyah: 40,000 eastern European Jews migrate to Palestine

1909 The first kibbutz is founded

1917 Balfour Declaration commits Britain to support a Jewish homeland in Palestine

1920–48 Britain rules Palestine as a League of Nations Mandate

1933–45 The Holocaust: Nazi genocide against European Jews

1939 Britain imposes limits on Jewish immigration to Palestine

1948 (14 May) Israeli declaration of independence

1948–9 Israeli war of independence against Arab states

1950 Israel introduces the Law of Return to encourage immigration

1967 Israel defeats the Arabs in the Six-Day War

1973 Israel defeats an Arab coalition in the Yom Kippur War

1985 Falashas (Ethiopian Jews) airlifted to Israel

1991 Mass migration of Russian Jews to Israel following fall of the Soviet Union

The Second World War and its Aftermath
1939–1972

The Second World War (1939–45) and its aftermath saw the greatest population movements in European history. The war created millions of refugees, who had fled to escape the fighting or been made homeless by bombing. Even greater numbers were forced to migrate by the Nazi and Soviet regimes and by border changes after the war.

In the areas occupied by Nazi Germany, over 6 million Jews were transported to concentration camps in Germany and Poland, where the majority were killed or died from maltreatment and disease. Nazi Germany also conscripted millions of eastern European civilians and prisoners of war – Poles, Czechs, Russians, Belorussians and Ukrainians – to work in Germany as slave labourers to support its war effort. In accordance with Nazi racial theories, these Slav peoples were treated as expendable 'sub-humans'. Millions of them died from overwork and abuse. French, Belgian and Italian civilians and POWs were also conscripted. Had Germany won the war, the Nazis planned to relocate the Slavs to Siberia to make *Lebensraum* ('living space') for the Germans. In preparation for this, Poland was divided between the Reichsgaue (provinces), which were to be resettled with Germans, and the General Government, which was to be a Polish settled labour camp. By 1944, 750,000 ethnic Germans from Nazi-occupied eastern Europe had been forcibly resettled in the Reichsgaue.

Forced migrations

The Soviet Union also organized forced migrations on a mass scale. After the Bolshevik Revolution millions of alleged counter-revolutionaries were deported to labour camps (GULags) in Siberia. Millions more were forced to migrate from rural areas to industrial cities following the collectivization of agriculture. After the Baltic states were annexed in 1939, Estonians, Latvians and Lithuanians were deported to Siberia and ethnic Russians were settled in the occupied countries to help 'russify' them. After occupying eastern Poland in alliance with Nazi Germany in September 1939, the Soviet authorities deported 750,000 Poles to labour camps.

Forced migrations reached their peak after Germany invaded the Soviet Union in 1941. To escape the advancing Germans, 1360 munitions factories and their workforces were relocated east of the Urals. Ethnic minorities whose loyalty was suspect, such as the

Crimean Tatars, Kalmyks, Chechens and the Volga Germans, were transported to Siberia and forced to live and work in appalling conditions. Estimates for the numbers of forced migrants vary considerably but probably exceeded 20 million.

The end of the war saw a devastated Europe teeming with displaced people. As the Soviet armies began to push back the Germans in 1943, millions of Cossack, Ukrainian, Latvian, Estonian and Lithuanian anti-Soviet collaborators were forced to flee west. Some found refuge in the West after the war but most were returned to the Soviet Union and almost certain death. As the vengeful Red Army advanced into Germany in the final months of the war, millions of Germans from East Prussia, Pomerania, Silesia and the Reichsgaue fled, hastened on their way by stories of atrocities enacted by Soviet troops.

None of these refugees could return home after the end of the war. Poland's borders were redrawn by the Allies. The Soviet Union was left in control of the Polish territory it had seized in 1939, while Poland was compensated with former German territory in East Prussia, Pomerania and Silesia. Those Germans who had not fled these areas were now expelled, to be resettled in Germany. Poles displaced from the east migrated west and settled the areas vacated by the Germans. The East Prussian port of Königsberg (now Kaliningrad) became part of the Soviet Union and its German population was also expelled and replaced with ethnic Russians. Other eastern European countries followed suit and expelled their German minorities. This included the Sudetenland Germans of Czechoslovakia. Hitler's annexation of this region in 1938 – greeted with wild enthusiasm by its German population – had been one of the milestones on the road to war. In total

Refugees cross a destroyed bridge on the River Elbe at Tangermünde, Germany, on 1 May, 1945. Retreating Germans troops had blown up the bridge a few days earlier.

around 12.5 million German refugees had to be resettled into a shrunken Germany. Centuries of German colonization in eastern Europe had been reversed in a matter of months.

The most important consequence of the war was the division of Europe into an eastern communist bloc dominated by the Soviet Union and a western democratic bloc allied to the US. Many Poles who had fled to the West to escape the Germans preferred to remain in exile rather than return to live under Soviet occupation. Germany was divided into American, British, French and Soviet occupation zones. So many Germans fled the Soviet zone that the Soviet authorities imposed travel restrictions and fortified the border. The resulting division of Germany into communist east and democratic west lasted until 1989. Russian ambitions to add Greece to its sphere of influence led it to support communist insurgents. In the ensuing civil war 10 percent of Greece's 7 million people became refugees. Most of the surviving 1.5 million eastern European Jews had no wish to return to their pre-war homes in anti-Semitic communities that had often collaborated with the Nazis. From temporary camps in Germany and France, most eventually emigrated to Israel or the US.

Post-war labour shortages

By the early 1950s the European economy was beginning to recover from the war and many countries were experiencing labour shortages. Britain's solution was to encourage immigration, and the Nationality Act of 1948 confirmed the right of all Commonwealth citizens and colonial subjects to unrestricted entry to the UK. Agents were used in the West Indies to recruit labour to fill vacancies in the transport system (and later the health services). In June 1948 the *Empire Windrush* docked in London carrying 492 immigrants from Jamaica. By 1951, 218,000 West Indians were working in Britain. Private companies organized recruitment drives in India and Pakistan to fill vacancies in textile and engineering factories in industrial cities in England. Little thought was given to the problem of assimilating immigrants into an ethnically homogeneous society – rising racial tensions led to restrictions on immigration in the 1960s. Germany, which encouraged Turkish 'guest workers', and France, which recruited North and West African labour, experienced similar problems.

IRELAND •Dublin

UNITED KINGDO

Londo

to the United States

Paris

FRANCE

Madrid•

•Lisbon

SPAIN

PORTUGAL

NORWAY
FINLAND
Helsinki
SWEDEN
Oslo
Stockholm
Estonia
Latvia
Riga
DENMARK
Lithuania
Copenhagen
Kaliningrad
(Königsberg)
Gdansk (Danzig)
NETHERLANDS
Amsterdam
Warsaw
Poles
Berlin
BELGIUM
GERMAN
POLAND
Brussels
DEMOCRATIC
Poles
Oder
REPUBLIC
Bonn
Rhine
Prague
FEDERAL
CZECHOSLOVAKIA
REPUBLIC
OF GERMANY
Dniester
Vienna
Berne
AUSTRIA
Budapest
SWITZERLAND
HUNGARY
ROMANIA
ITALY
Belgrade
Bucharest
Danube
YUGOSLAVIA
BULGARIA
Sofia
Rome
Istanbul
Tirane
to Israel
ALBANIA
GREECE
Athens
Mediterranean Sea

UNION OF SOVIET SOCIALIST REPUBLICS

Ukraine

Black Sea

TURKEY

pre-war border of Poland

communist-aligned countries

movement of Russians, 1945–50

movement of Germans, 1945–50

other movement of peoples, 1945–50

mass exodus of Jews, 1945–50

Soviet military intervention

A major casualty of the Second World War were the European colonial empires. Financially broken by war and facing growing independence movements, the European powers were compelled to grant independence to most of their colonies by the 1960s. Decolonization created serious refugee crises for France, the Netherlands and Britain. Many French citizens settled in France's North African colonies in the late 19th century. When they became independent (Tunisia and Morocco in 1956, Algeria in 1962), over 1 million French North Africans, fearful of a future under Muslim rule, fled en masse. Accustomed to a highly privileged lifestyle in the colonies, they found adjusting to life in France a difficult process. In the same period 300,000 white Dutch colonials were repatriated from Indonesia. By 1972 Britain had been forced to accept over 100,000 Asians expelled from its former colonies of Kenya, Tanzania and Uganda. Descendants of indentured labourers who had migrated to East Africa in the 19th century, their prosperity made them easy scapegoats for the failings of post-independence governments.

Map showing population displacement and migration patterns in post-war Europe, 1945–50.

243

The World on the Move

The great age of migration is now. Over three million people every year make the decision to emigrate to another country. Worldwide, there are over 150 million people who have permanently left the countries they were born in to make new lives for themselves abroad. Far greater numbers migrate within their birth countries. Though the scale of migration is unprecedented, its nature has not changed. Many migrants are fleeing war or political oppression, but the majority have economic motives, just as has been the case throughout history.

Passengers queuing at an airport check-in. Relatively cheap mass travel has facilitated the movement of people between continents, though cost and security measures mean that few illegal immigrants arrive by air.

Today, international economic migration is mainly from the developing world to the affluent countries of western Europe, North America and Australasia. Immigration presents governments with difficult policy choices. Large-scale immigration is usually unpopular with the host communities, who believe that immigrants reduce employment opportunities for the locals and depress wages, put pressure on housing and social services, and take advantage of social security and other taxpayer-funded benefits. Some also fear that their communities may be swamped by immigrants from alien cultures. This is often the case among relatively disadvantaged poor white communities in inner-city areas, where first-generation immigrants often settle. It is certainly true that European governments have awoken very late to the need to encourage immigrants to assimilate with the indigenous population. Instead of producing genuinely multicultural communities, lack of attention to this issue has often allowed communities to drift into *de facto* segregation. This is very pronounced in northern English industrial towns, many of which are starkly divided into white and Asian areas, with little interaction between them. The problems were brought sharply into focus in 2005 when disaffected young Muslim men rioted in Paris and carried out suicide bomb attacks on the London transport system. The USA, which has always been a nation of immigrants, and has 37 million foreign-born citizens, has generally coped with these problems much more successfully than Europe.

Calling for tough restrictions on immigration is an easy way for politicians to court popularity. However, most developed countries (the main exception being the USA) have low birth rates and aging populations, and economists believe that immigration, especially by young adults, is necessary to maintain the labour force. The situation is especially serious in Italy, which has the world's lowest birth rate with only 1.2 children per woman. By 2050 Italy will lose 28 percent of its population without immigration. If

there are to be enough taxpayers mid-century to fund present levels of retirement benefits, Italy needs annual immigration of 350,000 people. Immigration may be unpopular with the electorate but so is the prospect of raised retirement ages. Governments usually try to balance these conflicting priorities by attempting to restrict immigration to people whose skills are in short supply but this is exceptionally difficult to achieve in an age of mass travel and porous national borders.

The perils facing illegal immigrants

The development of cheap mass air travel since the 1970s has led to a great increase in mobility, for business and tourism even more than migration. Even so air fares are still beyond the means of many would-be economic migrants and air travel also has the problem for illegal migrants that it is well policed, making it difficult to avoid immigration controls. Knowing that the chances of gaining legal admission to Europe or North America are slight, illegal emigrants take terrifying risks. Unknown numbers drown attempting clandestine sea crossings in unseaworthy and overcrowded boats: across the straits between Cuba and Florida, across the Mediterranean from North Africa to Spain and southern Italy, West Africa to the Canary Islands (Spanish), and from the Horn of Africa across the Gulf of Aden to Arabia are all well-used routes. Another means, which often ends in suffocation, is to hide in a cargo container. In just one such tragedy, 58 Chinese migrants were found suffocated in a container truck at Dover, UK, in June 2000. Illegal immigrants trying to enter the USA from Mexico risk death from dehydration crossing the desert frontier. Migrants from sub-Saharan Africa take comparable risks crossing the Sahara Desert to reach the North African coast, from where they hope to be able to cross to Europe. People have even been known to chance almost certain death from cold and oxygen starvation at 35,000 feet (11,000 metres) by stowing away in the wheelbays of passenger aircraft.

A boat laden with asylum seekers from the long-running conflict between Ethiopia and Eritrea in the Horn of Africa, enters Italian waters after crossing the Mediterranean in June 2006.

The problems of illegal immigrants do not end when, or if, they reach their destination. Their illegal status makes them vulnerable to exploitation by unscrupulous employers. Others experience what amounts to debt slavery, while they pay back the costs of their journeys to traffickers. Young women, enticed to migrate by false job offers, may find themselves held captive and forced into prostitution. Illegal immigrants rarely complain to the authorities about their treatment because they know they would almost certainly be deported. Official amnesties, such as that proposed by President George W. Bush (b.1946) in the USA in 2004, would be effective ways to help illegal immigrants trapped in these circumstances but they are generally opposed by the public, who believe that they would simply encourage more illegal immigration.

Because of its clandestine nature, quantifying illegal immigration is almost impossible. In 2004 the US government estimated that there were eight to 12 million illegal immigrants in the USA but unofficial estimates, some politically motivated, range as high as 20 million. Most states devote considerable resources to combating illegal immigration but have little idea how effective their efforts are. To stem the waves of illegal immigrants from Latin America, the US government now plans to build a $2.2 billion wall along the Mexican border, with floodlights, surveillance cameras and motion detectors. India is planning a similar wall for its 2550 mile (4080 km) border with Bangladesh.

Internal migration

Despite its scale, it still takes an exceptional person to emigrate: only 2–3 percent of people are likely to take such a decision in their lifetimes. Vastly greater numbers take the less daunting step of migrating within their birth country. In China, the developing world's most dynamic economy, 200 million people, mainly single young men and women from poor peasant families migrated to the cities in the first five years of the 21st century alone, compared to about 250,000 who emigrated. Across the developing world an average of 160,000 people every day migrate from the countryside to the cities in search of better paid factory work. This repeats a pattern of internal migration experienced by all industrializing countries since the Industrial Revolution began in England in the 18th century. Growth in employment opportunities and wages generally lag behind the growth of the urban population and many migrants simply exchange rural poverty for urban poverty. Few countries now have internal frontiers of settlement, where pioneers can carve farms out of the wilderness. An important exception is Brazil, where every year farmers advance a little further into the Amazonian rainforest.

Economic migration within Europe has been made much easier by the European Union (EU). The EU allows free movement of labour between all its member states but language barriers have inhibited the growth of a fully mobile European labour force. The greatest increase in economic migration within the EU followed the admission of Poland, the Czech Republic and other

Immigrants from the poverty-stricken Caribbean island of Haiti picking beans in the southern US state of Florida.

former Communist Bloc countries in 2004. Within six months 400,000 Poles had emigrated to Britain to work in agriculture and construction for wages that were high by Polish standards. Eastern European migrants are mainly young single people who intend to return home once they have saved enough money to buy property or businesses.

The terrible plight of refugees

The collapse of the communist Bloc in 1989 was surprisingly peaceful in most eastern European countries but it fatally destabilized Yugoslavia. A federal multinational state, Yugoslavia had sat precariously between East and West throughout the Cold War, with a Communist government that refused to accept Soviet leadership. The breakup of Yugoslavia into its constituent republics in 1991–2 was followed by civil wars in Croatia, between Croats and Serbs, and Bosnia, between Serbs, Bosnian Muslims and Croats. The wars were marked by 'ethnic cleansing', attempts by the different national groups to drive ethnic minorities out of areas where they were in the majority. War crimes were committed by all sides, the worst being the massacre by Serbs of 6000 Bosnian Muslims at Srebrenica in 1995. Few of the refugees created by these atrocities have been able to return to their homes. When in 1999, Serbia attempted to drive the Albanian Muslim population out of Kosovo, NATO intervened. Since then most of Kosovo's Serbian minority have left. The collapse of the Soviet Union in 1991 also created its crop of refugees. The largest group were three to four million ethnic Russians who found themselves as ethnic minorities in newly independent former-Soviet republics. Most resettled in the Russian Federation.

Civil war, ethnic cleansing and genocide have caused far greater refugee movements in other parts of the world. The most notorious genocide of recent times was in Rwanda in 1994. Long-standing ethnic tensions erupted when the Hutu majority launched a government orchestrated attack on the country's Tutsi minority. Perhaps 500,000 Tutsis were killed, most with household tools such as machetes, and 700,000 fled the country. These refugees were soon able to return after a Tutsi-led Patriotic Front army overthrew the Hutu government. Fearing retribution for their part in the genocide, 1.75 million Hutu fled to DR Congo, Tanzania and Burundi, where most of them still remain. Hutu refugees proved a destabilizing influence in Congo, attacking ethnic Tutsis living in Congo and creating an internal refugee crisis. A new refugee crisis began in 2004 in the Darfur region of Sudan after government-backed Arab militias began genocidal attacks on villages of black Africans suspected of supporting a separatist movement. By 2007 almost three million people had been displaced by the conflict, and an unknown number killed. Most refugees were living in temporary camps in Sudan but over 200,000 had fled to neighbouring Chad, one of the world's poorest countries.

The burden of resettling refugees falls disproportionately on poor countries in the developing world. Refugees from conflicts or repressive regimes in the developing world often have to flee at short notice, with few possessions, and take the shortest route to safety, which is usually over the nearest international border, so leaving one developing country for another. Developed countries in the West are reluctant to accept refugees,

The conflict in Darfur, western Sudan, has created a massive refugee crisis that humanitarian agencies seem powerless to alleviate. Global political and economic considerations often thwart attempts to resolve such issues. For instance, in this case Sudan can afford to ignore Western condemnation since it has become a major supplier of oil to China.

usually described as 'asylum seekers', because they are often suspected of being economic refugees. Such is the case with refugees from Zimbabwe, where opponents of the government of Robert Mugabe (b.1924) run the serious risk of being imprisoned, beaten, tortured or killed by security forces. Unfortunately, Mugabe's government is not just oppressive, it is corrupt and incompetent, with the result that Zimbabwe's economy has collapsed. Widespread unemployment and hardship have led many Zimbabweans to emigrate to neighbouring countries, usually illegally, in search of work. Because these economic migrants sometimes falsely apply for political asylum, the claims of genuine political refugees are often disbelieved.

If the predicted consequences of climate change are fulfilled, then the 21st century may see a new class of migrant, the environmental refugee. A disproportionate percentage of the world's population lives in coastal areas that are potentially vulnerable to a rise in sea level. Some small island nations, such as the Maldives, are predicted to become uninhabitable by the end of the century. In low-lying Bangladesh more than half its 120 million population are vulnerable to flooding. This would create a refugee crisis of unprecedented proportions. Desertification in Africa, Asia and even southern Europe could create millions more refugees. Countries in high latitudes which may escape the worst effects of global warming will not be able to isolate themselves from these population movements. The challenge for governments in the 21st century will not be to stop migration, for that is impossible, but to manage it better.

Index

Further Reading

GENERAL
Chaliand, Gérard, *The Penguin Atlas of Diasporas* (New York, 1995)
Diamond, Jared, *Guns, Germs and Steel* (New York, 1997)
Manning, Patrick, *Migration in World History* (London & New York, 2005)
Olson, Steve, *Mapping Human History: Discovering the Past through our Genes* (London, 2002)

ANCIENT WORLD (human origins to *c.*AD 400)
Boardman, John, *The Greeks Overseas* (London, 1980)
Fagan, Brian, *The Great Journey: the Peopling of Ancient America* (Gainesville, FL., 2004)
Haywood, John, *Atlas of the Celtic World* (London and New York, 2001)
Mallory, J. P., *In Search of the Indo-Europeans* (London, 1989)
Markoe, Glenn, E., *The Phoenicians* (London, 2000)
Mulvaney, John and Kamminga, Johan, *Prehistoric Australia* (Washington, 1999)
Oppenheimer, Stephen, *Out of Eden: the Peopling of the World* (London, 2004)
Potok, Chaim, *Wanderings: a History of the Jews* (New York, 2003)

MEDIEVAL WORLD (*c.*400-1500)
Denoon, D., *The Cambridge History of the Pacific Islanders* (Cambridge, 2004)
Fraser, Angus, *The Gypsies* (Oxford, 1995)
Halsall, Guy, *Barbarian Migrations and the Roman West* (Cambridge, 2007)
Haywood, John, *The Penguin Historical Atlas of the Vikings* (London & New York, 1995)
Kennedy, Hugh, *The Great Arab Conquests: How the Spread of Islam Changed the World we Live in* (London, 2007)
McKie, Robin *The Face of Britain: How our Genes Reveal the History of Britain* (London, 2007)
Thompson, E. A., *The Huns* (Oxford, 1999)

EARLY MODERN WORLD (1500-1800)
Boxer, C. R., *The Portuguese Seaborne Empire* (London, 1991)
Hughes, Robert, *The Fatal Shore: the History of the Transportation of Convicts to Australia* (London, 2003)
McFarlane, Anthony, *The British in the Americas, 1480-1815* (London and New York, 1994)
Parry, J. H., *The Spanish Seaborne Empire* (London, 1977)
Pritchard, James, *In Search of Empire: the French in the Americas* (Cambridge, 2007)
Robinson, P. S., *The Plantation of Ulster* (Belfast 2000)
Thomas, Hugh, *The Slave Trade: the History of the Atlantic Slave Trade 1440-1870* (London, 2006)
Wood, Alan, *A History of Siberia* (London, 1991)

MODERN WORLD (1800-present)
Brown, Judith M., *Global South Asians* (Cambridge, 2006)
Coffey, M. and Golway, T., *The Irish in America* (London and New York, 2000)
Christopher, Emma, *Many Middle Passages: Forced Migration and the Making of the Modern World* (Berkeley, 2007)
Coleman, Terry, *Passage to America* (London, 1972)
Craig, D., *On the Crofters' Trail: In Search of the Clearance Highlanders* (London, 1990)
Gilbert, Martin, *Israel: a History* (London, 1999)
Hoerder, Dirk, *Cultures in Contact: World Migrations in the Second Millennium* (Durham, North Carolina, 2003)
McLynn, Frank, *Wagons West: the Epic Story of America's Overland Trails* (London, 2003)
O'Sullivan, P., *The Meaning of the Famine* (Leicester, 1997)
Polian, Pavel, *Against their Will: the History and Geography of Forced Migrations in the Soviet Union* (Budapest, 2003)

Picture Credits

First published in Great Britain in 2008 by

Quercus
21 Bloomsbury Square
London
WC1A 2NS

A CIP catalogue record for this book is available from the British Library

Cloth case edition: ISBN-978 1 84724 543 4

Printed case edition: ISBN-978 1 84724 187 0

Printed and bound in China

10 9 8 7 6 5 4 3 2 1

Designed and edited by BCS Publishing Limited, Oxford.